# The Portable Guide to Testifying in Court for Mental Health Professionals

## An A–Z Guide
### to
### *Being an Effective Witness*

Barton E. Bernstein, JD, LMSW
and
Thomas L. Hartsell, Jr., JD

**WILEY**

JOHN WILEY & SONS, INC.

*Authors' note:* Sample forms should be used only after careful review by a local lawyer. Jurisdictions differ in their technical and legal requirements, and every health professional should use forms specifically drafted for each individual practice, organization, or agency.

Published by John Wiley & Sons, Inc., Hoboken, New Jersey.
Published simultaneously in Canada.

For general information on our other products and services please contact our Customer Care Department within the United States at (800) 762-2974, outside the United States at (317) 572-3993 or fax (317) 572-4002.

Wiley also publishes its books in a variety of electronic formats. Some content that appears in print may not be available in electronic books. For more information about Wiley products, visit our web site at www.wiley.com.

*Library of Congress Cataloging-in-Publication Data:*

Bernstein, Barton E.
    The portable guide to testifying in court for mental health professionals : an A-Z guide to being an effective witness / Barton E. Bernstein and Thomas L. Hartsell, Jr.
        p. cm.
    ISBN-13 978-0-471-46552-2 (pbk. : alk. paper)
    ISBN-10 0-471-46552-6 (pbk. : alk. paper)
    1. Evidence, Expert—United States.   2. Forensic psychology—United States.   3. Mental health personnel—Legal status, laws, etc.—United States.   I. Hartsell, Thomas L. (Thomas Lee), 1955–   II. Title.

    KF8965.B47     2005
    347.73'67—dc22
                                                                2004065766

Printed in the United States of America.
10  9  8  7  6  5  4  3  2  1

# The Portable Guide to Testifying in Court for Mental Health Professionals

# Other Books by the Authors

*The Portable Lawyer for Mental Health Professionals: An A–Z Guide to Protecting Your Clients, Your Practice, and Yourself,* second edition (2004), John Wiley & Sons, Inc.

*The Portable Ethicist for Mental Health Professionals: An A–Z Guide to Responsible Practice* (2000), John Wiley & Sons, Inc.

*The Pocket Manual for Mental Health Professionals, a Compendium of Answers to Questions Most Frequently Asked by Professional Counselors, Social Workers, Psychologists, Marriage and Family Counselors, Family Therapists, Pastoral Counselors, Addictions Counselors, and Others* (2000), T. L. Hartsell Jr. and Barton E. Bernstein (214-363-0555, tlhartsell2@aol.com).

## Dedications

To my wife, Donna, for her constant inspiration and affection, with deepest love and appreciation.

To mental health professionals all over the world who dedicate themselves to alleviating stress, suffering, and personal difficulties.

To my children, Alon, the merchant; Talya Bernstein-Galaganov, the lawyer; and son-in-law Dr. Misha Galaganov, the musicologist. May they someday point out these books to my grandchildren and emphasize their contribution to the world, be it ever so humble.

To my sisters, Rona Mae Solberg and Berna Gae Haberman, and brother-in-law, Wolf (Bill) Haberman.

In loving memory of the past generation, my mother and father, Suetelle and Samuel Bernstein; my aunts and uncles, Anita and Irving Bloch and Miriam (Mickey) and Sidney Springer; and my late brother-in-law, Myron (Mike) Solberg.

To my good friend and colleague, Tom Hartsell, who took up the legal baton and ran with it to ever-lofty heights as an outstanding lawyer, professor, mediator, community leader, author, and role model for future generations.

BEB

To the mental health professionals who dedicate their lives to improving the human condition in the face of declining revenues, increased regulation, and administrative complexities. Unlike the IRS, the world is not becoming a kinder and gentler place, and the number of people in need of competent and caring mental health services is increasing every day. It has been our goal to assist the mental health community in a small way with the good work that it does. We want to help keep mental health professionals in business and providing the vital and underappreciated services our society so badly needs. So to all of you, this book is for you. Bless you.

To my mentor and friend, Bart Bernstein, who is 75 years young and still an inspiration. This book has been Bart's labor of love and a long time coming. Bart, I know I can never thank you enough or repay you for all you have done for me and taught me but know that I appreciate all of it and will be forever grateful. Signed, Your Greatest Admirer.

To my beautiful wife, Barbara, who knows only too well how much time and energy my professional life demands of me and our relationship, but who supports and comforts me and makes my life complete. Thank you, Darlin', from the bottom of my heart, for putting up with me and loving me.

To my parents, Tom and Julie Hartsell, I owe you everything. The best in me can be traced directly to you. I love you guys. May your golden years be blessed and happy.

To Ryan and Jason, my fine young sons, and Glenn and Chandler, my fine young stepsons, who have all become fine young men. The world is your oyster; relish it and revel in it.

To Bill and Paula Edwards, my wonderful inlaws, for their gift of Barbara, and all their friendship and support. I love you both. May your golden years be blessed and happy as well.

Last but not least, I want to give a big shout out to my pal Dexter, my Jack Russell (excuse me, Parson Russell) Terrier, who is asleep at my feet as I write this. Ol' Dex warms my heart with his every look and action. He puts meaning in the phrase "man's best friend" for me. He is my joy.

TLH

# Preface

When one of the authors, Bart Bernstein, began practicing law in the 1960s, the courtroom witness was treated with respect and kindness. After taking the witness stand and providing a brief introduction concerning his or her experience, the mental health professional proceeded to testify about the facts as he or she knew them and to offer an opinion concerning those facts. The lawyers, awed by the intellectual competence and knowledge of the expert, would rarely challenge the testimony of the learned specialist whose sage-like words, after a few perfunctory questions, would be accepted as gospel. Lawyers considered it bad taste to challenge the credentials, experience, education, or conclusions of experts. After all, if the expert had an opinion, stated with confidence and without the shadow of a doubt, what right had a lawyer, with a totally different orientation, to question that opinion? Often, the judge or jury, depending on who was to be the decision maker, accepted the expert testimony from the witness at face value, surrendering independent judgment without reservation and allowing the "expert" to determine the final outcome of the case by default. In contrast, in our current system, the jury or judge, depending on the case, is the final arbiter of disputes. Professional experts are *only one of the factors* that judges and juries consider when making judgments, reaching decisions, and pronouncing verdicts.

In the legal middle ages, the 1960s, the therapist in a custody case would take the witness stand and be sworn in. Then gentle examination such as the following would begin:

 What is your education?
What is your work history or employment since you received your advanced degree?

List your publications and any special studies.

How long have you treated Mr. and Mrs. Jones?

Have you interviewed the children and for how many sessions?

Describe the nature of the therapy offered to the Jones family.

Dr. Smith, as a result of your visits with the Jones family and considering your learning, training, education, and experience, have you an opinion concerning the best interest of the children? Would you recommend to the court that they reside primarily with Mr. Jones or Mrs. Jones?

The expert witness might reply:

"Yes, I do have an opinion. I would recommend that the children reside with _____ as that would be in their best interest."

LAWYER: "And what is your rationale or reason for this opinion?"

EXPERT WITNESS: "Based on my many years' experience in the field, my numerous cases and clients, and my education, research, and training, it is my professional opinion that _____ would act in their best interest because _____ ."

LAWYER: "Thank you!"

Today, taking the witness stand can be an experience from hell. Everything about the expert is subject to questioning. For example, questions may arise concerning:

- Your marital history.
- Your involvement with your children including support payments.
- Your grades in undergraduate and graduate school.
- Your involvement with professional organizations.
- Your credit and financial history if the lawyer can make it relevant.
- Your techniques of therapy or counseling.

- Outcome studies concerning your therapeutic techniques.
- Your treatment plans.

You could be asked questions such as:

State all the factors you considered in making your diagnosis.

State all the factors you considered in establishing your treatment plan.

State your initial prognosis and how it was altered or changed as new factors or considerations were taken into account.

Is your client taking any medications, and how does this affect the therapy or your client's behavior patterns?

If your client is taking prescription medication, is he taking it in the prescribed dosage?

Have you discussed the medication with the physician who prescribed it?

The preceding questions are not the only matters about which you might be cross-examined. They are examples of questions that set a tone or atmosphere for courtroom or deposition testimony indicating that, while mental health professionals are adequately prepared to be helping professionals, they are usually ill prepared to enter the legal arena. There are few graduate school courses that give more than a cursory look at what might happen in litigation, especially if the clinician is called into court in connection with a client's case.

Law schools have moot court, where law students are assigned cases and clients to represent before lawyers and judges to obtain courtroom practice and experience before they represent *real* clients. Mental health professionals have little opportunity to obtain such practice. Usually the first time they attend court is as a witness in a real case, involving real people in a real controversy, where the outcome affects individuals' lives and families.

This book makes the assumption that if the mental health professional is involved in his or her own litigation such as a business conflict or a malpractice case, the attorneys engaged will adequately prepare the professional for trial. We have included a chapter, however, that deals with a mental health professional as a party to a lawsuit.

This book can be most helpful when the litigation concerns clients engaged in their own disputes and the clinician is summoned into court either as an expert hired witness or when one of the disputants feels the testimony of his or her therapist, who is currently providing treatment or did so in the past, is vital to the case.

You can be called as a witness long after therapy has terminated. Once you have treated a client, you are always subject to subpoena if the client or the client's lawyer feels you know something relevant to the case and supportive of the client's position.

Although a witness may have nothing to gain from the court or deposition appearance, the client has a lot to lose if the witness is not prepared. The witness can be vulnerable in many circumstances, for example:

- Licensing board complaints have been filed against unprepared witnesses. Often, clients consider helpful and supportive testimony to be a part of the therapeutic process. They are devastated when a competent therapist of any discipline has taken one position in the therapeutic context and another under oath.
- Errors may be found in a clinical file or progress notes. Many clinical files are incomplete or too quickly written to be free of errors. Many clinicians do not review and appropriately correct files carefully before turning them over to clients or third parties.

It behooves every mental health professional to be competent in two specific areas: therapy and litigation. In the field of therapeutic services, competence in the offering of services is assumed. Degrees, licenses, experience, and education represent to the public that the clinician is proficient in the practice of mental health. Competence must be acquired through practice, familiarity, and formalized schooling.

When involved in any sort of contested litigation, first read the relevant chapters of this book; then review the contents with a lawyer or forensic expert. Examine all written material available concerning the client and the client's diagnosis, treatment plan, and prognosis. Role-play anticipated examination and cross-examination. Only then will you be technically prepared for trial. Being mentally prepared is another consideration. Brace yourself. It will be difficult until you get used to it. Remember, though, that the possibility of a courtroom appearance is part of the mental health practice.

We have created a trilogy of books to assist and educate the mental health professional. *The Portable Ethicist for Mental Health Professionals: An A–Z Guide to Responsible Practice* alerts the reader to ethical problems that can and will affect the therapist as the practice develops. *The Portable Lawyer for Mental Health Professionals: An A–Z Guide to Protecting Your Clients, Your Practice, and Yourself*, second edition, alerts the reader to legal problems that can and will affect the therapist as the practice develops and provides some of the forms that are essential to create a more risk-free practice. This book, *The Portable Guide to Testifying in Court for Mental Health Professionals: An A–Z Guide to Being an Effective Witness*, offers the practitioner a window into the forensic or courtroom scene. A court appearance without preparation is naïve and unfair to the client as well as to the service provider. This book will alert the mental health witness to the problems that are traditionally faced in the litigation context from initial engagement to ultimate posttrial termination of services.

# Acknowledgments

In the process of writing this book, we had many friends, acquaintances, and colleagues who provided inspiration, nurturing, and mentoring—all necessary for any work worthy of publication.

We want to thank John Wiley & Sons, Inc., for creating the idea and Kelly A. Franklin, our original editor, for her initial enthusiasm for the project. We also thank Tracey Belmont, senior editor, and Isabel Pratt, assistant editor, who helped to reorganize the chapters and who were able to digest legal concepts and help translate legalese into English as well as inspire additional publications. Thanks also to Linda Indig, senior production editor, and Pam Blackmon and the staff at Publications Development Company of Texas, who reviewed, organized, edited, and helped to make this book more useful.

Encouragement came from many special friends, some of whom we want to mention by name. James W. Callicutt, PhD, Graduate School of Social Work, University of Texas, Arlington, was Bart's mentor, initial source of inspiration, and first contact in the interactive field of law and mental health. He helped organize the first course in Law and Social Work and has facilitated the interaction ever since. Myron ("Mike") F. Weiner, MD, Department of Psychiatry, Southwestern Medical School, and a friend for over 30 years, bridged the gap between psychiatry and law, encouraging participation in the residents' program at the medical school and service on the adjunct faculty. Thanks to David Shriro and Martin Davidson, PhD (professor emeritus, North Texas State University), close friends and confidants for almost 40 years, for constantly encouraging (some might call it nagging) an addiction to writing and to Anthony Paul Picchioni, PhD, program director for the Alternative Dispute Resolution Program at Southern Methodist University, for emphasizing the need for continuing education in the area of ethics and malpractice and for his encouragement of all our endeavors.

BARTON BERNSTEIN/THOMAS L. HARTSELL JR.

*Dallas, Texas*

# Contents

## PART I
### THE JUDICIAL SYSTEM

1    Our System of Justice    3

2    Involvement in the Judicial System    18

3    Lawyers: Their Functions    24

4    The Expert Witness    32

## PART II
### TESTIMONY VERSUS THERAPY

5    Therapist: Two Different Roles    43

6    Ethics    49

7    Confidentiality    62

8    Resolving Conflicts before They Escalate    69

## PART III
### PREPARING FOR TESTIMONY

9    Subpoenas    79

10    Preparing for Discovery    90

11    Preparing "Ask Me" Questions for the Lawyer    97

12    Preparing for Deposition Testimony    105

13    Preparing for Courtroom Testimony    114

## PART IV

### IN THE COURTROOM

14   Testimony Tips   123

15   Lawyers' Tricks   133

16   Challenges to the Expert Witness: The *Daubert* Case   140

## PART V

### THE EXPERT WITNESS'S TOOLS

17   The Resume: Your Introduction to the Court   153

18   Contracts   158

19   Making Sure You Are Compensated   166

20   What to Do If You Are Sued   174

## PART VI

### OTHER EXPERT WITNESSES

21   The School Counselor as a Courtroom Witness   187

22   The Forensic Expert   198

APPENDIX A   Useful Web Sites   209

APPENDIX B   Useful Forms   211

   Example of a Motion to Quash Subpoena   211

   Example of a Motion for Entry of a Protective Order   213

   Example of a Qualified Protective Order   216

   Authorization for the Use and Disclosure of Protected
   Health Information   219

Checklist for Deposition Testimony   221

Checklist for Direct Examination for Courtroom Testimony   228

Checklist for Cross-Examination   235

List of Federal Cases Involving *Daubert* Challenges of Mental Health Professionals   238

Trial Vita (Sample Form)   240

Employee Evaluation Information and Consent Form   241

Home Study Information and Consent Form   245

Contract for Forensic Services and Information and Consent Form   249

INDEX   253

# PART I

# *THE JUDICIAL SYSTEM*

*When warring parents head to court to fight over child custody in New York, their lawyers often let them in on a little secret. The most powerful person in the process is not the judge. It is not the other parent, not the lawyers, not even the child.*

*No, the most important person in determining who gets custody, and on what terms, is frequently a court appointed forensic evaluator. Forensics, as they are often called, can be psychiatrists, psychologists or social workers; they interview the families and usually make detailed recommendations to judges, right down to who gets the children on Wednesdays and alternate weekends.*

*And the judges usually go along. (Emphasis added.)*

New York Times, Sunday, May 23, 2004, pp. 1, 25.

The preceding article emphasizes what lawyers have known all along and what every lawyer underscores to potential witnesses: The testimony of the forensic mental health professional is crucial, important, worthy of extensive preparation, and can affect the lives of an entire family immediately following the trial and for countless years into the future. Thus, it is imperative that the forensic witness be schooled in all the techniques necessary to prepare for evaluation, assessment, and court appearances.

The court appearance is the final report card. The grade is awarded by the judge or jury.

# 1

# Our System of Justice

*After practicing as counseling interns for two years and completing the requisite supervised hours, Karen and Jim became fully licensed counselors. They formed a partnership and opened a marriage and family counseling practice. Initially, business was slow, and they had to squeeze every ounce of revenue from the practice to keep the doors open. One unsettling day they each were served with a subpoena in a divorce case involving a couple they had counseled. Jim had provided individual counseling to the husband, and Karen had done so for the wife. Jim and Karen were obligated to appear to give depositions, and they did not know what to anticipate. They were also very upset at the loss of income that would result from their being away from the office.*

Even the most seasoned mental health professional can be unnerved by interaction with the legal system, especially the first time. Undergraduate and graduate mental health programs seldom offer courses that acquaint students with American jurisprudence. This chapter gives an overview of the legal process for the uninformed or novice mental health professional.

*The most seasoned mental health professional can be unnerved by interaction with the legal system.*

To say that there are many courts in the United States is an understatement. We are truly a country of law, litigation, and conflict, and we have the courts to prove it. There are city (municipal) courts, county courts, state courts, federal courts, appellate courts, courts of very specialized jurisdiction (e.g., bankruptcy and admiralty), administrative law courts, civil courts, and criminal courts. The military has its own courts, as do Native Americans.

The number of civil lawsuits filed today is extraordinary. If you consider just divorces and the fact that 50 percent of all first marriages and a still greater percentage of second marriages end in divorce, you can see how great the possibility is for a mental health professional to be involved in a civil lawsuit.

## The Process in Civil Litigation

Civil lawsuits seek recovery or redress for some wrong done to, or harm suffered by, the person bringing the suit. The recovery of a monetary award is most often the goal.

### Step One: Filing a Petition

To initiate a civil lawsuit, a party must file a *petition* (or a *complaint* in some jurisdictions) in the appropriate court, setting out the identity of the parties, reason(s) that the court has jurisdiction over the parties and the dispute, subject matter and appropriate facts of the dispute, and relief or damages requested. Defective filings are subject to attack and can be stricken, or the filing party can be ordered to file an amended petition.

### Step Two: Service of Process

After the suit has been filed, the opposing party, commonly referred to as the *respondent* or *defendant,* must be given notice of the suit and allowed to respond. A process server is sent to serve the opposing party with a copy of the suit (in some jurisdictions, service can be accomplished by mail). Courts require proof of such notice before allowing the suit to go forward. An opposing party can waive this right to service and enter an appearance in the suit.

### Step Three: Answer

The opposing party is usually required to file an *answer* or response to the suit within a short time period after receiving notice. A failure to file the answer can result in a default judgment being entered. In the answer, the opposing party can set forth defenses to the suit and file counterclaims against the person or party that brought the suit. Any defects in the complaint are generally raised at this time.

## Step Four: Preliminary Motions

In some suits, a court may need to address some matters quickly, and hearings may be conducted very early on by the court. This procedure is common in family law cases where a court is asked to decide temporary custody of children or use and possession of the family residence. In other kinds of cases, the court may need to enter injunctions to preserve or protect property or the rights of a party. Injunctions generally maintain the status quo until a more detailed hearing can be arranged or until the final hearing or trial.

## Step Five: Discovery

After the suit and the litigants have been engaged, the parties can implement procedures to help them prepare for trial. The goal is to avoid "trial by ambush" by allowing each side to learn as much about the dispute as possible before going to trial. Such procedures include interrogatories, depositions, request for records, and admissions.

*Interrogatories* are written questions that can be propounded to a party as well as to third persons who are not parties to the suit. These questions must be answered fully under oath (notarized) within a prescribed time period. Often this kind of discovery tool is referred to as a *deposition by written interrogatory.*

*Depositions* usually involve live, person-to-person questions and answers that are recorded by a court reporter and sometimes also videotaped. Depositions occur outside the courtroom and are usually conducted in an attorney's office. Both sides have the right to ask questions of the witness either directly or through their attorney.

*Requests for records* require production for inspection and copying of records or documents in the possession of a person or subject to

*Interrogatories are written questions that can be propounded to a party as well as to third persons who are not parties to the suit.*

*Depositions are usually conducted in an attorney's office.*

*Attempts to secure computer records and computer drives are very common in a party's search for evidence.*

that person's control. These kinds of requests can also be used to compel the production and inspection of any tangible item, not just written documents. Today, attempts to secure computer records and computer drives are very common in a party's search for evidence.

*Admissions* are requests for a party to admit or deny certain facts. Admissions can be very useful in establishing important case facts without introducing other proof at trial. Often, admissions can limit the scope of the trial.

### Step Six: Alternative Dispute Resolution

*The goal of ADR is to resolve the suit without having to go through a trial.*

*Alternative dispute resolution* (ADR) can occur at any point in the proceedings, even before the filing of a lawsuit. America's style of litigation can be very expensive for the parties, government, and society as a whole; thus, alternatives have become increasingly more attractive. ADR includes techniques such as arbitration, mediation, moderated settlement conferences, conciliation, negotiation, and summary jury trials. The goal of ADR is to resolve the suit without having to go through a trial and perhaps years of appeals. If the matter can be resolved through ADR, the case is usually concluded with less cost and in less time. The lawyers and the court typically control litigation while through ADR techniques, the process and outcome of the dispute can be put in the parties' hands.

### Step Seven: Trial

If the parties are unable to reach a settlement of the contested issues in the lawsuit, a *trial* will take place. Americans have always safeguarded the fundamental right to have an independent tribunal resolve disputes between its citizens. Cases are tried before a judge (bench trial) or a jury (jury trial). Either way, a decision is made and a final judgment (sometimes referred to as *decree* or *court order*) is then entered by the court.

A complete civil jury trial consists of six main phases:

1. **Selecting a jury:** Prospective jurors are generally provided minimal case information and then questioned to determine their ability to be fair and unbiased in determining the case. Each side in the case is given an opportunity to challenge jurors for ineligibility or bias and has a limited number of "strikes" to eliminate jurors for any reason. At the end of the process, a jury is seated to decide the issues submitted to it by the judge in the case.

2. **Opening statements:** Attorneys or litigants are allowed to address the jury directly in an opening statement providing an overview of the evidence they expect to present to the jury and their theory of the case.

3. **Witness testimony and cross-examination:** The party initiating the lawsuit is allowed to present evidence first, which consists primarily of calling witnesses to testify. In direct examination, a party calls a witness and begins asking questions of the witness. The opposing party is then allowed to ask questions of the witness, called *cross-examination*. When the initiating party has called all of his or her witnesses, the responding party goes forward with presenting his or her witnesses for direct and cross-examination.

4. **Closing arguments:** After all witnesses and evidence have been presented, each side is allowed to talk directly to the jury to summarize the case and present reasons that the jury should rule in a party's favor.

5. **Jury instruction:** After the parties have concluded their closing arguments, the judge gives the jury instructions on the decisions it will make with respect to the case. These instructions include the selection of a foreman and decisions on facts and the law that must be applied to these facts in rendering the verdict.

6. **Jury deliberation and verdict:** Jurors are required to deliberate until a verdict is reached or the court declares a mistrial because of deadlock. Either way, the jury is brought back into the courtroom, and the results of its deliberations are announced to the judge, parties, and lawyers in the case. The jury is then discharged, and members are free to leave the courtroom and to

discuss their experience if they choose to with the parties and lawyers.

### Step Eight: Postjudgment Motions

If a party is not satisfied with the outcome of the trial, postjudgment motions may be filed. Such motions include motions for new trial, motions for judgment notwithstanding the verdict, and motions for reconsideration. After the court has heard and rendered its decision on these types of motions, the judgment becomes final and appealable.

### Step Nine: Appeal

After the case is concluded at the trial court level, a party may appeal the case to an appropriate appellate court. Appellate proceedings usually include submission of a transcript of the trial, written briefs from each party, and oral argument to the appellate court.

An appellate court may affirm or reverse the trial court's judgment, in whole or in part, and may send the case back to the trial court for rehearing. The decisions of the first level of state appellate courts may be appealed to the state's highest court and ultimately to the U.S. Supreme Court. The decisions of the first level of federal appellate courts may also be appealed to the U.S. Supreme Court. A litigant generally has a right to appeal a case to the first level of appellate courts. State supreme courts and the U.S. Supreme Court have discretion in determining many of the cases they decide to hear. After all appeals have been exhausted, the case truly becomes final and the judgment is subject to enforcement.

## The Process in a Criminal Case

A criminal case is brought by a governmental authority to establish whether a crime has been committed and, if so, what the appropriate punishment should be—imprisonment, assessment of fines, or both can be the result.

## Step One: Arrest

A criminal case typically begins when a police officer places a person under arrest. An *arrest* occurs when a person has been taken into police custody and is no longer free to leave or move about. A police officer may usually arrest a person if the officer observes a crime; has a reasonable belief, based on facts and circumstances, that a person has committed or is about to commit a crime; or when an arrest warrant has been issued. An *arrest warrant* is a legal document issued by a judge or magistrate, usually after a police officer has submitted a sworn statement that sets out the basis for the arrest.

## Step Two: Booking

After arrest, a criminal suspect is usually taken into police custody and *booked,* or *processed.* During booking, personal information is recorded about the suspect; the suspect is searched, photographed, and fingerprinted; a criminal background search of the suspect is conducted; and the suspect is placed in a holding cell or local jail. Except when very serious crimes are charged, a suspect usually can obtain pretrial release through bail or *own recognizance* (the suspect is released after promising, in writing, to appear in court for all upcoming proceedings).

## Step Three: Bail

If a criminal suspect is not released on his or her own recognizance or pretrial release, then release can occur only through the bail process. *Bail* is a process through which an arrested criminal suspect is allowed to pay money in exchange for his or her release from police custody, usually after booking. As a condition of release, the suspect promises to appear in court for all scheduled criminal proceedings—including the arraignment, preliminary hearing, pretrial motions hearings, and trial. The bail amount may be predetermined through a bail schedule, or the judge may set a monetary figure based on the crime's seriousness, the suspect's criminal record, the danger the suspect's release may pose to the community, and the suspect's ties to family, community, and employment.

## Step Four: Arraignment

*Arraignment* is the first stage of courtroom-based proceedings during which a person who is charged with a crime is called before a criminal court judge. The judge reads the criminal charge to the suspect (now called the *defendant*), asks the defendant if an attorney has been retained or if he or she needs the assistance of a court-appointed attorney, and asks how the defendant answers or *pleads* to charges ("guilty," "not guilty," or "no contest"). Next, the judge decides whether the defendant can be released on his or her own recognizance or what bail amount is appropriate. Last, the judge announces dates of future proceedings in the case.

## Step Five: Plea Bargain

*In a plea bargain, the defendant agrees to plead guilty in exchange for a more lenient sentence.*

The vast majority of criminal cases are resolved through a *plea bargain* usually well before the case reaches trial. In a plea bargain, the defendant agrees to plead guilty, usually to a lesser charge than one for which the defendant could stand trial, in exchange for a more lenient sentence and/or so that certain related charges are dismissed. For both the government and the defendant, the decision to enter into (or not enter into) a plea bargain may be based on the seriousness of the alleged crime, the strength of the evidence in the case, and the prospects of a guilty verdict at trial. Plea bargains are generally encouraged by the court system and have become something of a necessity because of overburdened criminal court calendars and overcrowded jails.

## Step Six: Preliminary Hearing

Usually held soon after arraignment, a *preliminary hearing* can be described as a "trial before the trial" at which the judge decides *not* whether the defendant is guilty or not guilty, but whether there is enough evidence to force the defendant to stand trial. In making this determination, the judge uses the probable cause legal standard, deciding whether the government has produced enough evidence to convince a reasonable jury that the defendant committed the crime(s) as charged. A preliminary hearing may not be held in every criminal case in which a not guilty plea is entered. Some states conduct preliminary hearings only when a felony is charged, and other states use a *grand jury indictment* process in which a designated group of citizens decides whether, based on the government's evidence, the case should proceed to trial.

### Step Seven: Pretrial Motions

*Pretrial motions* are presented after the preliminary hearing and before the case goes to trial. Such pretrial motions often involve evidentiary issues about the admission or exclusion of certain evidence. They are tools used by the government and the defense in an effort to set the boundaries for trial, should one take place.

### Step Eight: Trial

In a criminal trial, a jury examines the evidence to decide whether, beyond a reasonable doubt, the defendant committed the crime in question. A trial is the government's opportunity to argue its case, in the hope of obtaining a guilty verdict and a conviction of the defendant. A trial also represents the defense's opportunity to refute the government's evidence and to offer its own in some cases. After both sides have presented their arguments, the jury considers as a group whether to find the defendant guilty or not guilty of the crime(s) charged. (Note: Although a trial is the most high-profile phase of the criminal justice process, the vast majority of criminal cases are resolved well before trial—through guilty or no contest pleas, plea bargains, or dismissal of charges.)

*The vast majority of criminal cases are resolved well before trial.*

A criminal trial consists of the same six main phases as a civil jury trial described earlier:

1. Choosing a jury.
2. Opening statements.
3. Witness testimony and cross-examination.
4. Closing arguments.
5. Jury instruction.
6. Jury deliberation and verdict.

### Step Nine: Sentencing

After a person is convicted of a crime, whether through a guilty plea, plea bargain, or jury verdict, the appropriate legal punishment is determined at the *sentencing* phase. The punishment that may be imposed on a convicted criminal defendant includes fines, incarceration in jail (shorter term), incarceration in prison (longer term), probation, a suspended sentence (which takes effect if conditions such as probation are violated), payment of restitution to crime victims, and community service.

### Step Ten: Appeals

*Both a state governor and the president have pardon authority.*

An individual who has been convicted of a crime may *appeal* his or her case, asking a higher court to review certain aspects of the case for legal error as to either the conviction itself or the sentence imposed. The government does not have the right to appeal a not guilty jury verdict. As in civil cases, there is an absolute right to a first level of appeal, but there is greater access to state supreme courts and to the U.S. Supreme Court for many criminal cases, especially death penalty cases. Both a state governor and the president have pardon authority and can be considered a final appeal option for the defendant who is not successful in having a criminal conviction reversed by the courts.

### Step Eleven: Expungement

*Expungement* is a process through which the legal record of a criminal conviction is *sealed*, or erased in the eyes of the law, after the passage of a certain amount of time or the fulfillment of certain conditions.

After expungement, a criminal conviction (and in some cases even an arrest) ordinarily need not be disclosed by the person convicted, and no arrest or conviction shows up if a potential employer, educational institution, or government agency conducts a background search of an individual's public records.

## The Juvenile Case

Just as adult crime has increased, so has the misconduct of our youth. Juvenile courts are handling increasingly higher caseloads, and juvenile detention facilities are overcrowded. With the emphasis on rehabilitation and continued monitoring, it is not difficult to envision the extensive involvement by mental health professionals in juvenile cases.

### Step One: Referral

A case can arise when the police apprehend a minor for violating a statute, but more commonly it begins when a school official, parent, or guardian refers a problem with a juvenile to the court. In this context, school counselors often are the first to recognize the genesis of criminal potential. Often the school counselor recognizes inappropriate behavior before the parent is willing to admit there is a problem.

The court intake officer then evaluates the case, sometimes called a *juvenile delinquency* case, to determine whether further action is necessary, the child should be referred to a social service agency, or the case should be formally heard in juvenile court. If the situation is serious enough, the juvenile may be detained in a juvenile correction facility pending resolution of the matter or be sent to an alternative placement facility, such as a shelter, group home, or foster home. Juveniles do not have the option to pay bail or post a bond to obtain their release.

### Step Two: Proceedings Determination

An intake officer makes an initial determination as to whether formal proceedings are necessary. If the intake officer decides that a formal hearing in juvenile court is not necessary, arrangements may be made for assistance for the child from school counselors, mental health services, or other youth service agencies. The intake officer considers a number of factors in deciding whether informal proceedings are appropriate, including the seriousness of the alleged crimes, the minor's delinquency and social history, and the level of remorse expressed by the minor.

If the intake officer decides that the case should be heard in juvenile court, a petition is filed with the court setting forth the statutes that the child is alleged to have violated. This petition is the equivalent of a criminal complaint in the adult criminal justice process.

In cases of serious offenses, such as rape and murder, the matter may be referred to the district or county attorney's office, after which the juvenile may be charged as an adult, tried in the criminal courts, and even sentenced to an adult correctional facility. Each state has a statutory age when a juvenile may be charged or certified as an adult for criminal law purposes.

## Step Three: Hearing

If the matter proceeds to juvenile court and the child admits to the allegations in the petition, a treatment plan or program is ordered. If the child denies the allegations in the petition, a hearing like the criminal trial of an adult is held. At this hearing the child enjoys both the Sixth Amendment right to counsel and the Fifth Amendment privilege against self-incrimination. Rather than try the case to a jury, however, a judge hears the matter and decides whether the juvenile has committed the acts alleged in the petition. If the allegations have not been proven to the court's satisfaction, the judge dismisses the case. If the judge decides that the allegations have been proven, he or she may rule that the child is a *status offender*, a *child in need of supervision*, or a *juvenile delinquent*.

## Step Four: Disposition

If the judge determines that the juvenile is a status offender or a delinquent, a second juvenile court hearing is held to determine the disposition of the matter. If the juvenile is not considered to be dangerous to others, he or she may be placed on probation. While on probation, the juvenile must follow the rules established by the court and report regularly to his or her probation officer. Serious offenders, however, may be sent to a juvenile correction or detention facility.

Other disposition options include community treatment, such as making restitution to the victim or performing community service; residential treatment, in which a juvenile is sent to a group home or work camp, with a focus on rehabilitation; and nonresidential community treatment, in which the juvenile continues to live at home or at a group home but is provided with services from mental health clinics and other social service agencies.

## Answers to Frequently Asked Questions About:

Civil suit involvement

Criminal prosecution involvement

### ? Question

*I am a counselor in private practice. I have been providing therapy to a client who is contemplating filing a civil lawsuit seeking money damages for injuries she sustained when a coworker assaulted her. In addition, a criminal case is pending against her assailant. The client initiated therapy with me when she began having panic attacks after the assault. When could I reasonably expect to be involved in her civil suit, and can I be asked to play a role in the criminal case? Will I be reimbursed for my time?*

### ! Answer

The most likely point at which your involvement might be requested in the civil suit is during the discovery phase of the lawsuit. You may be asked to provide copies of your records, give written responses to a deposition by written interrogatories, or give an oral deposition. You might also be requested to testify concerning mental status, seriousness of psychological damage, extent of emotional injury, permanence of psychological trauma, or the nature and expense of treatment of all the foregoing. It is also possible that one of the parties may wish to call you as a live and participatory witness at the trial in the case. Your client should have signed an intake and consent form that obligates the client to pay you a reasonable fee for your time spent in responding to any requests for your testimony or records. If the lawyer promises to pay or reimburse you, obtain that agreement in writing, signed by the lawyer. The form or letter should also indicate *when* you can expect to receive payment.

In connection with the criminal case, it is possible that both the state and the defendant could seek your records before trial. You could also expect to be called at trial as a witness and later during the sentencing phase of the case if the defendant is found guilty.

In either case, be sure you have written client consent or a court order before providing any records or information pertaining to your client.

## Legal Lightbulb

- If your involvement in a lawsuit is anticipated, carefully review your client file to be sure it is in good condition. Review it for accuracy, completeness, and proper order. Make at least three copies.

- Lawsuits are generally open to the general public, and a poor or inaccurate client record not only will be scrutinized by the parties and lawyers in the case but also could be accessed by any interested person.

- The mental health professional has the duty to disclose information from a client file or about a client only when legally allowed or permitted to do so or when court ordered to make a disclosure.

- The massive amount of litigation occurring in this country creates ever-increasing risks for all citizens, not just mental health professionals, to be drawn into legal proceedings.

## Summary

The sheer number of courts and the volume of litigation in our country virtually ensures that a practicing mental health professional will be involved with some clients' legal proceedings at least once, if not many times, while actively engaged in practice and even into retirement. It is simply a risk as well as a cost of being a mental health professional. There is no substitute for knowledge and preparation to make the court case experience as easy on the mental health professional as possible.

# 2

# Involvement in the Judicial System

*Susan never wanted to be involved in the judicial system. In fact, she did not like lawyers at all. She had entered the mental health profession to help individuals solve their interpersonal and intimate problems.*

*About two years after Susan entered private practice, two clients whom she had counseled in couples therapy decided to divorce. When both asked her to testify on their behalf, she declined. She clearly relayed that she had no concern with anything other than offering helpful therapy.*

*Imagine her surprise a few days later when a process server appeared and handed her a subpoena, commanding her to appear at the local courthouse to testify in the trial of her two clients.*

*Susan was shocked, angry, and upset. She wanted to offer therapy, not testimony. She wanted to help her clients, not be a partisan witness in a bitterly contested divorce. She knew that if she were on the witness stand and compelled to answer intimate questions about herself and her clients, the two-year trusting relationship she had developed with them would be over and the positive effects of therapy would be lost.*

*Jerry, another mental health professional, loved the courtroom scene. For years he had voluntarily appeared as what lawyers call a "hired gun" therapist. He would review a file, and if he could in good conscience testify in a manner supportive to the lawyer and the lawyer's client, financial arrangements would be made and preparations would begin. Most of his appearances were in bitterly contested cases such as child custody cases.*

The preceding examples illustrate the two types of mental health professional witnesses who become involved in the legal system. Susan is the most common type: a *reluctant treating professional* who is involuntarily compelled to participate in a legal proceeding involving a client or former client by providing records or testimony. Jerry is the kind of mental health professional witness who is often referred to as a *forensic expert*, a mental health professional who provides evaluations and testimony for a fee specifically to assist a party or the court in a legal proceeding.

## The Volunteer

A small professional cadre of specialized mental health experts, like Jerry, enjoys treating or evaluating clients either in therapy or as part of an individual or assessment team and then acting as witnesses in legal proceedings for a fee. These experts have a body of focused knowledge about a particular subject not possessed by the ordinary layman, and the general purpose of their testimony is to enlighten or educate the judge or jury in areas that might be otherwise difficult to comprehend. The principal difference between the volunteer or professional paid expert and the layperson is that the layperson typically testifies only about facts or matters personally observed or experienced, without being compensated for his or her time, while the professional paid witness is allowed to testify as to opinions that are material to the resolution of the dispute. Paid professional witnesses are allowed to answer hypothetical questions. They are involved in the legal system because they choose to be involved full time or as an adjunct to their office practice. All or part of their professional work consists of testifying in court. By contract, they are paid for their consultative time; the time spent in going to court, parking, waiting and testifying, researching and examining, reviewing files and the pertinent literature; and any other relevant time they spend on a case. They make or supplement their living in and about the court system, and they stand ready, willing, and able to take the stand, testify, and subject themselves to cross-examination. To these specialists, being in court is not a problem. They have mastered the techniques; understand the role of the lawyers, judges, and juries; and know the process. After several years' experience, taking the witness stand is like anyone

*A reluctant treating professional is involuntarily compelled to participate in a legal proceeding involving a client or former client by providing records or testimony. A forensic expert provides evaluations and testimony for a fee.*

*The layperson typically testifies only about facts or matters personally observed or experienced, without being compensated. The professional paid witness is allowed to testify for a fee.*

else going to the office—it is just another way to make a living. These "experts" can tolerate the hostility and verbal abuse of opposing counsel. In a sense, it is all part of the gamesmanship of litigation. After all, the courtroom is partly an ethereal search for truth in the philosophical sense and part theater.

## The Battle of the Experts

Judges and lawyers are accustomed to the battle of the experts, where two competent and educated individuals examine the same set of facts and circumstances and arrive at differing opinions. For example, two engineers might examine a piece of metal; one testifies that the accident in question was caused by metal fatigue while the other says it was not. Or, two aviation experts might determine that a crash was caused by different malfunctions.

So it is with mental health experts. Competent experts can reasonably differ when considering "the best interest of a child," whether a particular symptom was *caused* by a particular traumatic incident, or just *why* an individual breaks out into a cold sweat whenever he or she is in an enclosed space.

## The Reluctant Witness

The reluctant or involuntary witness, such as Susan, is the helping professional (whether psychologist, pastoral counselor, social worker, marriage and family therapist, addictions specialist, psychiatrist, physician, professional counselor, or mental health clinician) who has treated an individual and, because of the personal or evolving situation of that individual, finds himself or herself the focus of inquiry concerning the statements made to the therapist or the diagnosis, treatment plan, or prognosis of the client. This service professional, who probably entered the profession to serve the public, finds that such service includes being involved in the legal system and is caught in the middle of processes and procedures that are important in the lives of others but are not part of the mental health treatment plan of the individual client. What's more disturbing is that, unless the clinician has a lawyer-drafted and enforceable contract, the clinician will probably not be paid for the time, toil, and trouble spent testifying.

This book is about both kinds of witnesses, the volunteer professional and the reluctant therapist caught in the legal net who finds that the judicial process is demanding services without notice, preparation, or compensation. There is no option. When all the demands of proper legal service and notice have been complied with, the clinician must cancel all appointments, put on the latest professional attire, and appear ready to be sworn and testify. A subpoena or subpoena duces tecum (see Chapter 9) cannot be ignored.

*The clinician will probably not be paid for the time, toil, and trouble spent testifying.*

## Answers to Frequently Asked Questions About:

Contract *not* to testify

Payment for testimony

Service of process

### ❓ Question

*Because I hate to go to court, I have all new clients sign a consent form by which they agree they will not call me as a witness and, if an "expert" is needed, they will engage another clinician.*

*I currently am treating a woman in therapy who has signed this contract. However, when her husband filed for divorce, his lawyer had a subpoena issued and served on me to appear for a deposition at his office.*

*1. Is my "contract not to testify" binding on her husband?*
*2. I did not sign anything when the subpoena was served. Do I have to appear?*
*3. If I must testify, can I get paid for my time?*
*4. Will I always have to worry about being involved in the legal system?*

### ❗ Answer

Yes, you will always have to worry about being involved in the legal system. Your contract not to testify might serve to resist a subpoena served by your own client who signed the contract, but you must honor the subpoena served by a person who is not a signatory to the contract. There is even some question concerning whether every judge will honor the therapist-client contract itself, especially if the court feels you have information vital to the case and the judge wants to hear it or wants the jury to hear it. Thus, you would appear as requested. And no, you will not necessarily be paid for your time. You are no more immune to being called to court than any other citizen who is a witness to an event and who possesses evidence desired by a party to the litigation. If subpoenaed, you must appear. You can, however, file a motion for a protective order or a motion to quash (covered elsewhere in this book), but if overruled, you must appear. Court appearances in response to a subpoena are a responsibility of citizenship.

A subpoena does not have to be signed for by the witness. Rather, the process server has to find you, identify you, and deliver or touch

## Legal Lightbulb

- No one is totally immune from the judicial system.

- No clinician or therapist can practice in a manner that guarantees that he or she will never have to testify in court.

- A rare exception is a criminal act case in which the therapist wishes to claim the Fifth Amendment against self-incrimination.

- Another vulnerability area arises when the clinician testifies and either, both, or all parties to the litigation feel the testimony was not fully competent or properly prepared and file a licensing board complaint.

- Reluctance to go to court can be alleviated by role playing and thorough trial preparation. (See later chapters in this book.)

- An expert can be engaged as an expert witness for agreed-on, fair compensation. But if a subpoena is served, compensation is rare. The time lost without compensation is part of the cost of doing business.

you with the papers. Then you are served. There is no receipt as such. The service is documented on a copy of the subpoena, and the copy is filed with the court papers. Usually a service stamp is placed on the copy and signed or initialed by the server, who then deposits the copy of the served papers with the court.

## Summary

There is no "anticourt" insurance or a contract that can forever guarantee that the clinician won't be required to enter the arena of litigation. One cost of the business of providing mental health services is the possibility of becoming involved in litigation.

The solution is to learn, through education and the help of this book, the theory and basic procedures of litigation and the role of the professional in the litigation process. This knowledge will help desensitize the mental health professional to the process, and when the court calls, panic will not ensue. An informed and educated mental health professional has nothing to fear—rather, almost nothing.

# 3

# Lawyers: Their Functions

*Clarissa is unhappily married. She has consulted a therapist for counseling. The therapist talks with her concerning her feelings and mind-set within the marriage, the limits or risks of therapy, and the postdivorce effects of termination of a long-term marriage. The therapist then offers her the names of three attorneys whom she can consult, not for immediate representation, but for an informational consultation. How can a lawyer help Clarissa?*

## The Lawyer's Function as Counselor

The lawyer, if consulted at this stage of the relationship, *serves as counselor as opposed to advocate.* At this time, Clarissa is not asking for spirited, aggressive, partisan representation but, rather, legal information that she can use to determine her future actions. The lawyer would inform Clarissa about local law concerning divorce, division of property, disposition of children (if minor, disabled, or handicapped children are involved), provisions of state law concerning child support and alimony (if permissible under state statute), division of property, and any tax issues or consequences.

As a result of the lawyer-client conference, Clarissa should have a better understanding of her legal rights and options. At this point, it is possible that no action would be taken. The conference would educate the client concerning the realities of divorce.

## The Lawyer's Function in Preparing for Divorce

Armed with information on legal rights and options, the therapist and client might alter their clinical approach when discussing the unhappy marriage, making changes either as to timing, current activities, or therapeutic modalities. A fresh approach to confrontation, conciliation, or conversation might be suggested. The emerging reality of the current and postmarital situation could dictate a new method of dealing with the family system. While the therapist would treat the developing anxieties, the lawyer would point out some of the methods of preparing for divorce:

- Acquiring a marketable skill.
- Completing education.
- Putting aside a nest egg, "just in case."
- Accumulating a wardrobe suitable for social life, work outside the home, or chosen activities.
- Learning and being involved in family finances and investments.
- Acquiring a loyal group of social friends who will survive the divorce, should that occur.
- Creating a marital as well as a postmarital budget of projected income and expenses.
- Putting together a balance sheet of the accumulated assets and liabilities of the marriage, including assets owned before marriage and assets acquired during the marriage and how they were acquired.
- Noting the future opportunities for capital growth in the form of income, dividends, stock options, or bonuses.
- Assembling the preceding information into a complete family financial profile.

The same lawyer may advise the spouse to:

- Become more involved with the children and their activities.
- Start playing a more active role in the church community.
- Take firm control of the family's finances or, alternatively, train the spouse to fully participate in all the phases of family income, expenses, planning, and investments.

- Eliminate as much debt as possible even if it means liquidating assets.
- Encourage and assist the spouse in securing outside employment.
- Negotiate with an employer to delay a bonus or promotion until a later date.
- Switch jobs or careers if previously strongly considered. (It is better to have support obligations determined with a lesser paying job that you are happy in than being stuck in a job you hate because court-ordered obligations make it impossible for you to earn less money.)

## The Lawyer's Function as Advocate

*The final function of the lawyer in a domestic conflict is to represent the client in divorce proceedings.*

The final function of the lawyer in a domestic conflict is to represent the client in divorce proceedings. This function is the true advocacy role.

A divorce can be obtained by litigation or settlement, using conciliation, mediation, arbitration, or any other method of ADR. Judges and most lawyers, supported by the mental health professions, have encouraged all methods of ADR as an alternative to litigation. If a settlement cannot be reached, the final function of the lawyer is representation as an advocate of the client's position and objectives.

When the goals and strategy have been agreed on, the role of the lawyer is to achieve these goals insofar as that is possible. If a therapist is involved and he or she can testify as an effective witness, the therapist is called on to take the stand and testify in the trial or to serve in a supportive role during the trial and posttrial.

*As the needs of the client vary, so do the services of concerned and involved professionals.*

As with Clarissa, the roles of the therapist and the lawyer have changed considerably since the first interview. As situations develop, both have to respond to the changing needs of the client. The therapist may change from family systems counselor to a postdivorce supportive role, while the lawyer changes from advisor and educator to courtroom advocate. As the needs of the client vary, so do the services of concerned and involved professionals.

## Role of the Lawyer in a Lawyer-Mental Health Professional Relationship

*Dr. Jamieson has managed a counseling clinic at a local university for six years and now has decided to open a private practice in a nearby city. He has a following, a group of supportive professionals who will serve as an initial referral source, and an impeccable reputation that will ensure his acceptance as a provider for various managed care networks and panels.*

*In the past, he has needed a lawyer only to draft and execute his will. Now that he is entering the businessworld of private practice, he will require these legal documents:*

1. **Lease:** If he leases office space or purchases a building, he will need a lawyer to negotiate the lease or purchase, making sure it meets his requirements, including privacy, security, freedom from noise and interruptions, free parking for clients, options to renew the lease at specified terms and rates, easy access for handicapped or disabled clients, and public transportation under some circumstances. The therapist will list the requirements, and the lawyer will ensure that these important factors are included in the lease or purchase agreement.

2. **Managed care contracts:** Managed care contracts are designed to limit the liability of the managed care company by shifting responsibility to the actual provider of mental health services. These contracts must be reviewed carefully by a lawyer who can negotiate out unacceptable clauses and insert other provider-friendly verbiage. Especially onerous are "hold harmless" clauses and phrases that provide that the managed care company is protected if the provider is sued, whether the managed care company is liable or not. Another problematic clause is one that requires the treatment provider to refer clients only to the managed care company or to another treatment provider on the company's panel. The tricks are too numerous to list; thus, an attorney must carefully review every contract presented to an individual provider.

*An attorney must carefully review every contract presented to an individual provider.*

*The quickest path to conflict is the oral agreement that may be misinterpreted.*

3. **Association form:** Most therapists associate with other professionals during their practice. This association can be *occasional*, where they rent an office near one another or where they share part-time or full-time employees or coworkers. Other therapists operate in a loose association of independent contractors. Many do not have formalized agreements—a prescription for disaster. If the therapist is going to have associates, each should have a lawyer-drafted agreement that specifies the rights, duties, and obligations of all parties. The quickest path to conflict is an oral agreement that may be misinterpreted or reinterpreted as circumstances change. Dr. Jamieson should have his lawyer draft an association form for signature by those who choose to enter the practice. Changes, if required or requested and agreed to, can always be made to the basic form.

*Every treating provider must have a lawyer-drafted form that indicates what the provider will provide and how the provider will be compensated.*

4. **Intake and consent to treatment form:** Every treating provider must have a lawyer-drafted form that indicates what the provider will provide and how the provider will be compensated. The licensing boards of the various disciplines indicate what constitutes informed consent. Every intake form should include the exceptions to confidentiality; a statement of the goals, techniques, and methods of treatment; names of persons providing services; supervision, if any; licenses under which a provider operates; obligation for payment for noncancellation of missed sessions; provisions for third-party payments; and various other requisites. In addition to intake forms, therapists must have HIPAA-required forms, release of information forms, waiver of confidentiality forms, and numerous other working and workable forms ready to be produced as needed. (See *Portable Lawyer*, second edition, for intake forms and Appendix B of this book for examples of forms.)

5. **Malpractice or professional liability insurance:** Every practicing professional should have malpractice or professional liability insurance. While policies issued by sponsoring national organizations are generally adequate, certain coverages can be purchased or inserted, such as reimbursement for an attorney's appearance before licensing boards; protection if involved in the alleged negligence of an associate, supervisee, or employee; or additional policy limits in

the event a client harms himself or herself or others. While there is usually little negotiating space, there is some. Make sure your lawyer has protected you in all the areas where you are vulnerable.

6. **Forensic form:** The initial intake and consent form may or may not contain consent to testify at a trial if the client becomes a litigant. The therapist should have a form ready in case the client ever becomes a litigant and requires the testimony of the mental health professional. If called into court, the therapist should be compensated for his or her time, and the only way to obligate a client to compensate a therapist is to see that the obligation is in writing and signed by the client. On intake, the client should sign a form that indicates that the client will compensate the therapist for time and expenses incurred in the client's lawsuit.

*On intake, the client should sign a form that indicates that the client will compensate the therapist for time and expenses incurred in the client's lawsuit.*

7. **Specialized forms:** Depending on the nature of the practice, other forms may have to be created—for example, forms for group therapy, family therapy, minors, very young children, addictions therapy, as well as inpatient and outpatient care. All of these specialized forms require the professional input of a lawyer who understands contract law as well as mental health law.

## Answers to Frequently Asked Questions About:

Referrals to attorneys

Always a choice of three or more

Cultivating a list of specialized attorneys

### ❓ Question

*My general psychological practice consists of some deeply troubled individuals, but most clients are people who are functioning adequately for the most part. Many just want to talk about their financial worries. They are nervous about inheritance expectations or retirement savings, and I feel that these clients need legal advice in addition to therapy. Is it appropriate for me to make a referral, and to whom?*

**❗ *Answer***

Lawyers as well as therapy theory differ on this answer. Thus, we can offer only our opinions.

We have had mental health professionals refer to us for years. The benefit of such a referral, especially if accompanied by the client's permission to consult, is that a client-serving, interdisciplinary team results.

Assemble lists of legal colleagues and make referrals to individuals whose personalities and legal methods will, in the opinion of the therapist, blend or be consistent with that of the client and the problem at hand. For example, if a client wants a mediated settlement in a divorce, the referral *should not* be made to a legal firebrand who takes every case to trial.

Always make referrals to at least three competent attorneys. They should have knowledge of the problem or specialty at hand and have malpractice or professional liability insurance. On occasion, it is helpful to call the lawyer to determine whether he or she is still in business, has a current license, takes new clients, and stands ready, willing,

## *Legal Lightbulb*

- Cooperation between helping professionals can often assist the client in choosing the best path to take in difficult financial, legal, and emotional situations.

- Therapists can make referrals to lawyers and vice versa. The person to whom a referral is made must be competent, licensed, and capable of providing the services the client needs.

- When making a professional referral, be sure the referral has malpractice or professional liability insurance.

- Every therapist should have a number of attorneys to whom he or she can make referrals. Referrals should be suited to the client by temperament, disposition, and competence. To make an informed selection, the client should interview several lawyers.

and able to serve the type of clients you want to refer. A call to the state bar association or the state licensing agency will confirm current licensure and reveal any complaints lodged against him or her.

Remind your clients that your list is a limited list of professionals. The client should interview prospects so that he or she can make an informed decision. The final choice and responsibility belongs to the client.

## Summary

The function and role of the lawyer changes depending on the situation. In a divorce, the beginning role may be one of educating both the therapist and the client. Then the role changes, and the consultant lawyer plans an approach to the impending divorce. Finally, if the termination of the marriage is accomplished by either mediation or litigation, the lawyer serves as advisor and advocate.

When the mental health professional requires legal input, a lawyer advises, prepares documents, negotiates on behalf of the clinician, and sees that the final documentation is legally sound. Whether a plaintiff, defendant, petitioner, respondent or complainant, witness, or prospective witness, the lawyer should be consulted for trial preparation and trial representation.

# 4

# The Expert Witness

*Jason had a checkered past before he became a psychologist: He was arrested at 18. He has now been retained to testify as an expert witness in a case, and the client's lawyer has asked him if there are any blemishes on his record. Jason told the lawyer about the arrest. When Jason testified in court, the attorney discussed the facts surrounding the arrest and had Jason explain how it was a life-altering experience that was directly responsible for his becoming a psychologist. The client was pleased with Jason's testimony and the outcome of the case. Had the attorney not been made aware of Jason's past and it had been brought out during cross-examination by the opposing counsel, Jason could have been discredited as an expert witness.*

There are numerous kinds of *expert witnesses*. For example, an auto mechanic with no degree but with a lifetime of experience repairing and restoring vehicles might qualify as an expert on automobiles manufactured before 2000. The judge allows him to qualify as an expert.

An MIT graduate with a PhD in aeronautical engineering and 10 years' experience examining jet airplanes and arranging for their repair might qualify as an expert in metal fatigue or some other aspect of metallurgy. The judge determines that her qualifications exceed that of the average layperson and believes that she will help him or the jury arrive at a fair and informed judgment.

A psychologist who has visited with families in family systems therapy, has published widely, has completed numerous home studies, and is used by child protective services as their mental health professional of choice when complex family issues are to be determined might qualify as an expert witness. The psychologist's education, his numerous books and articles, the seminars he has presented and attended, and his experience in the courtroom qualify him to testify concerning the best interest of the children in the case.

Although the expert might offer an opinion to the court, he or she is a witness only and does not make the final determination in any given case. The judge or jury, not the experts, make the final decision.

In general, for a person to qualify as an expert witness: (1) the subject matter must be beyond the knowledge of the average layperson, and (2) the witness must offer special knowledge or experience in a particular field so that his or her opinion will assist the judge or jury.

The expert's special knowledge endows him or her with the right to testify concerning hypothetical questions; that is, the expert can be asked to assume certain facts (usually facts in the case) and then can testify concerning his or her opinion based on these facts. The background of the witness can be helpful to the judge or jury even if the expert does not have firsthand knowledge of all the facts in the case.

*The judge or jury, not the experts, make the final decision.*

*For a person to qualify as an expert witness, the subject matter must be beyond the knowledge of the average layperson, and the witness must offer special knowledge or experience in a particular field so that his or her opinion will assist the judge or jury.*

## The Lay (Nonexpert) Witness

The lay or nonexpert witness observes an event and then testifies from the witness stand about that observation by recalling the facts that were observed. The lay witness cannot offer opinions, nor can the lay witness answer hypothetical questions. Rather, the lay witness can testify concerning only what he or she experienced through the senses. For example, the lay witness can testify that:

- He saw a person hitting a child, but not that it was child abuse.
- She knew that the mother never took the child to the doctor, but not that such a lack of attention was child abuse or neglect.
- Dad always took the children to football games, to PTA meetings, and to teacher conferences, but not that the best interest of the children would be served if they lived with their dad.
- Dad had an occasional drink and periodically came home wobbly, but not that the dad was an alcoholic.

*Conclusions as to abuse, neglect, the best interest of a child, addiction, or alcoholism are not in the domain of the layperson.*

In each of the preceding examples, the testimony of the nonexpert witness is limited to what was personally, physically observed or experienced. Conclusions as to abuse, neglect, the best interest of a child, addiction, or alcoholism are not in the domain of the layperson. The expert could draw conclusions and answer questions concerning those conclusions, while the nonexpert is limited to personal observations.

## Differing Roles of the Expert Witness

An expert mental health professional has many roles to play and can serve the legal and general community in numerous valuable positions. The expert witness can:

- Visit with the potential plaintiff, petitioner, defendant, respondent, witness, or complainant before trial and determine what kind of witness that person will make and the best manner to prepare that witness for trial (e.g., determine how the witness will stand up under examination and cross-examination and whether the potential recovery is worth the stress and strain of participating in the litigation process).
- Assist in pretrial selection of effective witnesses and prepare them for trial (i.e., eliminate those whose fear of the courtroom will render them ineffective witnesses even though they possess valuable information).
- Calm and prepare witnesses for effectiveness in the courtroom.
- Assist lawyers in picking a jury (i.e., help the lawyers select jurors who are most likely to be sympathetic to their case).
- Point out to attorneys mannerisms that might be annoying to the judge or jury and those that seem to be regarded favorably (e.g., screaming and shouting versus using a more moderated, modulated voice).
- Help the lawyer prepare the witness in vocabulary, demeanor, and manner of dress in the courtroom. (We once asked a client to wear a suit to court and the client complied. The jury later commented that the client looked as though he had stopped at a department store on the way to court, bought a suit off the rack, and stuffed himself into it.) Witnesses should dress appropriately and look natural.

- Offer to be available for posttrial debriefing so witnesses or litigants will not feel abandoned, and offer future support, therapy, or mental rehabilitation.

## What the Expert Can Expect When Taking the Stand

The expert witness must be prepared for two phases in the courtroom: examination and cross-examination.

### Examination

*Examination* is the friendly eliciting of information from a side's own witness. Generally, although the question and answer format is used, the questions are well known and customary and the lawyer asking the questions already knows the answers to all the questions. A well-known sequence of questions leads to the final, bottom-line question whereby the lawyer asks the expert witness if he or she has formed an opinion concerning the matter at hand. The witness answers "yes."

The lawyer then asks the expert to give that opinion, which the witness provides in short, concise, informative sentences. The lawyer next asks what led the witness to that opinion or conclusion. The witness states the rationale, justification, or grounds for the opinion. In theory, the rationale should be so solidly based that the case is made, subject only to the contradictory testimony of opposing counsel's expert witness.

The sequence of examination may vary from lawyer to lawyer, with each attorney acquiring a technique that is suitable to his or her own style of presentation. However, the mental health professional entering into the litigation field can expect to provide:

- Personal identification.
- The nature of his or her employment and the method or methods used when studying the subject that is the topic of this litigation. (*Note:* Testimony should emphasize that employment and payment are not in any way connected with the outcome of the case or the amount of damages that may or may not be recovered.)

*Examination is the friendly eliciting of information from a side's own witness.*

- Data and literature that support the witness's opinion and data and literature that might arrive at a different conclusion and how to distinguish between the two sets of information.
- Literature that substantiates the procedures used in this case as generally accepted in the mental health professional community. (*Note:* Gone are the days when testifying, "My 30 years' experience have led me to conclude that. . . ." is sufficient. Today, scientific basis is helpful, and empirical studies should be made available to the court.)
- Both the scientific and historic bases and background for tests used and relied on in reaching conclusions.

The witness should:

- Avoid technical terms, jargon, argot, and psychobabble.
- Explain technical terms in plain and simple language for the judge and jury.
- Stop talking after answering the questions and stating an opinion. Testimony is at the discretion of the judge and lawyers. (*Note:* Often the witness feels that with just a few more sentences, the matter could be explained. *Resist the temptation.* Lawyers' anecdotal conversations are filled with stories of witnesses who lost cases for their clients with that last irrelevant, inappropriate, voluntary, harmful remark. Let the lawyers do the asking.)
- Provide brief answers. It is the lawyer's responsibility to clear up or clarify ambiguities. Although it is *possible* to ask the lawyer for permission to explain further, it is rarely a good idea. Let the lawyer, who has law school and trial experience, decide whether to ask a particular question. (A good way to help the lawyer know what to ask is to deliver "ask me about" questions to him or her before examination begins. If the lawyer feels the information to be elicited will be in the best interest of the client, the question will be asked. For example, you might suggest to the lawyer: "Ask me about the bruise I observed on the child's arm after a visit with her mother on June 23.")

## Cross-Examination

*Cross-examination* is totally different from examination. It is usually hostile and unpleasant and can be brutal and vicious, especially if you have been an effective witness in favor of the lawyer's adversary. It is the duty of the cross-examining attorney to minimize you and any evidence you have offered that supports the opponent in the litigation. You can be attacked in the following ways:

*Cross-examination is usually hostile and unpleasant.*

- Your education and experience may be challenged.
- Your resume or vita will be reviewed with microscopic clarity, and errors will be highlighted. If there are any overstatements of experience or academic credentials, count on those being questioned in the most embarrassing manner possible.
- The lawyer may argue that you are taking a position that is inconsistent with previous public positions or testimony.
- Your negative credit history, criminal record, child support payments records, records of litigation, marital and legal history, and all matters of public record are fair game for cross-examining lawyers.

## Answers to Frequently Asked Questions About:

The expert in a child custody case

Collateral research in difficult areas

Reference to research

### ❓ Question

*I have been engaged to testify in a custody case involving several children. I have an opinion as to what would be in the best interest of the children, but a collateral issue involves the possible alcoholism and drug abuse of the father. This does not seem to be a problem when I talk to the father, neighbors, or children, but the mother insists he has a serious drinking and drug problem. While I feel confident in matters of family therapy, I feel a little less confident when it comes to matters of alcoholism and the misuse of controlled substances, although there are ample written materials that I feel*

*I could master and about which I could testify credibly. Can I do my home-work and then qualify as an expert?*

### ⚠ Answer

Yes, if you are thorough and persuasive. The expert is qualified on the basis of learning, training, education, and experience. Many professionals have limited personal experience in specific technical fields, but they have extensive research experience and have studied their subject extensively and in depth. Do a computer search and review the literature. Bring the literature with you to the courtroom and index it. Then be prepared to produce the references that support your position. Be prepared to supply copies of your research to the judge and opposing counsel. Education is not all in the classroom, it can be serious study and continuing education classes. The technical requirement is that the judge is convinced you are knowledgeable beyond that

## Legal Lightbulb

- Examination is the friendly eliciting of information from a side's own witness.

- Cross-examination is the often-hostile attempt of the opposing attorney to minimize your testimony.

- The expert must submit evidence of expertise to the judge.

- The judge determines whether or not the proffered expert is, in fact, an expert.

- If the judge determines the witness is an expert, the witness may: (1) offer opinion evidence and (2) answer hypothetical questions.

- Usually the judge's ruling regarding an expert cannot be appealed.

- Even if an expert offers an opinion, the judge and jury may disregard it.

- The "battle of the experts" is increasingly troublesome to juries and judges when considering mental health issues, such as competence and best interest of children.

- Final decisions are made by the judge or jury.

of the average layperson. If you have read widely and absorbed texts concerning the effects of alcoholism and drugs sufficiently to impress the court, the judge will allow you to testify. Whether you are credible or not depends on how you are received and perceived by the judge and the jury.

## Summary

The role of the expert witness is varied and exciting. In the beginning of a conflict, the forensic expert might be consulted to determine whether a case is worth pursuing, whether the parties are credible, and whether they can testify in a manner that will have persuasive power and weight. The expert can advise the lawyers, principals, and potential witnesses concerning the viability of the case. Later, if the case is filed, the expert witness can be a catalyst for settlement.

The expert is expected to be prepared, professional, and effective. The special knowledge that the expert brings before the court is helpful because it enables the court to understand difficult concepts and information that have taken the expert years to master. The expert helps the court to make an informed decision or judgment.

Posttrial, the forensic expert can help to either rehabilitate the client or make a referral to another therapist to further treat the client. From beginning to end, the expert's role is critical to courts, clients, lawyers, and the reputation of the mental health profession.

# PART II

# *TESTIMONY VERSUS THERAPY*

Most forensic therapists that we have encountered over the years did not enter graduate school with the intent to do forensic work. Rather, the goal was to become a helping mental health professional who would improve the human condition by providing quality therapy. Late in their graduate school education or soon after entering professional practice, these therapists became exposed to and intrigued by the legal system and the role they could play in that world as mental health professionals. Many were attracted by the financial opportunities forensic work presented.

They all reported, however, how different they found the legal system to be from the world of mental health treatment. Many were unprepared for their first experience—their baptism by fire—in a courtroom and the intense cross-examination they were subjected to. In the therapy room, clients rarely question the mental health professional, but in the courtroom, the therapist may be vigorously challenged by skeptical attorneys and judges about their qualifications, the evaluation performed, the treatment provided, and the opinions they attempt to offer.

Providing treatment and offering testimony are two vastly different roles filled by mental health professionals, and just because a therapist is good at one will not ensure success in the other.

# 5

# Therapist: Two Different Roles

*Susan has marital problems that she thinks affect her minor child. She does not want to consider or discuss a divorce at this time, but the thought of marriage dissolution is foreseeable.*

*If she and her husband seek marriage counseling, whom should they select? There are many suggested therapists with excellent credentials. If she and her husband try counseling but still ultimately seek a divorce and should custody be a bitterly contested issue, will the therapist stand ready, willing, and able to capably testify? Will the therapist be a credible, competent, and reliable witness if so requested? There is a profound difference between excellent therapy and excellent testimony.*

*Jim is a forensic psychologist. He is not interested in offering long- or short-term therapy and refuses to apply to managed care panels. Rather, he offers his services to lawyers who are in the process of selecting a jury and want the jury panel to consist of the potentially most favorable jurors. Just how will lawyers seek his services?*

## The Treating Therapist

The client who *might* require a mental health professional to testify in court should make this possibility clear during the initial interview. The clinician who *might be willing* to go to court should make his or her willingness known during the initial interview so that both are clear as to the expectations of the other. A client who assumes that he or she has made a favorable impression on a therapist and that the therapist would be willing to go to court should a dispute evolve into litigation will be distraught to discover at the last moment that the clinician who was so supportive during therapy sessions is terrified of the courtroom and is reluctant to take the witness stand.

The skills necessary to treat clients are very different from the skills necessary to testify competently, credibly, and believably in court. The compassionate therapist who guides the distraught client through life's traumas needs to be technically competent and knowledgeable in the area of mental health. This person must have some chemistry with the client, be able to listen and relate to the client's problems and circumstances as they unfold, and assist the client in dealing with these problems and circumstances. Often, in today's managed care environment, the treatment must be accomplished in a relatively short period of time.

The connection between the client and the therapist is one of a professional relationship. For the relationship to succeed, the client and provider must have a cooperative and respectful dialog, in which the situation of the client is clinically evaluated, an appropriate diagnosis is determined, and a treatment plan is established. When the treatment has reached the stage where the client's mental health is as good as it can be, treatment is terminated subject to the continuing future needs of the client. The door usually remains open for future treatment either by this therapist or a subsequent therapist if necessary. The client's file, with the permission of the client, can be made available to the new treatment provider. Indeed, professional standards require that each provider have in place a plan that provides for the continued confidentiality of the file in the event of the death, disability, or retirement of the client or the therapist.

## The Forensic Therapist

The forensic therapist specialist is a rather new concept in the field of mental health. The forensic therapist testifies in a legal proceeding, and his or her testimony is admissible as evidence in a court of law.

The forensic expert dedicates all or a good part of his or her practice to attending litigation proceedings and testifying for one side or another. The expert may or may not have a private practice and may or may not treat individuals or offer therapy.

A good forensic therapist will be a trained and licensed mental health professional who enjoys interacting with lawyers and judges and testifying in court. This professional will be a good communicator presenting well, both visually and orally, and will be unflappable when under fire from cross-examining lawyers. A forensic therapist may function in a background role assisting a lawyer with jury selection, evaluating evidence or witnesses, or play a primary role as a testifying expert favorably advancing a client's position in the lawsuit.

If the forensic therapist is to testify as a witness, this person must first be:

- Able to demonstrate specialized knowledge by learning, training, education, or experience that will allow a judge to qualify the person as an expert witness.
- Available in the sense that there will be no scheduling conflicts when the trial is set.
- Comfortable with the point of view desired by the client and the client's attorney and willing to testify effectively to that point.
- Willing to testify for a fee agreeable to the client.
- Ready, willing, and able to do the necessary research and to spend the time necessary to prepare thoroughly for trial.
- Available to the client's attorney for consultation if needed during trial preparation and the trial itself.

If the forensic therapist is to assist the lawyer with examination or cross-examination of witnesses or with evaluating witnesses, evidence, the judge, or the jury, then this person must:

- Be able to serve in a support capacity when needed by the lawyer as the case is being prepared for trial.

*The forensic therapist testifies in a legal proceeding, and his or her testimony is admissible as evidence in a court of law.*

- Suggest questions to be asked on examination and cross-examination of witnesses.
- Suggest which prospective jurors or seated jurors might or might not be favorable to the client or the client's case.
- Observe, while the lawyer is taking notes and preparing questions, activities taking place during the trial that might impact the client's case.
- Be available to help the lawyer during recesses and evenings during the trial to prepare for subsequent proceedings.

A lawyer will often select a forensic therapist by reputation by talking to other attorneys or judges to find out whom they would recommend on a particular issue or case. What will be of most importance to the lawyer is the therapist's professional qualifications and experience, how the judge or jury will view that person, whether or not favorable testimony can be expected, and what fees the therapist will charge. An attorney may interview several prospective forensic therapists before making a decision on whom to engage on behalf of the client.

## Answers to Frequently Asked Questions About:

Obligation to testify

Obligation to render an opinion

Methods of dealing with assertive clients

### ❓ Question

*I am treating a couple in therapy. They have one child and now have decided to seek a divorce. Each understood at the beginning of therapy that one risk of therapy is that a divorce might be the result. Each wants custody of the child, and both want me to testify on their behalf. Although I have been supportive in my remarks to both parents over their months in therapy and although I do have a "leaning," I do not have a clinical opinion concerning what would be in the best interest of the child. I know either or both of them may summon me to court. After being sworn, what should I say?*

## ! Answer

This answer is clear. You can emphasize to either counsel that both parents indicate they love the child and the ultimate decision is up to the judge or jury. Do not let either lawyer, your client, or the judge lead or badger you into stating conclusions you cannot clinically support. Tell them only what you know, not what you "feel." Make only statements you can back up with clinically supportive data. The forensic witness need not always have an opinion as to the ultimate issue in every case. Sometimes clients will try to threaten you into testifying favorably about them or for them. Be firm and offer only testimony that can be adequately supported by your own evaluation, observations, research, and corroborated collateral sources.

### Legal Lightbulb

- It is not necessary to testify about a conclusion or opinion you have not personally and clinically determined.

- If you do arrive at a conclusion, make sure it is substantiated by supporting data, a substantial body of professionally accepted literature, or empirical studies.

- There is no harm in indicating to the court that either parent would be competent, loving, and appropriate.

- It is not necessary to be critical from the witness stand. Resist the attorney's tendency to goad you into reaching inappropriate conclusions or making statements you prefer not to make.

- It is easy to state the parties' good points and weaknesses without evaluating or comparing the parents.

## Summary

The skills necessary to treat clients are very different from the skills necessary to testify competently, credibly, and believably in court. The treating therapist must be compassionate, technically competent, and knowledgeable in the area of mental health. The forensic therapist must have expertise in the relevant subject matter, be a presentable and effective communicator, and be able to stay calm and focused under trying circumstances. Above all else, this person must be likeable, believable, and persuasive.

The treating therapist's willingness to testify in court on behalf of the client should be discussed during the initial interview with the client. The forensic therapist, a rather new concept in the field of mental health, specializes in testifying in legal proceedings. Competency and effectiveness in offering therapy will not guarantee success when testifying in court.

# 6

## Ethics

Suzanne, a licensed psychologist, is working with a 10-year-old who had become withdrawn and depressed and had started wetting her bed at night. The girl's mother accused her ex-husband of abusing the girl during his visitation periods. During the course of several months, the girl's problems did not seem to improve and Suzanne became convinced something indeed was happening at her dad's. Although the child made no outcry about any abusive behaviors and had not said anything negative about her father, Suzanne urged the mother to pursue legal action. The mother filed suit to restrict the dad's access to the child and called Suzanne as a witness. Suzanne voluntarily and eagerly appeared in court. Suzanne was shredded on cross-examination, and the court dismissed the mother's suit. The judge sternly lectured the mother and advised her that she was fortunate that the court did not change custody in favor of the father. The girl's mother was livid after the trial and filed a complaint against Suzanne with the state board.

While working as a licensed counselor, Brad provided individual and marital counseling to a couple that attended his church. Brad had inter-action with the husband on occasion at church meetings and activities but tried to keep as much distance as possible between himself and the husband on those occasions. In spite of these efforts, the husband always perceived their interaction as very cordial and believed that he and Brad were friends. When the wife filed a suit for divorce, Brad was asked to appear in court on her behalf. Brad ended up disclosing observations and information that were unfavorable to the husband. After the case was concluded, with the *wife prevailing on all disputed issues, Brad continued to provide individual therapy to the wife. The husband eventually filed a complaint against Brad with the state licensing board.*

State licensing boards receive a significant number of complaints from disgruntled litigants complaining about mental health professionals who have testified in their lawsuits. If lawsuits are lost from a litigants' perspective, they often refuse to place blame where it usually belongs—on themselves or the weakness of their case or position. Clients look for a reason to blame the testifying therapist. Judges, except for misconduct, cannot be sanctioned. It is difficult to pursue attorneys, but mental health professionals are sitting ducks. The ease with which a client can file a licensing board complaint is disconcerting. This chapter discusses some of the more common ethical issues that can confront a mental health professional when testifying in court.

## Informed Consent

*Mental health professionals are bound to advise clients of the possibility of disclosure to third parties of the information provided during the treatment and evaluation process.*

Mental health professionals are bound to advise clients of the possibility of disclosure to third parties of the information provided during the treatment process. Even mental health professionals who are hired as experts to provide evaluation and courtroom testimony must advise the evaluee of the potential for disclosure of confidential information. Failure to advise constitutes a breach of the mental health professional's ethical obligation to the client or evaluee.

As discussed in earlier chapters, all exceptions to confidentiality and the limitations on confidentiality should be provided to a client in writing, and the client should be given an opportunity to discuss this information with the therapist. The *Code of Ethics of the National Association of Social Workers* (approved by the 1996 NASW Delegate Assembly and revised by the 1999 NASW Delegate Assembly) contains the following section:

> 1.07 Privacy and Confidentiality (e) Social workers should discuss with clients and other interested parties the nature of confidentiality and limitations of clients' right to confidentiality. Social workers should review with clients, circumstances where confidential information may be requested and where disclosure of confidential information may be legally required. This discussion should

occur as soon as possible in the social worker-client relationship and as needed throughout the course of the relationship.

Although clients or evaluees are properly advised of all potential disclosures and this fact is documented in writing, they may not like the fact that the mental health professional testifies and provides unfavorable information in a lawsuit. However, if they have been fully informed in writing, they will not be able to prevail on a complaint alleging failure to secure informed consent. If you do not advise the client that you could be compelled to provide intimate and confidential testimony that would be harmful to the client, you can be assured that the client will do whatever he or she can to cause you harm when the case is concluded.

## Breach of Confidentiality

There are very limited circumstances that will allow a mental health professional to disclose confidential information to third parties (see Chapters 7 and 10). Licensing acts and ethical canons prohibit improper disclosures of a client's mental health information, including the fact that the client is a client and a recipient of mental health services. The American Psychological Association's *Ethical Principles of Psychologists and Code of Conduct* (2002) contains this disclosures clause:

> 4. *Privacy and Confidentiality* 4.05 Disclosures
> (b) Psychologists disclose confidential information without the consent of the individual only as mandated by law, or where permitted by law for a valid purpose such as to (1) provide needed professional services; (2) obtain appropriate professional consultations; (3) protect the client/patient, psychologist, or others from harm; or (4) obtain payment for services from a client/patient, in which instance disclosure is limited to the minimum that is necessary to achieve the purpose.

If a mental health professional wrongfully assumes that a legal basis exists for disclosing a client's protected health information, he or she will have committed an ethical violation. We have been involved in or been consulted in several cases where information was provided to the client's attorney who requested records or issued a subpoena. Client consent or a court order should ordinarily be obtained even if it is the client's own attorney requesting the information. Do not assume that the attorney representing the client has the client's consent. When any doubt exists, get legal advice from your own attorney prior to disclosure.

## Avoiding Harm

Mental health professionals enter into the profession with the desire to help people and to improve their functioning and lives. Harming a client is totally contradictory to this goal and violates ethical canons. The American Psychological Association's *Ethical Principles of Psychologists and Code of Conduct* (2002) provides the following clause:

> 3.04 Avoiding Harm
>
> Psychologists take reasonable steps to avoid harming their clients/patients, students, supervisees, research participants, organizational clients, and others with whom they work, and to minimize harm where it is foreseeable and unavoidable.

*If mental health professionals know that their testimony will be harmful to a client, an effort should be made to block the disclosure.*

To sit in a courtroom and listen to a trusted mental health professional reveal intimate and personal details about himself or herself can be devastating for a client. Clients' lives, reputations, and liberty can be severely impacted by what a mental health professional knows and reveals. If mental health professionals know that their testimony will be harmful to a client, an effort should be made to block the disclosure.

The *Code of Ethics of the National Association of Social Workers* (approved by the 1996 NASW Delegate Assembly and revised by the 1999 NASW Delegate Assembly) contains this clause on blocking disclosures:

> Ethical Standards
>
> (j) Social workers should protect the confidentiality of clients during legal proceedings to the extent permitted by law. When a court of law or other legally authorized body orders social workers to disclose confidential or privileged information without a client's consent and such disclosure could cause harm to the client, social workers should request that the court withdraw the order or limit the order as narrowly as possible or maintain the records under seal, unavailable for public inspection.

It may be appropriate to work with the client's attorney or for the mental health professional to hire his or her own lawyer to move the court for a protective order to prevent any information from being disclosed or to at least limit the disclosure as much as possible. Mental health professionals must do all that is legally and ethically within their power to avoid harming clients. Failure to do so can lead to an ethical violation and sanctioning.

## Conflict of Interest/Dual Roles

When a treating therapist participates in a client's legal proceeding, a potential conflict of interest arises and the therapist operates in a dual role. The roles of helping professional and testifying witness will have very different outcomes and may be diametrically opposed to each other. Ethical canons universally prohibit dual relationships unless they cannot be avoided.

*Ethical canons universally prohibit dual relationships unless they cannot be avoided.*

The American Counseling Association's *Code of Ethics* (1995) offers this advice on dual relationships:

> A.6. Dual Relationships: Avoid when possible. Counselors are aware of their influential positions with respect to clients, and they avoid exploiting the trust and dependency of clients. Counselors make every effort to avoid dual relationships with clients that could impair professional judgment or increase the risk of harm to clients. (Examples of such relationships include, but are not limited to, familial, social, financial, business, or close personal relationships with clients.) When a dual relationship cannot be avoided, counselors take appropriate professional precautions such as informed consent, consultation, supervision, and documentation to ensure that judgment is not impaired and no exploitation occurs.

The *Code of Ethics of the National Association of Social Workers* (approved by the 1996 NASW Delegate Assembly and revised by the 1999 NASW Delegate Assembly) contains the following clauses about conflicts of interest:

> (a) Social workers should be alert to and avoid conflicts of interest that interfere with the exercise of professional discretion and impartial judgment. Social workers should inform clients when a real or potential conflict of interest arises and take reasonable steps to resolve the issue in a manner that makes the clients' interests primary and protects clients' interests to the greatest extent possible. In some cases, protecting clients' interests may require termination of the professional relationship with proper referral of the client . . .

> (c) Social workers should not engage in dual or multiple relationships with clients or former clients in which there is a risk of exploitation or potential

harm to the client. In instances when dual or multiple relationships are unavoidable, social workers should take steps to protect clients and are responsible for setting clear, appropriate, and culturally sensitive boundaries. (Dual or multiple relationships occur when social workers relate to clients in more than one relationship, whether professional, social, or business. Dual or multiple relationships can occur simultaneously or consecutively.)

Avoiding participation in a client's lawsuit and disclosing confidential information may not, in the long run, be possible. A mental health professional must then address whether he or she as the testifying expert can continue in the role as treating therapist. The client must be advised that continuation in the treating professional role may not be possible after testimony is given. The client should also be made fully aware of any negative information the therapist may have to disclose. If the client then pursues obtaining the testimony of the treating professional, he or she will have little chance of proving an ethical violation after the lawsuit is concluded, win or lose. Clients must be informed fully that while they can, to some extent, control what is asked of a witness by their own counsel, clients cannot control the questions asked by opposing counsel.

Recall the situation of Brad, the church counselor who provided marital therapy to a couple. When Brad voluntarily agreed to appear and testify for the wife, he found himself taking action that harmed the husband. Brad did not discuss with the husband the potentially harmful information that was going to be disclosed. When the trial was concluded, Brad continued to provide individual therapy to the wife, an act the husband could have perceived as a further betrayal. When the trial was announced, Brad should have declined to testify and should have discontinued all therapy with this couple and made appropriate referrals.

## Lack of Competence

Mental health professionals should not exceed their level of competence when services are being provided. The American Psychological Association's *Ethical Principles of Psychologists and Code of Conduct* (2002) provides this section on competence:

2. <u>Competence</u> 2.01 Boundaries of Competence

(a) Psychologists provide services, teach, and conduct research with populations and in areas only within the boundaries of their competence, based on their education, training, supervised experience, consultation, study, or professional experience.

The American Counseling Association's *Code of Ethics* (1995) contains:

C.2. Professional Competence. A. Boundaries of Competence. Counselors practice only within the boundaries of their competence, based on their education, training, supervised experience, state and national professional credentials, and appropriate professional experience. Counselors will demonstrate a commitment to gain knowledge, personal awareness, sensitivity, and skills pertinent to working with a diverse client population.

The *Code of Ethics of the National Association of Social Workers* (approved by the 1996 NASW Delegate Assembly and revised by the 1999 NASW Delegate Assembly) also includes advice on competence:

1.04 Competence (a) Social workers should provide services and represent themselves as competent only within the boundaries of their education, training, license, certification, consultation received, supervised experience, or other relevant professional experience.

If the mental health professional does not have the training and experience necessary for a case, treatment should not be provided and the client should be referred to a competent therapist. Voluntarily testifying in a lawsuit about treatment that a therapist is not competent to provide and rendering opinions the therapist is not competent to offer only compound the problem. Suzanne, the psychologist in the first example at the beginning of the chapter, did not have the experience necessary to competently treat the child, and her inexperience and lack of training were made obvious to the court. It is not difficult to understand why the mother became angry with Suzanne after the lawsuit was finalized. Clients often become angry when their expectations, even if unreasonable, are not fulfilled.

It is clearly an ethical violation for mental health professionals to exceed their level of competence in whatever service they provide to their clients, including courtroom testimony. Mental health professionals who are not comfortable testifying in court and do not

*Clients often become angry when their expectations, even if unreasonable, are not fulfilled.*

perform well under pressure should not volunteer to participate in a client's lawsuit. If the mental health professional does volunteer, the client is entitled to competent, effective testimony.

Mental health professionals have gotten into trouble for offering opinions for which they had an inadequate basis. In essence, they offered opinions they were not competent to render or that had no basis in either fact or the literature. Consider the following provisions from the American Psychological Association's *Ethical Principles of Psychologists and Code of Conduct* (2002):

9. Assessment. 9.01 Bases for Assessments

(a) Psychologists base the opinions contained in their recommendations, reports, and diagnostic or evaluative statements, including forensic testimony, on information and techniques sufficient to substantiate their findings.

(b) Except as noted in 9.01c, psychologists provide opinions of the psychological characteristics of individuals only after they have conducted an examination of the individuals adequate to support their statements or conclusions. When, despite reasonable efforts, such an examination is not practical, psychologists document the efforts they made and the result of those efforts, clarify the probable impact of their limited information on the reliability and validity of their opinions, and appropriately limit the nature and extent of their conclusions or recommendations.

(c) When psychologists conduct a record review or provide consultation or supervision and an individual examination is not warranted or necessary for the opinion, psychologists explain this and the sources of information on which they based their conclusions and recommendations.

*The mental health professional should carefully consider any opinion expressed, and when there is an inadequate basis to support the opinion, it should not be given.*

The mental health professional should carefully consider any opinion expressed, and when there is an inadequate basis to support the opinion, it should not be given. For example, if a mental health professional is asked to state whether a mother should be awarded the exclusive right to establish the child's primary residence and the father has never been evaluated or even spoken to, it is inappropriate to give an opinion on this issue. A court may press the mental health professional for an opinion. Under those circumstances, the opinion should be qualified. The therapist may respond by saying, "Your Honor, I have not had an opportunity to evaluate the father or even speak to him. However, if you want an opinion, I will say that if everything the mother has told me about the father is true, and I have set forth her allegations in my report and testimony, then under those circumstances, I would have to conclude that the mother should be awarded the exclusive right to establish the child's residence."

## Loss of Objectivity or Impartial Judgment

Mental health professionals are required to avoid situations or relationships with clients that negatively impact on their professional decision making and judgment. The *Code of Ethics of the National Association of Social Workers* (approved by the 1996 NASW Delegate Assembly and revised by the 1999 NASW Delegate Assembly) contains the following provision:

> 1.06 Conflicts of Interest. (a) Social workers should be alert to and avoid conflicts of interest that interfere with the exercise of professional discretion and impartial judgment. Social workers should inform clients when a real or potential conflict of interest arises and take reasonable steps to resolve the issue in a manner that makes the clients' interests primary and protects clients' interests to the greatest extent possible. In some cases, protecting clients' interests may require termination of the professional relationship with proper referral of the client.

In many cases, therapists act unprofessionally when they lose their objectivity. This situation seems to occur more frequently with mental health professionals who work with children. They sometimes perceive themselves as child advocates and lose their ability to be objective. A lack of objectivity can cause the mental health professional to render an opinion for which there is not sufficient support or information. Lack of objectivity has also caused mental health professionals to be difficult when asked to provide records and reports to parents or other third parties who were legally entitled to the information. Clients, courts, and attorneys have a right to review files and progress notes when the proper request is made. The mental health professional who refuses to furnish a copy of the records does so at his or her own peril.

*Lack of objectivity can cause the mental health professional to render an opinion for which there is not sufficient support or information.*

It is helpful to stay focused on the primary mission, which is to provide quality and competent treatment to the client. Worrying about the outcome of the client's lawsuit should be secondary to the mental health professional's treatment responsibilities.

*Answers to Frequently Asked Questions About:*

Confidentiality

Conflict of interest

Courtroom testimony

### ❓ *Question*

*Last spring I saw a husband and wife for marital counseling. During our joint sessions and later during individual sessions, the parties described the incident that prompted them to seek counseling. There were two sides to the story, but they agreed that the wife hit the husband several times with a baseball bat and then threatened to smash in the windows on his car. The husband responded by pointing a handgun at the wife and threatening to kill her if she hit the car. He later claimed to have known that the gun was not loaded, but his wife insists that the gun was loaded and that he fired one shot into the air. The parties are now in the midst of a divorce case. I recently received a subpoena from the wife's attorney to appear at their trial next week. I called the wife's attorney and advised him that I thought my testimony could be just as harmful to the wife as to the husband. I shared with him matters the wife had revealed to me but refused to tell him anything that I had been told by the husband. The wife's attorney still wants me to testify about what I know about the gun incident.*

*I really don't want to testify. Our center's intake form (which both clients signed) contains a provision that the marital therapist will not be called by either participant as a witness in any legal proceedings between the participants. Is this form enough to get me out of testifying? I have an appointment for individual therapy with the wife scheduled for the week after the trial. Is there any reason I should not continue providing individual therapy to her?*

### ❗ *Answer*

First, you did not indicate if you obtained consent from the wife to share information with her attorney. You should never assume that just because a subpoena is issued by the client's attorney the client is aware the subpoena was issued. You should always secure client consent to share confidential information, even with his or her attorney. Even though you did not reveal anything the husband told you to the attorney, if you made remarks that confirmed or identified the husband as a client, you may have breached confidentiality. Before you reveal any more information, you should attempt to secure the written consent of both the husband and the wife. If you are unable to do so, you should wait until you are court ordered to answer any question that requires disclosure of protected health information.

The contractual agreement you have with this couple not to call you as a witness in any legal proceedings *can* serve as a basis for a motion for protective order. You may wish to consult an attorney to file such a motion and have the court rule on it prior to your scheduled court appearance. If you do not have the time or the ability to do this, you can certainly call it to the court's attention when you are called to the witness stand. Bring a copy of the contract to the court and have it available. Orally move the court to release you from the subpoena based on the parties' contractual agreement. It is possible the court will let you leave without disclosing any protected health information. If not, the court will order you to testify; then you will have the legal basis you need to disclose confidential information about the parties.

You should not continue to provide individual services to the wife. Doing so will have the potential to inflame the husband, who was also your client, and there is no way to predict what may result from your testimony. You have an obligation not to take action that can be harmful to a client if you can reasonably avoid doing so. Treating the wife under these circumstances could be harmful to the husband. The fact that you are scheduled to continue treating the wife posttrial is an area the husband's lawyer may use to try to discredit your testimony or show bias toward the wife if your testimony is perceived to be adverse to the husband. There is no reason to give the lawyer this opportunity. We can think of no compelling reason for you to continue to provide services to the wife. It would be best if you contact the wife before your scheduled court appearance and advise her that under these circumstances she should pursue individual counseling with another therapist.

## Legal Lightbulb

- Decide early on your response if litigation does come to pass for a client, and let the client know what you will do or won't do.

- Deciding to continue with just one of the participants in individual therapy could be emotionally upsetting and, therefore, harmful to the other participant you will not be treating.

- Contractual provisions whereby clients agree not to call the therapist as a witness in their lawsuits give the therapist a basis for a motion for a protective order. Depending on case issues, the court may still require testimony.

- The duty to avoid conflicts and harm to clients makes it difficult in many cases to continue providing therapy to clients once the mental health professional testifies in the client's lawsuit.

- Mental health professionals must never exceed their level of competence when providing mental health services, including forensic work.

- When the mental health professional voluntarily participates in a client's lawsuit, the client has the right to expect professional and competent testimony.

- Losing objectivity makes the mental health professional vulnerable to rendering opinions for which there is insufficient basis and support.

- It is essential and ethically and legally appropriate for every therapist to enter into the courtroom fully prepared for trial.

## Summary

Very few lawsuits end with both sides feeling like winners. Often they are "winner take all" cases, and the losing party is very upset at the loss and the time and expense incurred in obtaining an unsatisfactory result. Because lawyers, judges, and jurors are not easily punished for any perceived mistakes, the mental health professional bears the brunt of the losing client's fury. State licensing boards field large numbers of complaints from disgruntled litigants. The majority of these complaints do not have merit, but many times they do present an ethical violation. Until the mental health professional has acquired extensive experience with the legal system, he or she should approach each request or subpoena as the very first received and assume nothing. The first order of business should be to secure independent and competent legal advice before responding in any way. An ethical violation can put the mental health professional out of business and must be avoided. A call to your lawyer, a learned colleague, or your malpractice insurance carrier might prevent a mistake and save a career and a license.

# 7

# Confidentiality

When Jane first went to counseling, she was a little reticent to tell her "whole" story. She held back until it was obvious that progress could not be made unless she made a full disclosure of everything bothering her. She spoke about her parents, her husband, her neighbors, and all the other assorted contacts she felt had injured her psychologically. She also spoke about how, after years of love, attention, and affection, she had an agonizing and serious falling out with her wealthy grandmother when the grandmother had become complaining, remote, and was focusing her attention on a distant niece.

After about a year of therapy, the treatment was successfully terminated. Jane felt better having talked about her relationships and having them all put in perspective.

After the grandmother died some three years later and the will was probated, she was astounded to discover that her name was conspicuously omitted. Jane filed a will contest alleging fraud and undue influence when the old will was revoked and the new will, omitting her, executed. She testified, under oath, that she was a loving grandchild and the entire grandmother-grandchild relationship was always mutually supportive and loving. She admitted she had been to a counselor and had to, under oath, disclose the identity of the therapist. Conveniently, she forgot the part of the therapy that concerned the differences she had with her grandmother that might have given the grandmother grounds or reason to omit her from the will. Inconveniently, the counselor had recorded the differences in the session notes because they were germane to the therapy.

*The session notes and the clinical file were presumably relevant to the grandmother's state of mind and motivation in changing the will. Jane's session notes were subpoenaed, and the deposition of the counselor became part of the court record. The notes totally discredited Jane's testimony about her relationship with her grandmother.*

*Were the notes confidential?*

## Confidentiality between Therapist and Client

Confidentiality does exist between therapist and client. Every mental health ethical code and many state statutes provide that what is said to a counselor is sacred, not to be repeated. However, all clients must be informed (as part of informed consent to treatment) that certain exceptions and limitations exist. Clients are entitled to be informed of *all* exceptions to confidentiality at or before the time treatment begins so that they can select *what to reveal* and *what not to reveal* in therapy sessions. A client can never complain that the exceptions and limitations to confidentiality were unknown if they are printed in a document signed by the client.

*A client can never complain that the exceptions and limitations to confidentiality were unknown if they are printed in a document signed by the client.*

## Exceptions to Confidentiality

Certain exceptions to confidentiality are almost universally consistent but vary from state to state in the vocabulary used to describe them. It is important to check with a local lawyer to determine if the point at issue is confidential and not subject to disclosure in your area. Exceptions to confidentiality include, but are not limited to:

1. **Child abuse:** All states have child abuse reporting statutes. Whenever abuse is suspected or indicated, the therapist must report to appropriate authorities. When a child abuse report is made, the person making the report in good faith is immune from civil and criminal penalties.
2. **Elder abuse, abuse of the disabled:** Statutes have been passed in most states to protect the elderly (sometimes defined as over 65), the infirm, and the legally disabled. Observed or suspected

*Check with a local lawyer to determine if the point at issue is confidential and not subject to disclosure in your area.*

abuse or neglect of these individuals must be reported. There are both criminal sanctions and civil liability for failure to report.

3. **Consent in writing:** Consent in writing is the most common exception to confidentiality between client and therapist. Once the client consents to the release of information from the clinical file, the consent becomes part of the file and the provider may release such documents and information as are authorized in the release.

4. **Office staff, secretaries, and legal assistants:** It is not a breach of confidentiality that files are perused by accountants when billing, by lawyers should litigation be instigated, and by research personnel or others who are part of the therapeutic or legal team. Only the minimum amount of confidential information necessary for these individuals to fulfill their duties or functions should be shared. If these service providers are not employees of the mental health professional, the HIPAA Privacy Rule requires that a business associate contract be executed (see *Portable Lawyer*, second edition).

5. **Duty to warn:** Most states either by common law and case precedents or by statute mandate a duty to warn an identifiable, intended victim of a possible imminent threat of harm as well as law enforcement personnel. Even the few states that do not impose a mandatory duty to warn the identified victim require or permit a mental health professional to contact medical or law enforcement personnel. It is important that providers know the local state guidelines as soon as they begin practice, and it is equally important to stay current as time passes.

6. **Mental health or condition:** Whenever the mental health or condition of a client is an issue in a legal proceeding, the client's file and confidential information are subject to disclosure, for example, will contests, competency hearings in criminal cases, and civil suits seeking recovery for emotional damages.

7. **Parent-child relationship:** If custody or visitation of children becomes contested, the clinical notes and testimony of the mental health professional treating the parents or the child can be subpoenaed into court.

8. **School counselors:** Under the education codes of many states, school counselors have the right to breach absolute confidentiality under restricted circumstances on a "need to know" basis. Thus, school counselors can inform teachers if children in their class need special attention or care, and they can inform the school principal or nurse if there are conditions that would indicate that the nurse or the principal should be informed about matters that concern the general welfare of the school. Likewise, where there is a danger to the child or others, parents are entitled to be informed and brought up to date about happenings in the school, and documentation should be entered in the record indicating who was informed and about what.

9. **Criminal cases and investigations:** Law enforcement officials have a right to inquire about clients of therapists as part of their investigation. When a crime is being investigated, every citizen, including therapists, is legally bound to cooperate with investigating officers.

10. **Group and couples or family therapy:** Participants in group, couples, or family therapy cannot be guaranteed confidentiality. The facilitator can guarantee that the facilitator will not waive or breach confidentiality and can insist that group members sign a confidentiality pledge, but a group leader cannot guarantee that every member of the group will be honorable and not repeat what was revealed in the group setting. To achieve some assurance that conversations will remain confidential, it is best to have a confidentiality pledge backed by a hold harmless agreement that makes the participants personally liable if they breach confidentiality.

11. **Subpoena and response to a subpoena:** Once litigation has begun, subpoenas are sure to follow. It is possible to resist a subpoena by means of legal tools such as motions to quash or dismiss, motions to suppress, motions for protective orders, or other motions depending on the jurisdiction, but should all these defensive motions fail and should the judge order the clinician to testify, the clinician must testify.

12. **Malpractice suits and complaints before the licensing board:** When a client sues a mental health professional, files a complaint against the therapist with the licensing board, or files a complaint with a national organization, the client waives confidentiality. After all, how can the professional defend himself or herself or prepare an adequate defense if the documentation in the file cannot be used in a trial or hearing? Clients need to be told prior to beginning therapy that should the client file a suit against the therapist or lodge a complaint with a licensing board, the file is no longer confidential.

13. **Confidentiality survives death:** Every mental health professional must have a death or disability plan in place. This plan includes providing for the continued confidentiality, preservation, and maintenance of the clinical file of each client. The ethical standards provide for the number of years (usually from 5 to 10 years after the last treatment or from 5 to 10 years after a child reaches legal majority if the client was a minor) the files must be secured and preserved. In the event of the death of the client, the confidentiality of the file remains. The contents can be disclosed only to the legally appointed representative of the deceased.

## Answers to Frequently Asked Questions About:

Confidentiality

Exceptions and limitations

Oral explanations

Understanding of the average client

### ▉ Question

*I have attended numerous seminars, all of which inform me that a new client has a right to know all the exceptions and limitations to confidentiality at or before the first session and before therapy commences. When I start explaining my understanding of these exceptions, the client becomes so nervous I have to stop. Is there an easier way to have an informed client without spending huge amounts of time educating clients concerning exceptions to confidentiality?*

 **Answer**

You should never undertake to orally explain the exceptions to confidentiality. List the exceptions and limitations to confidentiality in your notice of privacy practices as required by the HIPAA Privacy Rule. This same information should be included or referenced in the initial intake and consent to treatment form signed by the client. Give a copy to the client with the recommendation that he or she take it home, read it over, and ask any questions at the next session. If the client asks a specific question, the clinician should answer it fully.

## Legal Lightbulb

- Protection of the therapist includes a disclosure of the exceptions and limitations to confidentiality as determined by state laws and the ethical canons of the profession.

- If a client refuses to acknowledge informed consent to the exceptions to confidentiality, don't treat the client.

- There are mandatory breaches of confidentiality, such as child abuse, elder abuse, and duty to warn in some jurisdictions. There are permissive disclosures in other jurisdictions such as the permissive right to call the police or a medical facility when a person presents an imminent threat of harm to self or others.

## Summary

It is generally assumed that from the inception of therapy to ultimate termination the matters shared between clinician and client are confidential. This assumption is true to the extent that what is revealed to the therapist cannot become part of community knowledge, gossip, or other general information without the *clear, unambiguous consent of the client.* This principle includes spouses, lovers, family, and close friends who would *love to hear about your most bizarre and exotic cases.*

Breach of confidentiality is a common ethical complaint as well as grounds for a malpractice suit. Confidentiality rules become cloudy when the law or litigation is part of the equation. The statutes fluctuate and are periodically amended by courts and legislative bodies, and many differences exist between state and federal law.

# 8

## Resolving Conflicts before They Escalate

*Horatio Smith was a good therapeutic witness. He had reviewed his clinical notes carefully before trial. He knew the facts of the case and had carefully noted the dates and sequences of events and their import. Before the trial, Dr. Smith visited with the attorney and handed her a carefully considered list of suggested questions to be asked and, further, made himself available for consultation prior to the trial and during the protracted litigation.*

*The jury, after careful deliberation, determined that the opposing counsel and the opposing party were also well prepared and had better facts to work with. Well-organized cases can be lost when the facts are against a client. Efficient and competent lawyers, presenting the best there is to offer, can lose.*

*The client was furious and blamed Dr. Smith for the loss.*

### The Angry Client

The best place to handle the angry client is in the therapist's office, with a support staff available and in a calm atmosphere where adequate time is committed. The worst place is immediately after the trial in a public space such as the courtroom corridor or cafeteria.

Let the client vent as much as possible. Allow that perhaps a different approach "might" have been helpful, but remember that absolutely

*The best place to handle the angry client is in the therapist's office. The worst place is immediately after the trial in a public space.*

nothing would guarantee a change in result. If appropriate, delicately remind the client that the overall case strategy was the result of the input of the client, the lawyer, other witnesses, and the therapist, and the presentation was the best possible under the circumstances. If it does not violate the rules of delicacy, suggest that the case and the case result is to some extent the result of the client's behavior and the client remains somewhat responsible for the consequences of that behavior.

*With a genuinely angry client, risk management is the goal of posttrial conferences.*

With a genuinely angry client, risk management is the goal of post-trial conferences. *The angry client has several options:*

1. **The client can vent and then forget it.** The client might tell friends what a "raw deal" he or she got, receive sympathy and compassion, and put the matter behind him or her. Most litigants are able to accept the loss of a case as an unpleasant experience that can be overcome. Most understand justice is not always perfectly administered.

2. **The client can file a malpractice suit against the testifying mental health professional.** In this scenario, the client either has to prove that the testimony contained an act of omission (not testifying to all or most of what *could have* been said) or an act of commission (testifying incorrectly or negligently concerning what *was* said). Then, the client must prove that this witness's testimony was the proximate cause for the case being lost. It is difficult for a client to prevail when suing a testifying mental health professional client for alleged acts of negligence related to the testimony. Most attorneys are reluctant to take on this kind of case. Any particular witness is only a portion of the complete body of evidence submitted to and considered by the court. A forensic specialist may be formidable but is not always a provable *determining* factor in any given litigation. To win a malpractice case against the mental health witness, the client must prove by a preponderance of credible evidence that had the witness testified as he or she could and should have, the client would have won the case. Rarely can a client show or prove that a case would have turned out differently had any one witness testified differently.

3. **The client can file a complaint with the licensing board.** Use of this option is becoming more widespread. Complaints can be filed for failure to prepare adequately and professionally for trial, for unprofessional conduct with the lawyers while in the courtroom, for failure to cooperate with the clients and the lawyers in trial preparation and participation, for offering testimony that is different from what was represented to the client before trial, or for having an inadequate basis for the opinions stated in court or in a report submitted to the court. Complaints have also been filed when the client rightly assumed that the forensic witness had a complete and accurate set of clinical notes, only to find that the notes were not up to clinical or ethical standards or were incomplete, inaccurate, sloppy, or illegible.

> *Complaints to the licensing board are becoming more widespread.*

Complaints are convenient and easy because they are free to the client. The state licensing board is obligated to investigate complaints and to take appropriate action. In many states the toll-free number of every state licensing board must be conspicuously posted in every provider's office. If the complaint, taken as true, sets out a violation of an ethical standard or guideline, the state board begins an investigation and asks the therapist to formally respond to the allegations. If the state board then determines that an infraction has occurred, it will generally pursue sanctions against the therapist. The client will have sought and obtained some satisfaction with minimum effort and no expense. A complaint to the licensing board can give satisfaction to the client although it does not change the ultimate outcome of the case.

4. **Angry clients may attack mental health professionals by insulting their competence, professionalism, and personal life.** Should there be remarks or written materials that fall short of libel and slander (which are actionable civil causes of action), there is little the professional can do about it. If a client attacks you in this manner, consult with an attorney who specializes in this type of case. Do not take it on yourself to respond by assuming that a good, aggressive offense is the best defense. The professional has to contend with professional ethics and rules of confidentiality and privilege

*Much more can be gained from ameliorating the problem in mediation than by engaging in hostile conflict.*

that circumscribe what can be publicly said to and about a client. The professional also may have the need to continue practicing in the community. Much more can be gained from ameliorating the problem in mediation or other alternative conflict resolution methods than by engaging in hostile conflict and gaining the upper hand.

## The Bottom Line

The angry client may be rational or irrational, reasonable or unreasonable, approachable or unapproachable. The manifestation of anger may be overt and blatantly hostile, a quiet innuendo, or a subtle dig. Whichever manner is employed, it must be handled in a manner that diffuses the difficulty quickly and easily, managing potential risk effectively. Some methods of diffusion are:

- A *lawyer-supervised and carefully drafted* letter to the client that does not admit wrongdoing or fault but communicates to the client the therapist's sincere sorrow over the outcome of the case.
- Office visit(s) with a third party present, if necessary.
- Formalized mediation or other ADR. Often, uninvolved and unemotional third-party professionals can ameliorate the problem whereas emotionally involved participants cannot.

*Do not offer to return fees paid by the complaining client.*

Do not offer to return fees paid by the complaining client. Such an offer could result in perceived admission of wrongdoing or negligence, continuing demands by the client for additional funds or therapy, or other unimagined creative demands.

## Resolving Posttrial Conflicts

The treating therapist called to court as a witness will find that the diagnosis, treatment plan, and ongoing prognosis for a case shift with every trial. The particular problem originally contemplated in therapy sessions will be affected by trial preparation, trial participation, and the aftermath of the trial. Continued therapy is appropriate, shifting the diagnosis gradually as the trial evolves and then draws to conclusion. Therapy should continue as long after the trial as necessary for the client to accommodate to his or her new realities. It may take a while.

## File Review

Review every file periodically to be sure it conforms to ethical standards of the profession as determined by the licensing boards and to determine whether it contains required consent forms concerning both treatment and the right to share information. When a client is angry or upset, extra care and caution should be paid to all progress notes and exhibits in the client file. Files should include:

*Review every file periodically to be sure it conforms to ethical standards.*

- Periodic case or progress notes.
- Clearly defined diagnosis, a treatment plan appropriate to the diagnosis, and a prognosis that is updated from time to time as the treatment plan is implemented.
- All necessary consents and revocations of consents.
- All required HIPAA Privacy Rule forms including a notice of privacy practices and a log of disclosures.
- All correspondence such as requests for information that was included in any reports or used in testifying.
- If there has been a change in the principal therapist, supervisor, or intern, the notes of these professionals.
- Copies of notifications to insurers if the client has threatened either a complaint to the licensing board or a malpractice suit.

The original purpose of the clinical notes might have been to document the therapy and for the use of future providers of services. Progress notes are viewed differently when reviewed for a licensing complaint or a malpractice suit.

*Progress notes are viewed differently when reviewed for a licensing complaint or a malpractice suit.*

*Answers to Frequently Asked Questions About:*

Clients who threaten

Depressed clients who don't get better

Clients who want to blame someone

### ? Question

*I have been treating a depressed client for about one year. She and I discussed at the beginning of therapy that, in her case, we were in a "holding pattern" in the sense that she was making progress if her symptoms remained somewhat constant. I made no guarantees and told her so but offered competent therapy for her various problems, and she maintained her stability during the treatment period.*

*About six months ago, she and her husband divorced, and, following a contested trial, custody of their children was awarded to her husband. Now, without a husband, her children, and income, she is becoming even more depressed.*

*In her last conversation, she threatened me with undisclosed accusations. She wants me to reimburse her for the therapy because she did not get better and needs the money to live on. In addition, she feels that her increased depression because of her loss of children and income is partially my fault because my courtroom testimony, although generally supportive, was not as strong as she felt it should have been. Her status or life position is not good, but I don't feel responsible for the result of the litigation. What should I do?*

### ! Answer

This client has to be handled gingerly, with compassion and delicacy, *but firmly.* A therapist promises a client competent therapy, which is all that can be promised or offered. Often, competent therapy results in the client "not getting worse" rather than getting better. In this case perhaps the benefit to the client was that the status quo was maintained and her mental health did not deteriorate. Every client must be told that when there is litigation, the judge or jury makes the final determination.

A therapist may treat a client as long as the client is ready, willing, and able to pay for therapy. When the client is no longer able to pay for sessions, the therapist should locate three or more local community services, where the cost is either free or offered on a sliding scale, and make a referral. As long as the therapist does not abandon the client without making a sensible referral, the therapist has acted ethically.

The process of termination of services and referral to an agency or community service should be explained and documented in the file. If possible, have the client acknowledge in writing an understanding of the circumstances of the situation and a willingness to contact community services. Offer to cooperate, with the client's permission, with subsequent therapists and wish the client well. Perhaps offer a free termination interview.

## Summary

There is no way to practice in the field of mental health without *ever* having an occasional unhappy or complaining client. Whether the complaint is reasonable or not, it cannot be ignored. The wise therapist

### Legal Lightbulb

- Make sure nothing in the original contract of engagement guarantees a certain result or a specific outcome.

- A threat from an upset client is adequate grounds for termination of treatment. Remember, clients already have problems, and the clinician wants to help the client with the problems, *not become one of the problems.*

- While in most cases the best defense is a good offense, when it comes to a conflict between clients and mental health professionals, the professional has limited means by which to respond or to defend. Attacking the client can be counterproductive and possibly unethical.

listens to the complaint, determines whether there is any feasible solution, and, if possible, seeks to implement a peaceful resolution. Some compromise may be possible through the ADR processes of mediation, arbitration, negotiation, or other methods of agreeable conflict resolution. What is to be avoided at all costs is a public confrontation or litigation. When the differences reach this stage, the professional loses even if the case or conflict is won.

# PART III

# *PREPARING FOR TESTIMONY*

As with most things in life, preparation is the key to success. A mental health professional who does not take seriously an impending court appearance could face daunting consequences. Even a treating mental health professional who is compelled into court by subpoena is expected to testify competently and professionally. Licensing board complaints, malpractice suits, embarrassment, and loss of reputation are some of the problems that mental health professionals can face if they do a poor job in court. It is unlikely that a person who practices a mental health discipline for any length of time can completely avoid contact with our legal system.

With preparation and an understanding of the legal system, even a treating therapist who is required to make a rare court appearance can competently testify and avoid any negative consequences.

# 9

# Subpoenas

*Kevin, a social worker, had been in private practice for a year when he was served with a subpoena to appear for a deposition with his client's file. Kevin appeared at the deposition, testified, and allowed his client's file to be copied, marked as an exhibit, and made part of the deposition transcript.*

*In Kevin's state, a subpoena issued in a civil case does not in and of itself give rise to an exception to confidentiality, and his unhappy client filed a complaint with the state licensing board. Kevin received a public reprimand from the licensing board and spent an anxious 2 years waiting for the statute of limitation period for filing a malpractice suit to expire.*

*On receipt of a subpoena from the attorney for the husband of her client, Susan, a licensed mental health professional, immediately contacted her client to discuss the matter. She found out that her client did not want her to testify under any circumstance. Susan then began contacting colleagues and her licensing board but became frustrated when she was unable to get specific direction.*

We receive more calls from panicked therapists about subpoenas than any other issue confronting mental health professionals in their practices. Even mental health professionals with extensive professional experience can become unnerved by a subpoena and unsure how to respond or proceed. The danger, as Kevin found out, is in wrongfully disclosing a client's confidential information, which can lead to serious consequences for the mental health professional. Improperly breaching

*We receive more calls from panicked therapists about subpoenas than any other issue.*

confidentiality can result in licensing board sanctioning, the imposition of penalties by the Office of Civil Rights for violating the HIPAA Privacy Rule (45 CFR Parts 160 and 164), and damages in a malpractice lawsuit.

Susan's predicament underscores the widespread confusion among mental health professionals about how to respond to a subpoena. It is no wonder that mental health professionals become anxious when served with a subpoena.

Pursuant to the HIPAA Privacy Rule Section 164.508 (a), a mental health professional may not use or disclose protected health information without a valid client authorization. The use or disclosure of psychotherapy notes requires a more specific authorization. (See *Portable Lawyer*, second edition, for a more thorough discussion of the Privacy Rule and HIPAA-related forms, including authorizations. See also a sample authorization for the use and disclosure of protected health information in Appendix B of this book.) *Psychotherapy notes* are defined as:

> . . . notes recorded (in any medium) by a health care provider who is a mental health professional documenting or analyzing the contents of conversations during a private counseling session or a group, joint, or family counseling session and that are separated from the rest of the individual's record. *Psychotherapy notes* excludes medication prescription and monitoring, counseling session start and stop times, the modalities and frequencies of treatment furnished, results of clinical tests, and any summary of the following items: diagnosis, functional status, the treatment plan, symptoms, prognosis, and progress to date.
>
> —Section 164.501

Most of the "good stuff" a lawyer is seeking when issuing a subpoena is found in the therapist's psychotherapy notes. The Privacy Rule requires a written authorization signed by a client that specifically allows for the disclosure of the information in the psychotherapy notes before compliance with a subpoena can occur (Section 164.508 (2)). Or does it?

Unfortunately, the Privacy Rule backs in the exceptions to confidentiality that are required or permitted by federal and state law. Section 164.512 (a) (1) provides: "A covered entity may use or disclose protected health information to the extent that such use or disclosure is required by law and the use or disclosure complies with the relevant requirements of such law." Is a subpoena in and of itself an exception to confidentiality allowing for disclosure? State laws vary, but generally, the subpoena itself is not an exception. The underlying issues in a lawsuit may give rise to an exception and allow for or mandate disclosure of confidential information, but the subpoena itself is not the exception.

Section 164.512 (f) (1) (ii) of the Privacy Rule provides:

> A covered entity **may** disclose protected health information . . . in compliance with and as limited by the relevant requirements of:
>     A . . . court-ordered warrant, or a subpoena or summons issued by a judicial officer . . .
>     An administrative request, including an administrative subpoena or summons . . .

We consider such subpoenas to be the equivalent of a court order because the testimony or record production is being compelled directly by the court or tribunal. Even though this section of the Privacy Rule uses the word *may*, we contend that subpoenas issued by a court or administrative tribunal should be complied with in all respects. Failure to do so could easily result in sanctions against the offending mental health professional that could include incarceration for contempt.

The general rule is that a subpoena in and of itself does not permit disclosure of confidential information except if the subpoena is issued directly by a court or administrative tribunal. Most subpoenas are not issued directly by a court or administrative tribunal but by a clerk, notary, court reporter, or an attorney in the case. Before disclosure of confidential information can occur after receipt of a subpoena issued by one of these persons, there must be a legal basis for disclosure. It is usually a sound and safe practice to require client consent or a court order before disclosing any confidential information in response to a subpoena. In fact, in most cases client consent or a court order is the only legal basis that allows disclosure of confidential information. Remember, the HIPAA Privacy Rule requires written authorization from a client before confidential information can be disclosed and a more

*A subpoena in and of itself does not permit disclosure of confidential information except if issued directly by a court or administrative tribunal.*

*In most cases client consent or a court order is the only legal basis that allows disclosure of confidential information.*

specific authorization before psychotherapy notes can be revealed. Section 164.512 (e) (1) (i) deals with court orders and provides, "a covered entity may disclose protected health information in the course of any judicial or administrative proceeding: (1) in response to an order of a court or administrative tribunal . . ."

The Privacy Rule does provide a mechanism that will allow for disclosure of protected health information in any judicial or administrative proceedings in response to a subpoena, a discovery request, or other lawful process that is not accompanied by an order of a court or administrative tribunal. A covered entity may disclose protected health information in these circumstances if:

> (A) The covered entity receives satisfactory assurance . . . from the party seeking the information that reasonable efforts have been made by such party to ensure that the individual who is the subject of the protected health information that has been requested has been given notice of the request; or
>
> The covered entity receives satisfactory assurance . . . from the party seeking the information that reasonable efforts have been made by such party to secure a qualified protective order . . .
>
> —Section 164. 512, (e) (ii)

With respect to the notice requirement, the Rule provides that a mental health professional will have "received satisfactory assurance" if he or she receives from the party seeking the information a written statement and accompanying documentation that:

> (A) The party requesting the information has made a good faith attempt to provide written notice to the individual (or, if the individual's location is unknown, to mail a notice to the individual's last known address);
>
> (C) The notice included sufficient information about the litigation or proceeding in which the protected health information is requested to permit the individual to raise an objection to the court or administrative tribunal; and
>
> (D) The time for the individual to raise objections to the court or administrative tribunal has elapsed; and
>
> (1) No objections were filed; or
>
> (2) All objections filed by the individual have been resolved by the court or administrative tribunal and the disclosures being sought are consistent with such resolution.

With respect to the qualified protective order requirement, the Rule provides that a mental health professional will have "received satisfactory assurance" if he or she receives from the party seeking the information a written statement and accompanying documentation that:

(A) The parties to the dispute giving rise to the request for information have agreed to a qualified protective order and have presented it to the court or administrative tribunal with jurisdiction over the dispute; or

(B) The party seeking the protected health information has requested a qualified protective order from such court or administrative tribunal.

A *qualified protective order* is an order from a court or administrative tribunal that prohibits the parties from using the protected health information for any purpose other than the litigation or proceeding for which the information was requested and requires the return or destruction of the protected health information (including all copies made) at the end of the litigation. (See the sample qualified protective order included in Appendix B.)

This Rule further provides that in the absence of being provided with "satisfactory assurance," a mental health professional may make reasonable efforts to provide the client with notice as set out in the Rule or seek a qualified protective order directly.

Many states (e.g., Maryland) have laws with provisions that put the burden on the client to take steps to block the disclosure of their confidential information. Not all state laws provide for this kind of approach (e.g., Texas), and it is imperative that you be familiar with your state's law. If your state law does not allow disclosure of mental health records consistent with the satisfactory assurance provisions of the Privacy Rule, you must comply with the more protective laws of your state.

Remember, if you are served with a subpoena that is not accompanied by an order of a court or administrative tribunal, the HIPAA Privacy Rule permits disclosure of protected health information without client consent if satisfactory assurance is given that the client was notified and given enough time to seek to block disclosure or a qualified protective order was entered. In the absence of satisfactory assurance, a mental health professional can provide the client with the notice or personally seek a qualified protective order (i.e., filing a motion for a protective order). However, more protective state laws may not allow for a mental health professional to disclose confidential information when the mental health professional personally advises the client that a subpoena has been received.

## Kinds of Subpoenas

The technical requirements for the different types of subpoenas vary in each state. A subpoena may be unenforceable if it does not comply with all state requirements. Many states require a transportation fee (tender) to be attached to the subpoena. There may be a distance rule beyond which a person is not subject to subpoena. You should check with an attorney in your state before making a determination that compliance with a subpoena is not required due to a technical deficiency.

*A plain subpoena requires a witness to appear at the time and location specified in the subpoena. A subpoena duces tecum requires the witness to appear at the time and location specified in the subpoena and to produce at that same time and location identified documents.*

A subpoena may be a *plain* subpoena or a subpoena *duces tecum*. A plain subpoena requires a witness to appear at the time and location specified in the subpoena. A subpoena duces tecum requires the witness to appear at the time and location specified in the subpoena and to produce at that same time and location identified documents. The majority of subpoenas issued and served on a mental health professional are subpoena duces tecums requiring the witness to appear with client records.

## Recommended Procedure When Served with a Subpoena

We recommend that you follow these procedures when you are served with a subpoena:

1. Carefully review the subpoena and determine the client, extent of information requested, and terms of any qualified protective order attached to the subpoena.

2. Contact the client and seek written authorization to respond to the subpoena even if a qualified protective order is attached. If the client provides the authorization, prepare to testify and to produce any records requested. If the client will not provide you with written authorization *and* if a qualified protective order accompanies the subpoena, comply fully but consistently with the qualified protective order. Do not provide more information than the order directs you to provide. Attempt to keep the client informed during all phases of the proceedings.

3. Have a waiver of confidentiality form handy. When a client suggests that the professional share mental health information, the client should first sign an original and a copy of the waiver form, with the duplicate original placed in the client file and the other original placed in an envelope and delivered to the client.

4. If state law is *not* more restrictive than the HIPAA Privacy Rule, a qualified protective order is not attached, and the client cannot be contacted, determine if sufficient written confirmation (satisfactory assurance) that the client was notified of the subpoena and the information requested and had time to make an attempt to block disclosure (filing a motion to quash the subpoena) accompanies the subpoena. If the time has elapsed for the client to block disclosure, you may proceed with disclosure. Because the HIPAA Privacy Rule does use the word *may,* you have the option of not disclosing the confidential information until specifically authorized by the client or ordered to do so by a judge.

5. If the client cannot be contacted or will not give consent to the disclosure *and* the subpoena was not accompanied by satisfactory assurance or a qualified protective order and the law in your state is *not* more protective than the HIPAA Privacy Rule, you may consider personally providing the appropriate notice to the client and then responding to the subpoena or seeking a protective order or ruling from the court and abiding by the court's ruling.

6. If client consent, satisfactory assurance, or a qualified protective order has not been obtained, you must appear at the time, date,

and place required by the subpoena. Once in attendance, no personally identifiable client information should be disclosed until a court specifically orders the disclosure. The approach varies slightly depending on which of the following kinds of subpoenas is issued:

—**Record subpoena or discovery request:** This subpoena compels you to produce specific client records. Appear at the time and place directed but do not provide the records requested. Do not even identify the subject person as a client. Firmly respond to questions that would cause improper disclosure with, "I am sorry but without client consent or a court order, I am not in a position to respond to these types of questions." You may have to repeat this answer several times.

—**Deposition subpoena:** This subpoena compels you to appear and give oral testimony outside court. Appear at the time and place directed. If the subpoena requested that you produce records, bring them with you but do not allow anyone but the client to access them. (Client consent or court directive may be obtained before your arrival or during the deposition, so make sure you have the records.) Until such time as client consent or a court order is obtained, you must not disclose any personally identifiable information about your client, including the fact that the person was or is a client. Respond as appropriate with, "I am sorry but without client consent or a court order, I am not in a position to respond to these types of questions."

—**Court appearance (trial) subpoena:** This subpoena compels you to appear and give oral testimony in court. Appearing in court might cause more anxiety but is the safest and easiest subpoena to deal with under these circumstances. Appear at the time and place directed in the subpoena, and bring any records requested but do not answer any questions or surrender any records to anyone until you are on the witness stand and the court specifically orders you to do so. When you are asked to disclose confidential information, turn to the judge and say, "Your Honor, without client consent I am not comfortable answering this question." If the judge directs you to answer the question, you should do so. A directive from a judge issued in open court, although verbal, is a court order and you must comply.

Attorneys try to intimidate the mental health professional, but unless you are certain that there is a legal basis for you to disclose confidential information, insist on client consent or a court order. When in doubt, consult with a knowledgeable attorney before responding.

*Unless you are certain that there is a legal basis for you to disclose confidential information, insist on client consent or a court order.*

## Answers to Frequently Asked Questions About:

Responding to a subpoena

Confidentiality of drug and alcohol treatment records

Attachment of witness

### ❓ Question

*I am a licensed addictions counselor and received a subpoena commanding me to appear in court to testify and to produce records of a client who voluntarily came to me for treatment for his alcohol problem. I called the attorney who issued the subpoena and learned that he represents my client's wife and the case involves child custody issues and divorce. I advised the attorney that I am not able to breach confidentiality with respect to clients who have voluntarily come to me for drug or alcohol treatment. The attorney's response was, "So it's true, then, that Mr. Smith came to you for treatment of alcohol and drug problems?" I told him I wasn't saying that but was only stating my ethical duty as an addictions counselor as I understand it to be. He made me very uncomfortable and said that because the case involved child custody it created an exception to confidentiality and that I had to testify and produce the subpoenaed records. I contacted my client, who does not want me to testify or turn over any information in his file. What should I do?*

### ❗ Answer

For patients who voluntarily enter into drug or alcohol treatment, federal law (42 CFR Part 2—Confidentiality of Alcohol and Drug Abuse

Patient Records) precludes disclosure, without patient consent, of patient identifying information, the affirmative verification of another person's communication of patient identifying information, or the communication of any information from the record of a patient who has been identified. This law further provides that responses to requests for information cannot acknowledge a patient's past, present, or future status as a patient. The client's protected health information may not be used in any civil, criminal, administrative, or legislative proceeding. Furthermore, the HIPAA Privacy Rule does not allow disclosure under these circumstances.

You have been placed in a precarious position. You have two choices as we see it. One, you can appear in court at the time designated in the subpoena and assert the position that federal law prohibits you from answering questions that even identify a person as a client. However, if the judge orders you to answer, you will have to answer. We do not recommend you violate a direct order from the judge.

Or, you can hire an attorney or have the client's attorney file a motion to quash the subpoena or a protective order limiting the use and disclosure of the information you are being asked to provide. If you fail

## Legal Lightbulb

- Attorneys seeking disclosure of health care information should not be trusted to provide you with accurate information about *your* duties and obligations.

- Seek *competent* legal advice when confronted with a subpoena before responding.

- Without a protective order or order quashing the subpoena, you must appear in court, but do not disclose confidential information or produce records until the judge orders you to do so.

- Securing competent legal advice is crucial to ethically and legally responding to a subpoena.

- When confronted with a court order, comply fully but consistently with the order. Be careful not to disclose information not called for by the protective order.

to take this step, it will be necessary for you to appear in court at the time designated in the subpoena and raise the confidentiality issue with the judge when you are called to the witness stand. If you fail to file a motion to quash or for protective order and fail to appear, the attorney can seek an attachment order (like an arrest warrant) from the court directing a law enforcement officer to take you into custody and to escort you, by force if necessary, to the courthouse.

You may want to secure your client's consent to allow you to talk to his attorney directly. If there is no basis in the attorney's mind for blocking your court appearance and testimony, insist on spending time with the attorney to prepare for your court appearance. If you cannot get cooperation from the client's lawyer, you have a right to secure your own legal representation and you should do so.

## Summary

As confusing and complicated as responding to subpoenas may be, a simple approach can alleviate all the anguish and stress: Unless you secure client consent to the disclosure being sought, it will take a court order for you to provide the information. It should not be the responsibility of the mental health professional to sort out all the federal and state laws in this area. If the mental health professional chooses to go forward with disclosure in the absence of client consent or a court order, he or she should do so only with competent legal advice and with certainty that there is a legal basis for the disclosure. If an attorney advises you there is a legal basis for disclosure, get it in writing.

# 10

## Preparing for Discovery

*During the past several years of therapy, Susie had noticed that the therapist took copious notes during her sessions. She had also taken psychological tests and, over the years, sent notes, cards, and letters to the therapist. When she received a threatening letter from a rejected suitor, she dutifully copied it and sent the copy to the therapist together with written notes transcribed during frightening phone calls.*

*When Susie became involved in litigation wherein her mental health status was an issue, her therapist received a subpoena duces tecum for a deposition plus a motion for the production of documents. It seemed that the whole paper trail was about to become a matter of public record.*

*After a lengthy conference with her lawyer, Susie realized, much to her dismay, that when mental health is an issue in a case, the client's whole clinical file is subject to discovery.*

### A Little History

There was a time when "trial by ambush" was common. Most of the information and evidence that would come before the court would come out at trial, and lawyers were surprised and upset when secret witnesses, documents, or circumstances suddenly appeared in the middle of a formal hearing, completely throwing counsel and clients off balance. Today that scenario is almost impossible. The rules of discovery are such that litigants can discover the other party's lay and expert witnesses, documents to be introduced at the trial, physical evidence that will enter the court as demonstrative evidence, and, indeed, almost every circumstance on which either litigant bases his or her case.

Gone are the days when one lawyer could ambush another by hiding or concealing evidence or when a secret witness could sit disguised in the corridor to be brought into the court and sworn in much to the astonishment of the other lawyer or party to the suit. Today the thorough, diligent, and careful lawyer, by using discovery methods, can determine the evidence that will be presented in court.

Proper discovery brings to the attention of a litigant the entire case that will be offered by the adversary when the case comes to trial.

## The Deposition and Deposition with Subpoena Duces Tecum

The deposition subpoena duces tecum is probably the most common legal device the mental health professional will face in practice. The subpoena for a deposition commands the therapist to appear in person, usually at an attorney's office, and answer questions concerning a party litigant. The litigant is usually a former or present client of the therapist or might be a witness or prospective witness. The principal parties may be present as well as the lawyers, together with a court reporter and, if videos are to be made of the deposition, a video technician. The witness is sworn so all testimony is under oath. The lawyer asks questions and the witness answers. All testimony may be recorded, transcribed, or a combination of both. At the end of the deposition, the written record is submitted to the witness, who has the obligation to read the entire transcript, check it for accuracy, and make any corrections needed. The final product is the accurate record of what the witness said, as corrected, if there are errors in transcription.

*Proper discovery brings to the attention of a litigant the entire case that will be offered by the adversary when the case comes to trial.*

If *a plain subpoena* is issued, only the witness has to appear. This is a personal command to appear at the time and place designated, be sworn, and answer questions from memory. After the deposition is complete, the transcript is submitted to the witness for signature.

If *a subpoena duces tecum* is issued, the witness must appear at the time and place designated and bring all the documents specifically itemized or listed in the subpoena. Every lawyer has a boilerplate list for mental health professionals. For example, the witness must bring to the deposition:

- All clinical records, psychotherapy notes, memoranda, letters, communications, telephone logs, or other documents that in any way pertain to the client, together with all billing records, records of payments, correspondence, or other communications.
- All tests, test records, photographs, letters received, copies of letters sent, and memoranda of conferences with any individual who has knowledge of the case or with any consultants used or conferred with in connection with the case.
- Medical records used for consideration when making the diagnosis or treatment plan and any correspondence concerning the physical health of the party to the litigation.
- All items that will be submitted as evidence in the trial as either direct evidence or as anticipated rebuttal evidence.

## Motion for Production of Documents

A motion for production of documents, usually accompanied by a record production subpoena, commands the recipient to make documents available for examination and copying. This directive can be brought alone or in conjunction with a subpoena for a deposition.

For example, a litigant knows that a series of therapists have treated a client. The lawyer for the litigant does not know exactly what transpired in the sessions but is savvy enough to know that every professional must keep session notes. Therefore, the lawyer knows that with a motion to discover the contents of the documents, the lawyer can trace the therapy progress from initial intake to ultimate termination or to the current date. Although this procedure can be handled at the time of deposition, there are pressures of time, interruptions, other lawyers, perhaps clients looking on, and no privacy. However, with a motion for the production of documents, the lawyer can look over the documents, make copies leisurely, and, having examined all relevant documentation, arrange for a deposition and/or interrogatories or requests for admissions.

If documents are to be produced by a witness, the witness should, prior to the time the deposition is taken, name and number the exhibits so that references to documents are clear.

## Interrogatories

Interrogatories are questions, usually a series of 30 that can be expanded to another 30, that are propounded to the litigants or witnesses. The questions are intended to save deposition costs and solidify testimony before the trial begins.

*Interrogatories are questions that are propounded to the litigants or witnesses.*

 Interrogatories usually begin with questions such as:

What is your name?

What is your work history?

What is your marriage history?

The first series of questions is designed to determine some facts of the case and what the witness knows about them. If the answers require more clarification, additional questions can be asked.

In responding to interrogatories, the usual method is for the lawyer to send the questions to the witness to answer "in the rough." Then, before submitting the answers to the other party, the attorney checks them. No answer should be offered without advice of counsel, just as no answer should be blurted out in either the courthouse or in a deposition. Answers given without advice frequently return to haunt the witness. After the questions have been understood, answered with advice of counsel, and forwarded to opposing lawyers, they are or can become a part of the court record.

*Answers given without advice frequently return to haunt the witness.*

## Requests for Admissions

Requests for admissions are questions put in a "yes" or "no" format, for example:

 Request: "Admit or deny that you met John Jones on January 1, 2004."

Answer: "Denied."

If the question cannot be either admitted or denied, it must be stated and the reason given, for example: "I cannot either admit or deny I met John Jones on January 1, 2004, because I have no immediate recollection of that date."

As with interrogatories, it is advisable to consult with an attorney before responding to requests for admissions. Discuss proposed answers to the requests for admissions. Are your answers accurate, or could there be an interpretation that is totally different from your intended response? Are the answers enough to satisfy the question yet not subject you to challenge and attack?

## Extra Legal Discovery

There is often substantial discovery *about* a witness, especially a forensic expert or well-known community mental health professional. Often, when the name of an expert appears on a witness list, opposing counsel immediately sends out feelers in the community to learn about the expert informally.

*Just about anything a professional person has accomplished in a lifetime is recorded somewhere in cyberspace.*

Just about anything a professional person has accomplished in a lifetime is recorded somewhere in cyberspace and can be easily reviewed with the help of a search engine such as Google. Before accepting involvement in the litigation process, check out the cyberspace possibilities. See where you are listed and how. Then assume opposing counsel has the same investigative potential, and be prepared to explain your history and writings, especially if there is anything potentially embarrassing or contradictory in your file. Assume that embarrassing and pointed questions will be asked; have explanations ready.

## Answers to Frequently Asked Questions About:

Consultation

Compensation for consultation

Discovery

### ? Question

*An attorney asked me to consult with a married client who discovered that her husband was a homosexual and had liaisons with other men. The couple has two young children. The husband has now announced that he wants a divorce so he can "come out." If I am asked to participate in the divorce case, what can I expect?*

### ! Answer

If custody or visitation is an issue in the case, you will probably be compelled to participate in the discovery phase of the trial and be asked to testify in court. During discovery, you could be served with a request for production pursuant to which you would be asked to provide a copy of your client file. You could also be served with a deposition subpoena and requested to appear at a lawyer's office to give oral testimony and to produce the client's file. You should anticipate these events and secure from your client her written authorization for you to disclose her confidential information in response to all discovery requests and deposition or trial subpoenas served on you in connection with her divorce case. It would also be a good idea to bring up the matter of how you will be compensated for your time in responding to requests and subpoenas and get your client's written commitment to pay you.

## Summary

In today's mental health workplace, there are mandated clinical records for every mental health discipline. Numerous psychological tests and privacy forms are part of therapists' practice. The therapist

## Legal Lightbulb

- Experts can be discovered before trial and deposed.

- The deposition can be for testimony only or duces tecum, together with all documentation in the file.

- Almost all documents in a clinical file are subject to examination by opposing counsel. Disclosure can be resisted by motions to quash or motions for a protective order filed by an attorney. However, if the judge feels the documents are admissible evidence, they can be discovered.

cannot guarantee the client that the contents of the file will not be the object of prying eyes, regardless of the steps taken to protect the file.

If there is litigation, the therapist is subject to being served with a subpoena or subpoena duces tecum, which might make the entire file and all supporting documents available for examination by the other party. If opposing counsel or parties do not want the expense of a deposition, a motion for production of documents can be issued, which requires that certain documents be produced for copying or examination. Then, if desired, requests for admissions or interrogatories can be issued compelling the therapist to admit or deny matters under oath or answer numerous questions that are then filed in court papers. Whichever the method, once a therapist undertakes to treat a client, under most court rules, should a client be involved in litigation, the client file is subject to discovery. Diagnosis, treatment plans, supporting documents, and clinical notes cannot be concealed unless they come under a specific rule of evidence that grants them a defined privilege.

If clients are involved in litigation, very little information in their file is sacred. Discovery can pry open the most intimate secrets from progress notes and documented therapy. Clients must be warned of this possibility. Indeed, ethical codes require that clients be fully informed of the exceptions to client confidentiality before therapy commences.

# 11

# Preparing "Ask Me" Questions for the Lawyer

*Dr. Redding, a well-known psychiatrist, was engaged in a custody battle for his 8-year-old son. During the trial Dr. Redding's ex-wife testified as to her love for the child, her competence, and her plan for the child's future welfare, as well as her ability to care for and nurture the child. She was calm, never rattled, and came across as the "perfect mom."*

*Dr. Redding was peculiar, but still a capable dad. However, the judge was more impressed by the wife's demeanor. When the trial was over, he admonished Dr. Redding's lawyer: "This woman seemed to be a perfect mother. Why did you waste my time with a case like this?"*

*A few days after the trial, one of the expert witnesses called Dr. Redding's lawyer. "Why didn't you ask me about her medication?" he asked. "If you had only asked, I could have testified that she took enough Valium to sedate an army. Of course, she was calm and unflappable; she was practically anesthetized. I had this answer ready, but you never asked."*

It is easy to make the assumption that every lawyer goes into court completely prepared with a thorough knowledge of the law, plus all the facts, circumstances, and theories of a given case. It is also easy to optimistically assume that the lawyer has read and digested the entire available file, including the reports of mental health professionals, and has a handle on the entire panorama of all the large and small issues presented in the case. Another assumption might be that the lawyer knows all there is to know about the mental health history of

*One way to conserve time and expense is for the testifying mental health professional to prepare a list of questions for the lawyer to ask him or her when testifying.*

*Furnishing questions to the lawyer is a win-win event.*

the client or the opposing party, is technically well schooled in psychology or mental health treatment and law, and is in a position to ask all the "right" questions. Unfortunately, these assumptions aren't usually valid.

Every method that will save lawyer time and client expense is helpful. One way to conserve time and expense is for the testifying mental health professional to prepare a list of questions for the lawyer to ask him or her when testifying. After all, the mental health professional has the most intimate knowledge of the mental health of the client or the client's adversary, knows what should be asked, and has an in-depth knowledge of the answers to the proposed questions.

The experienced courtroom lawyer can frame the questions into legitimate, admissible questions and then propound these questions to the therapist. The trial lawyer will have offered into evidence all the important testimony, and the mental health professional will leave the courtroom knowing that whatever should have been said was said in the proper manner. Furnishing questions to the lawyer in advance of trial is a win-win event.

The worst feeling for a lawyer is to walk out of the courtroom and have a therapist ask: "Why didn't you ask me about . . . ? It would have clinched the case."

Therapists generally have one primary concern: the betterment of the mental health of their client and the relief of psychological pain and suffering. The process in a consulting office practice is intimate and confidential. When mental health professionals are involved in the legal system and are asked to testify, they must make a mind-set shift to that of *advocate for* their client, and in this context they work with the client's lawyer to present to the judge or jury evidence in the best interest of the client as perceived by the client with the advice of the lawyer. The job of the lawyer is to present the most favorable evidence in the most favorable light. The clinician assists the lawyer in selecting the most favorable evidence and suggests to the lawyer which evidence might be unfavorable and how this unfavorable evidence can be presented in the *least unfavorable manner*. In civil cases, the ruling is by a preponderance of the evidence; that is, one grain of sand on the scales of justice can determine whether the client wins or loses a case.

This fact should underscore the importance of sorting through, selecting, and presenting every possible piece of favorable evidence in the case and then determining and defining the critical position of the professional when introducing this evidence.

In the vignette at the beginning of this chapter, the testifying therapist could have prepared the following suggestions for Dr. Redding's attorney:

 "Ask the witness which medications she has ingested in the past 24 hours."

"Ask the witness which medications she now takes and her history of taking them."

Either of these questions might have changed the attitude of the court and the outcome of the case. Remember, all you have to do is set the stage. The lawyer will take your few words and fashion the admissible question you will be asked. Just hand the lawyer the list with as much advance notice as possible. The lawyer creates the questions to ask you.

## Main Categories of Questions

Questions can be divided into three main categories:

1. **Specific professional qualifications, studies, or training:** Most professionals have advanced degrees. Occasionally, a professional has some specific ability or particularized training that sets that professional above and apart from the general class of equally educated individuals. This ability or training might be a special study commissioned by the government, a prestigious university or an internship with an internationally known expert, or an international study in another country or culture that affords special insight into the problem before the court. It might be a dissertation or thesis that is directly on point with the issues in the case at hand. In this situation, ask the lawyer to ask you about:

My study of _____ commissioned by
_____ University.

My dissertation concerning _____.

My studies with Dr._____ in Spain.

My internship with the department of mental health in Washington.

The year I spent in Africa studying AIDS.

My thesis titled _____.

My work on the _____ case.

My time with the police department of _____.

The year I studied in Sweden with Dr. _____.

My year with Child Protective Services in _____.

My four years in the hospital corps in Vietnam.

My military experience in this area of conflict.

*Think about what you want to say that will be helpful to your client, and then furnish key words to your lawyer so you will be asked about these important factors.*

Before the trial begins and you are called to the witness stand, think about what you want to say that will be helpful to your client, and then furnish key words to your lawyer so you will be asked about these important factors.

2. **Critical or exceptional events:** The therapeutic process often includes the recitation of critical events that shape impressions and opinions for years to come. Sometimes these are in the nature of flashbacks that dramatically affect the thinking process of your client. Other times they are in the form of odors, external feelings, or approaches to problems that are profoundly affected by a significant dramatic event. A momentous event may have been only seconds in terms of time elapsed (e.g., an auto collision or being shot), but the memory exists as if it happened yesterday and is played over and over in the person's mind and will never be forgotten. This episode is dramatic in its impact and future control over the thinking process of the individual. The lawyer must be reminded to ask you about them. For example, tell the lawyer to ask you about:

The automobile crash of August 2004.

My first contact with this client and what impressed me most about the encounter.

The client's bout with a terminal illness, which turned out to be a false alarm.

The client's fear of flying/drowning/falling/suffocating.

The client's fear of intimacy.

The client's feelings when she received her advanced degree.

The emotional impact about being laid off or downsized.

Different reflective events affect every person, and not all events are entitled to a high priority. This is the time to sort out the experiences in a person's life that affect this litigation and determine which of those events could affect the outcome of the trial. Ask the lawyer if they are relevant and part of the lawyer's grand plan for the case. If so, the lawyer will be thrilled you brought them to his or her attention.

3. **Outstanding traits of the client:** It is not possible to lead the witness in direct examination and suggest answers to questions. For example, it would not be admissible to ask, "Isn't the client a hyperactive person?" or "Doesn't the client have a remarkable memory?" or "Isn't the client very excitable?" These are leading questions in that they imply certain expected or anticipated answers. However, the lawyer in direct examination can ask:

Is there any peculiar trait of the client that stands out?

Is there anything about the client's memory that struck you as unusual?

What was the client's demeanor when confronted with a challenging event?

These questions are not leading in that they do not tell the witness what the expected answer should be. Rather, they are general questions. From the case itself, the role playing prior to trial, and the lawyer-therapist consultations, the answers become obvious. The flow of testimony has to have the *appearance of spontaneity*.

## Other Categories of Questions

There are numerous other categories that can be developed by the expert professional witness when preparing for a case. Because each circumstance is different, the therapist witness will have to sort through myriad case notes and observations to determine which particular items of information will be helpful or redundant, relevant or immaterial. Additional categories include:

- The diagnosis and how it changed as time went on.
- Significant dates and sensations to remember.
- Any dramatic visual images or piercing sounds to remember.
- Any common threads of the investigation.

The therapist should create a general listing of categories and implement them for each trial. Perhaps the best method is to first ponder priorities. What are the most important issues? Which are the least? Then offer the lawyer prioritized suggestions.

## Answers to Frequently Asked Questions About:

Questions to be asked

Questions that are not asked

Questions about payment for testifying in court

Questions such as, "Did your lawyer tell you what to say?"

**?** *Question*

*I am a counselor and have been asked to testify for a client in a lawsuit. I want to be as helpful as I can and have been advised by a colleague to prepare questions for my client's attorney. How do I prepare the list of questions to be asked, and what do I do if I have information and the question is never asked? Is it tricky to be asked questions about payment? And will I always be asked about lawyer-clinician preparation time before court?*

### ❗ Answer

There is no formula that can instantly produce the questions that the therapist wishes to be asked on direct examination. Rather, the therapist has to review the client's goals in the litigation, mentally sort through all the clinical evidence available, and then determine which questions should be asked that will best support the client's perception of the case. Often, the resulting questions will be the synthesis of the client's input with that of the lawyer and the therapist. With cooperation and compromise, the resulting questions should illustrate most of the salient points that are important to the case.

Nothing can be done when questions considered critical by the clinician are not asked. The witness cannot volunteer the answers or appeal to the court to interrogate him or her. Unfortunately, when the witness feels there are burning questions that have not been asked, the only outlet is to take a deep breath and hope for the best. Assume the lawyer has reasons for not asking these questions.

The therapist should be paid for testifying in court, including preparation time, travel and expenses, waiting time, consultative time, research, and any other expenses that are reasonably necessary to the prosecution of the litigation. The clinician can and should tell the court exactly what he or she is being paid for testimony. Be prepared to make an open disclosure of fees and fee computation. If you are asked, "Did your lawyer tell you what to say?" answer, "No, he told me to tell the truth and let the chips fall where they may."

At this point it is not helpful to become defensive, belligerent, or resentful. Tell the truth with confidence, cordiality, and consideration. Let the opposing lawyer do what he or she can to shake your confidence. Stay calm and serene. Sooner or later, the lawyer will go on to the next topic.

## Legal Lightbulb

- If a reminder to the lawyer is necessary (e.g., a memo or a picture), attach it to the question list, appropriately identified.

- Work with the lawyer to anticipate a question about your pretrial preparation, payment for court time, and involvement in the case. Practice the answers with studied casualness.

- Testimony is not a complete recapitulation of all the therapy. Advise your lawyer of all the significant items, and work with the lawyer to determine which will be most persuasive to a jury or judge.

- Most therapists have some special aptitude or field of exceptional expertise. The judge or jury should be made aware of these areas of interest and proficiency.

- The lawyer's job as an advocate is to present the known evidence in the most favorable light. Once the lawyer has total command of the facts, the lawyer can select those relevant and favorable to the client's case and make sure, if possible, they are brought before the court.

### Summary

Usually, the client has one day in court to make his or her case, so it is in the best interest of the client and the witness to be fully prepared for trial.

Being prepared includes a consideration of the persuasive evidence in possession of and within the knowledge base of the mental health professional. Make a list of what you feel is important to the case and what you want to be asked about by the client's lawyer during the trial. Submit these questions to the lawyer and discuss them, letting the lawyer determine, within the parameters set by the court, what is to be illustrated in court and what is to be eliminated.

The lawyer has the final word, with the advice and consent of the client. Sometimes one suggestion to the attorney can make the difference in the outcome of the case.

# 12

# Preparing for
# Deposition Testimony

*After successfully traversing the long road through graduate school, super-
vision, and licensing, Susan Jones set about doing quality therapy and pos-
itively impacting the lives of her clients. After 2 years in private practice,
she walked out of her office after a long day to find a process server waiting
next to her car. She was served with a subpoena to appear for a deposition
the following week. The subpoena was issued by an attorney for the husband of a client she had treated. Her client had discontinued coming to
therapy 3 months earlier without any communication. Susan had never
been subpoenaed or deposed and had only a vague idea of what to expect.
Furthermore, she was unsure if she had to appear or what she could law-
fully say. How should she prepare?*

The most common call we receive is from a mental health professional
who has received a subpoena, often for a deposition. A *deposition* is a
common discovery tool available to litigants that typically occurs in
the office of the attorney taking the deposition. In addition to the witness, a court reporter, the parties to the lawsuit, the attorneys involved
in the suit, and, if the deposition will be videotaped, a videographer
are present. The witness is sworn in and asked questions by each side
in the lawsuit with the side requesting the deposition going first.

The court reporter takes down all testimony, all the questions and
answers, and any objections or discussions that take place on the
record and generates a transcript of the proceedings. Any exhibits

marked during the deposition are attached to the deposition transcript. The witness then is given an opportunity to review the original transcript and make any necessary corrections before signing it in front of a notary and returning it to the court reporter. The deposition, subject to rulings on objections by the court, can be introduced into evidence at any court proceeding in the case.

In some respects, depositions should cause more anxiety for the witness than courtroom testimony. Depositions take place outside the presence of the judge, and the questioning can be much broader than what would occur at trial. The general rule is that any relevant question or any question that could lead to the discovery of relevant information can be asked of the witness. Questions intended solely to harass, intimidate, or embarrass the witness are clearly not proper, but attorneys are allowed wide latitude when probing a witness for bias. For example, if a mental health professional is testifying about the effects the death of a 6-year-old child can cause to the mental and emotional health of a parent, asking about the therapist's sexual orientation would be inappropriate. However, if the mental health professional is testifying on behalf of a gay client who is seeking custody of a child, inquiring about the therapist's sexual orientation might be appropriate.

*The witness usually spends more time in the deposition than giving courtroom testimony.*

The witness usually spends more time in the deposition than giving courtroom testimony because of the wide latitude attorneys have in questioning the witness in a deposition. Attorneys often use more devious and tricky tactics than they would in the courtroom and try to provoke, embarrass, or confuse the witness just to see how he or she will react. Another goal is to pin the witness down to a set of facts or opinions so any deviance at trial can be used against the witness. Eliciting testimony that is favorable to his or her client's position in the case is also a primary goal of each attorney even from witnesses adverse to their client.

Susan, and every mental health professional, should approach a deposition with caution and seriousness, taking the following suggestions into consideration:

**1. Be clear on your ability to disclose confidential information.**
Remember, a subpoena that is not issued by a court is almost never an

exception to confidentiality. In many states, court reporters and even attorneys can issue deposition subpoenas. Just because a mental health professional has been summoned to a deposition does not mean that answers to questions that reveal confidential information can be given. Ordinarily, client consent or a specific court order is required to do so. On receipt of the subpoena, a mental health professional should contact the client to find out whether the client will consent to disclosure of protected health information at the deposition. (See Chapter 10 for a discussion of this issue in greater detail.) Assuming client consent or other authority to disclose confidential information exists, be sure to document this proof or analysis in your client's file. When it comes to confidentiality issues, oral consents should always be noted in the progress notes and written consents inserted in the clinical file.

If you do not have legal authority to disclose client information, you still must appear at the deposition but cannot answer any question that would cause you to disclose the client's protected health information. In most cases, this restriction includes even admitting that you provided professional services to the client. You can answer the usual preliminary questions, such as your name, address, and occupation. When you are asked, "Have you had occasion at any time to provide professional services to Mr. Adams?" you should respond, "I'm sorry, but without client consent, a court order, or other legal authority, I am not in a position to answer." If the attorney persists in pressuring you for an answer, stick to your guns and respectfully decline to answer. The attorney will then be forced to seek a court order compelling your answer, which is just what you need in the absence of client consent to answer.

**2. Carefully review the client file.** It is a rare case that a mental health professional is not asked to bring documents or client records to a deposition. As with courtroom testimony, it is critical to carefully review the client record before the deposition. The client file should be free from error, organized, and in proper sequence. Properly correct any mistakes you find in the file. Create an index of the file if it is voluminous so relevant information can be located quickly. Bring only the records that you are asked to bring. Bring at least one copy of the records with you so you can substitute the copy for the original and return to your office with your original records. As with testimony, do not turn over client records unless you have client consent, a court order, or other legal authority. Come to the deposition with the records in hand, but do not let anyone look at them until you have a legal basis for doing so.

*Clients should be contacted in an attempt to secure authorization to testify.*

**3. Consult.** Typically, the treating mental health professional is surprised by the deposition request. Myriad questions will run through his or her mind, including a curiosity about the litigation. Clients should be contacted in an attempt to secure authorization to testify, and it is appropriate as well to ask them questions about the lawsuit. Ask for names of all the parties' attorneys. Try to learn what the disputed issues are and what the client and the opposing party each want to achieve in the case to help you anticipate the kinds of questions that might be asked by the attorneys during the deposition. Try to determine what the client is expecting from you. If clients are horrified over the prospect of what might be disclosed, have them contact their attorney about pursuing limiting motions such as a motion to quash or a protective order from the court.

Get permission from the client, and contact the lawyer yourself. Try to force the attorney to spend time with you reviewing the file and discussing the case, especially any negative information about the client. Learn if a protective order is desirable or achievable. Ask the attorney to role-play with you questions that each attorney is most likely to ask. Have the attorney describe for you the personality and tendencies of the opposing lawyer in the case. Ask him or her to answer any questions you might have about the deposition process.

*You have the right to consult with your own attorney in preparation for the deposition.*

A witness has the right to be represented by his or her own attorney at the deposition. You also have the right to consult with your own attorney in preparation for the deposition. However, you still must have client consent to disclose protected health information to this lawyer. If the client consents, remember to enter into a business associates agreement with the attorney as required by the HIPAA Privacy Rule. (See *Portable Lawyer*, second edition, for a discussion of business associate agreements and sample forms.) If the client will not authorize disclosure, you can still ask the attorney about the process and the kinds of questions that might be asked of you in the deposition.

Consult with colleagues—being careful not to identify your client. Ask about their deposition experiences and any contact they have had with the lawyers in the case. If there are difficult treatment issues, review those issues with your colleagues and ask their professional opinion and advice.

Consult the literature and relevant and important research and studies. Be prepared to defend the diagnosis and treatment provided to the client. If the mental health or condition of a client is an issue in the lawsuit, both sides will want to examine you on what was or is wrong with the client, how you went about treating the problem, why you selected the technique or method you used, the treatment effect, the client's current state of mental health, and the client's prognosis. Proving how appropriate, good, and ethical your professional services were will help you if a licensing board or malpractice claim is brought against you by a client who loses the case and is upset with you.

**4. Deal with problem issues for the client.** On initial review of the client file, a mental health professional might realize that some information would be harmful to the client or the client's lawsuit. Under these circumstances, be proactive in bringing the problem to the attention of the client and, with client consent, to the client's attorney. The client will be less likely to hold the mental health professional accountable later if the client knows all efforts were made to protect him or her. If the information is really harmful, keeping the information or the mental health professional out of the case must be considered. That is the job of the attorney for the client, who can best assess the appropriateness and success of motions to quash the deposition subpoena or a motion for a protective order. Let the client's attorney advise the client that, as bad as the information may be, there is no way to keep the therapist from having to disclose it.

With advance knowledge and time to prepare, there may be a way to soften the impact of the negative information.

**5. Deal with logistical problems.** Most states allow for the filing of motions for protective orders if a deposition subpoena will cause an undue hardship, expense, or burden on the witness. The witness might be asked to testify on a day when she and her husband are scheduled to depart for a long-awaited vacation. Or, perhaps the deposition falls on a date when the therapist has an unusually large number of clients to see with little time to reschedule. It is possible that the witness has recently had surgery and is unable to travel across town to the lawyer's office. In these circumstances, contact the attorney taking the deposition to see if he or she will voluntarily agree to reschedule the deposition for a better date and time or location. If the attorney refuses, contact the other lawyer in the case to see if he or she can help. If you strike out with both lawyers, consider hiring your own attorney and seek protection from the court. Judges are usually sympathetic to such requests for protection if the requests are reasonable.

Remember that unless the noticing attorney agrees otherwise or a motion for protective order is filed, the witness is required to appear at the time and date set forth in the deposition. Failure to do so can result in sanctions being issued by the court.

Under these circumstances, can you get paid for your time in preparing for and giving the deposition? If the client initially (on entering therapy) contracted to pay fees for responding to subpoenas, the client can be billed for the mental health professional's time. If the witness is a forensic expert hired for purposes of the lawsuit, this contingency should be covered in the engagement contract requiring the client or the client's attorney to pay the fees. But what if neither of these scenarios is true? Does the therapist who must cancel an entire income-producing day have any recourse?

There remains the possibility of seeking a protective order from the court asserting undue expense. It is possible for the court to enter an order for payment of fees to compensate the witness for the cost of lost income when giving the deposition. The expense to the witness in giving the deposition should be great enough to offset the cost of engaging an attorney to prepare, file, and argue the motion on the witness's behalf.

We also recommend a clause in the client's intake and consent form that obligates the client to pay fees to the therapist in the event the therapist is subpoenaed.

**6. Deal with problem issues for the mental health professional.** Mental health professionals are not immune to making mistakes, and being asked to testify in a client's case could bring a mistake to light.

Failing to generate notes or to maintain the physical integrity of a client's file would most certainly present problems if the offending therapist's deposition and client file were requested. Miscoding or misdiagnosing a client condition to ensure third-party reimbursement could lead to criminal prosecution.

When these kinds of serious problems arise, it is imperative that the therapist engage his or her own private attorney. There may be a way to work around the issue and protect the therapist or at least lessen the severity of the impact or consequences. Be careful about approaching colleagues who will have an ethical duty to report you to your licensing board if you have fallen short of your duties or obligations. An attorney will not have such a duty and may be able to help finesse you through the difficult dilemma and the deposition.

**7. Role-play.** As with live courtroom testimony, there is no better preparation for a deposition than to role-play questions and answers. Role playing should be done with an attorney for the client but, if not, with an attorney engaged by the witness for this purpose.

This session is also an opportunity for a mental health professional to provide the client's attorney with the "ask me about" questions that should be asked by the attorney. It is a time to perfect answers to the anticipated difficult questions. While perfection may be an unreachable goal, certainly being better prepared is realistic.

## Answers to Frequently Asked Questions About:

Depositions

Who pays for my time?

Who pays for copies of my records?

How long can it last?

### ❓ Question

*I have received a subpoena to give a deposition in a case involving one of my clients, whom I have been treating for 5 years. I have been asked to produce a copy of my client's file, which is huge. Who has to pay for the copies and my time? How long will the deposition last?*

**!** *Answer*

Most jurisdictions have restrictions in place that limit overall deposition time in a case and may restrict the amount of time that can be spent in deposing an individual witness. Other rules provide that depositions should take place during normal business hours and on nonholiday weekdays. You should consult with a lawyer in your state for the specifics.

Most states also have statutes that provide for the recovery of reasonable charges for record production to include a cost per page (usually not to exceed 25 cents per page) and an administrative charge ($15 or so per each request).

Getting paid for your testimony and preparation time is a more problematic issue. The general presumption is that witnesses should not get paid for their testimony. However, you can contract with your client before starting therapy, obligating the client to pay a fee if you are ever compelled to give testimony. If there is no contractual agreement, you

## Legal Lightbulb

- Even if the prospect of getting paid for time and expense in preparing for and giving the deposition in your jurisdiction is slim or nonexistent, play dumb and ask the noticing attorney about your fees.

- No judge is present to assist the witness at a deposition.

- The scope of questioning in a deposition is very broad, especially when probing a witness for bias.

- If you believe that you are at risk because of something you did or failed to do (negligent acts of omission or commission), consult with your own attorney as quickly as possible before the deposition.

- A subpoena to give a deposition is ordinarily in and of itself not an exception to confidentiality. Careful consideration must be given to whether a legal basis exists to disclose protected health information.

may consider filing a motion for a protective order due to the unfair expense the deposition will cost you. This is a matter of judicial discretion, and an attorney in your area should be able to tell you the likelihood of success for such motion.

## Summary

As with research for trial, preparation for a deposition requires many of the same techniques to prepare for an attorney's questions and answers. It is necessary to learn all that can reasonably be known about the facts of a case, the literature surrounding the problem at hand, the individuals involved, and the community attitudes about the circumstances unfolding in the litigation. Only then is the witness being deposed fully prepared to have the deposition taken. (See a checklist for deposition testimony in Appendix B.)

# 13

## Preparing for Courtroom Testimony

*Melissa Burns, a dedicated social worker, has been investigating the Rodriguez family. She has decided, clinically, that it is in the best interest of this family that the children be placed in a foster home for a while (perhaps 6 months or so) until the family can "get their act together." The attorney for the Rodriguez family has contested this decision and a suit is pending. The attorney has issued a subpoena duces tecum for Ms. Burns. What should she do?*

### Trial Preparation

To prepare for courtroom testimony, clinicians should:

**1. Review the record of the client.** Every clinician must have a clinical file that contains the progress notes of each client. This file must be reviewed microscopically to correct spelling errors and typographical mistakes, clarify statements that could be misread or misinterpreted, and, if needed, add an addendum to the file that makes it clearer and more complete. Use accepted methods of correction, such as lining out, dating, and initialing. Computer-generated records can be altered as long as the initial entry can still be read clearly and the new entry is initialed and dated.

**2. Organize the file.** In the perfect world, every client file is meticulously maintained, indexed, and filed in a manner that allows for instant retrieval. In the real world, some files are maintained more casually. Before trial, the file must be organized in chronological sequence, indexed as to subject matter, referenced if there are documents that pertain to the file but are not part of the file, and assembled. If there are letters, memoranda, notations from other therapists, audiotapes, videotapes, movies, photographs, drawings, test scores, or comments from other individuals such as teachers, counselors, principals, physicians, or nurses, these items should be listed in a table of contents.

*Before trial, the file must be organized.*

Likewise, if there has been selected research concerning the file, a bibliography should be available, especially if the therapist relied on a particular study in forming an opinion. Whatever professional literature or scientific or semiscientific data contributed to the ultimate conclusion should be part of a supplementary file, available for examination.

**3. Contact the client.** You might presume that every client has an attorney and every attorney has kept his or her client fully informed concerning the litigation and the involvement of the mental health professional in the case. Another presumption is that the client is fully informed as to the ramifications of mental health testimony and how such testimony can affect the postlitigation life of the client. While these are comfortable presumptions, they are not necessarily reality. Sometimes, lawyers, awash in problems of their own, do not keep clients fully informed as to all the implications of litigation, including what might or might not be part of a court or trial transcript. Witnesses can say what they intend to say and can be maneuvered into saying things they never meant. Make sure the client is fully informed by means of a lawyer-drafted waiver of confidentiality form that fully indicates to the client that the information about which you testify will become part of the public domain and the therapist is not responsible for how this information may be used by third parties.

**4. Copy the record.** After reviewing the clinical record, make at least two or three copies—one for the lawyer for the client and another for opposing counsel, if requested. A third copy might be required for the court. Generally, the best idea is to copy the file and ask the court's permission to substitute a "true and correct" copy for the original. This request is universally granted, and the witness keeps the original file while the copy is introduced into evidence and becomes an exhibit in the case.

**5. Comply with and review production requests.** Often, as part of the discovery process, opposing counsel will request that the therapist produce documents for examination and copying. After the documents are produced, they may be used in the litigation depending on the relevance of the evidence and the usefulness of the material. It is important that prospective witnesses review each document so they are familiar with its contents. Often there is a phrase in a letter, an error in a memorandum, a position in a mental health status report, or a typographical error in a clinical file that needs correction and explanation at the time of trial. The therapist must be cognizant of this circumstance *before* the trial begins.

**6. Review requests for admissions, interrogatories, and depositions.** In the nature of trial practice, there may be a considerable time lapse between the date a deposition was taken, admissions were propounded, or interrogatories were answered and a court appearance. Reviewing the discovery documents before the trial is critical so that memories are refreshed and so that no one is attacked in the courtroom by testimony that is considered a "prior inconsistent statement." Do not rely on your memory of a deposition taken years ago. Review. Is it still correct, or does it require up-to-date clarification?

**7. Consider protective orders.** Several protective motions are available to witnesses and clients when they are subpoenaed to court. One is a motion to quash, which is usually used when there is a technical error in the subpoena itself. In a motion for a protective order, after a hearing, the court may rule that all or certain of the items or documents subpoenaed into court are not germane to the case or are irrelevant or immaterial. When a subpoena is served, if in the considered judgment of the client and the attorney, the testimony or the clinical file should be protected in some way, a lawyer files these motions to guard and protect either the witness or the file or both. Whether to file these motions is part of the strategy of counsel with the advice and consent of the client. Protective motions are not always used, but they should always be considered.

**8. Attend a pretrial lawyer conference and role-play.** Many busy lawyers review the clinical file and then call the clinician, saying, "I see nothing damaging to my client in the file. Just go to court and tell the truth." This is good advice but at a bad time. An effective witness should not go to court without role-playing the testimony with the lawyer. Although direct examination is usually simple and straightforward, cross-examination can be brutal. Everything can be challenged, including background, diagnosis, treatment, periodic prognosis, and just about everything else in the client file or alleged from the witness stand. It is important to anticipate all the direct examination questions and have prepared and rehearsed answers. It is also important to review the facts of the case with the lawyer and anticipate tricky, sometimes manipulative, cross-examination questions. These kinds of questions can be handled effectively only if they are considered in advance and if preparation is made. It is somewhat like a college exam. No one knows for sure what the professor will ask, but with planning and time, most questions are predictable and sensibly answerable.

*It is important to anticipate all the direct examination questions and have prepared and rehearsed answers.*

**9. Expect certain questions in cross-examination.** You may be asked questions such as:

Do you have the requisite learning, education, experience, and training to treat this client?

Does your opinion or conclusion result from scientifically based facts or evidence, or is it based on general, unsupported opinion?

If you have based your conclusions and opinions on studies and literature, are they still current and supported by the latest science in the field?

Who do you consider the prevailing authorities in this particular field at this particular time?

How much are you being paid for this testimony?

How much time did you spend with your lawyers preparing for this case?

Did your lawyers tell you what to say or how to testify?

Have you ever been arrested, divorced, convicted of a crime, caught cheating on an exam, expelled from a college or university, denied a professional license, or denied professional liability insurance, or have you had professional disciplinary action taken against you? *Note:* While these questions are asked *as if* seeking answers, the realistic possibility is that the inquiring lawyer has already investigated thoroughly and is quietly waiting for you to deny a fact that is known to him or her. The "hiding behind a log" attorney would love for you to deny you were ever married and then produce two or three divorce decrees.

Were you engaged just to come to court today or did you previously clinically treat this client?

Did you role-play direct and cross-examination with the plaintiff/defendant's lawyer? If so, what was the nature of the role play?

You used the word *paranoid*. Can you define the word? What are the ramifications of this particular problem? What are the side effects?

You noted in the file that the client took certain medications. How did these medications affect "talking therapy?"

There were certain corrections in the file. Was the file initially inaccurate? And if so, why?

You testified in your deposition that _____, yet today you have told us something different. These positions are inconsistent. Can you explain?

*Whenever there may be ramifications that may affect your life, separate from this case, consult with a private attorney.*

**10. Engage a personal lawyer.** On occasion it is important to engage a personal lawyer to represent you, especially if there is any hint of a *conflict of interest* between any of the parties and you. Whenever there may be ramifications that may affect your life, separate from this case, consult with a private attorney.

*Answers to Frequently Asked Questions About:*

Contract

Getting paid

Exercising legal remedies

### Question

*My client signed a lawyer-drafted, legally enforceable contract of engagement when she commenced therapy in which she agreed to compensate me at my usual hourly rate for all the time that I spent on her behalf, including any court or deposition time. Both she and her lawyer promised orally to honor this commitment when my deposition was scheduled and taken and later when I was asked to testify in court. Now, after some 15 hours in deposition time and 3 hours in court time, both refuse to answer my calls or respond to my invoices. What should I do?*

### Answer

There is no question that compensation should be paid. However, as practicing lawyers, we must suggest that if letters and calls do not produce a voluntary payment, write it off as a business risk and in the future demand a down payment prior to any court appearance or the taking of a deposition. Usually, referring an account receivable such as this to a collection agency, a lawyer for collection, or filing a suit in small claims court brings forth a counter claim for malpractice, a complaint to the licensing board, and letters to your national professional organization. This type of problem occurs often, especially if the client or the client's lawyer can find or create any fault with your treatment. This is an expensive lesson, which normally only has to be learned once.

## Summary

The effective witness begins to prepare for trial from the date of the engagement. Reviewing client records and all relevant documents and

## Legal Lightbulb

- Preparing for trial includes the review of all documents that affect your testimony in any way.

- Role-play your part of the trial with the client's lawyer.

- Legally justified and available protective motions should be used if appropriate.

role-playing examination and cross-examination with the client's attorney are crucial aspects of preparation. The client, the court, and the witness are best served when a witness presents competent and effective testimony in the case. Anything less than that can result in disciplinary action or a malpractice case for the mental health professional who takes the witness stand unprepared. (See the checklist for courtroom testimony in Appendix B.)

# PART IV

# *IN THE COURTROOM*

A treating therapist designs and equips the space in which therapy will be offered to clients. Within this world, the therapist is in control, comfortable, and confident. Once inside the courtroom, however, the therapist will encounter a much different world where judges and lawyers are in control, and one in which the therapist may experience discomfort and a lack of confidence. Becoming familiar with this environment is just as essential to gaining ease and confidence in testifying as solid preparation. The more one knows about the system, the environment, and the players involved, the more effective that person will be as a witness.

# 14

## Testimony Tips

*Kevin, a social worker, confidently walked to the witness stand in a malpractice case filed against the social services agency that employed him. Although he was not personally named as a defendant in the suit, his testimony was considered crucial by both sides. With 25 years of clinical experience, Kevin was sure that he would convince the jury to exonerate the agency in all respects. He previously had blown off attempts by the agency's attorneys to go over his testimony and prepare him for his courtroom appearance. What transpired was a disaster: The agency was found liable, and damages were assessed at $350,000. The agency then terminated Kevin's services. On questioning jurors, the agency's attorneys learned that jurors were unanimously turned off by Kevin's arrogance and his insistence that absolutely nothing wrong had been done by the agency, its staff, or anyone associated with this case.*

In deciding cases, jurors and judges are influenced by their perception of the witness's mannerisms, demeanor, and appearance. These things can be as important as what the witness has to say. By following a few common sense rules, witnesses can cause judges and jurors to have a more favorable perception of them.

*By following a few common sense rules, witnesses can cause judges and jurors to have a more favorable perception of them.*

### Tell the Truth

Lying under oath is perjury and can result in criminal prosecution and loss of your professional license and reputation. Even being evasive will leave the judge or jury with a very negative impression, and often the entire testimony of the witness is either discounted or disregarded.

## Testify from Your Own Knowledge or Observation unless Asked Otherwise

A mental health professional is always on much safer and stronger ground if his or her testimony is based on actual observations of the client and personal knowledge of the facts. Stick to what you know. Avoid testifying in the "we" mode; for example, "We always record this." "We always do it this way." Using the "we mode" makes the witness seem less credible, as if the witness has something to hide or is trying to spread blame around. When asked what you do, answer, "I do things this way, and here's why." Taking responsibility for what you do, have done, and what you have said will improve your overall effectiveness as a witness.

## Listen to the Question

The courtroom can be an intimidating place with lots of distractions. Force yourself to actively listen and to focus your attention on the person asking the question. Try to block out everything but the face and mouth of the person questioning you. Don't try to answer a question you think you heard. Ask for it to be repeated, concentrating fully on the questioner and the specific question the second time.

*It is better to give a precise and concise response to a question that you understand than to try to speculate and give information you think is being asked of you.*

## Answer Only the Question That Is Asked of You, and If You Don't Understand the Question Ask That It Be Repeated or Rephrased

You won't get demerits for politely indicating that you did not understand the question. It is better to give a precise and concise response to a question that you understand than to try to speculate and give information you think is being asked of you. It is critical in

a deposition that you understand the question because you will probably be given an admonishment at the onset such as, "If you answer
a question, it will be implied that you understood it." Giving the
wrong answer to a misunderstood question can spell disaster.

## You Are Not Taking a Test

"Right" or "wrong" answers are not an issue in a lawsuit. Truth is the
only important consideration. Professionals are commonly reluctant,
even fearful, of responding to a question with, "I don't know" or "I
can't recall." Assuming one of these responses is the truth, then it is
the correct answer. If you find yourself being forced to repeatedly answer that you cannot recall or you don't know, it helps to vary your
verbal and nonverbal responses to this line of questioning. Try to look
more thoughtful, pause, and then say, "I honestly can't remember." If
appropriate, qualify the response to appear more honest by saying, "I
wasn't in a position to observe the client on that occasion; therefore,
I can't answer your question."

## Unless You Personally Recorded an Event at the Time, All Dates Are Approximate

Use phrases such as "on or about" or "estimated to be." Qualify nu-
merical and descriptive items in your testimony because they are the
basis for fruitful cross-examination. For example, if you testify at trial
that you saw the client in your office on Monday, June 1, and you previously testified in a deposition that you saw the client in your office
on Tuesday, June 2, you have given your cross-examiner an opening. If
you had testified that you saw the client *on or about* June 1," the dis-
crepancy is more easily explained and the judge or jury will be more
comfortable with your time frame. This method of answering becomes
even more critical if there is a long lapse of time between a deposition
and the courtroom appearance. Your memory is likely to fade, and you
can improve your credibility and performance with this kind of qualification in your answers.

## Do Not Guess

If you approximate, say so. If you are asked the question, "For how long a period of time did Mr. Jones exhibit symptoms of depression?" do not say, "Three months," unless you are absolutely certain that is accurate. It is better to state something like, "To the best of my recollection, it was approximately 3 months." Don't be forced into giving a specific response if you are not certain of your answer. Attorneys are always looking for inconsistencies and inaccuracies in their cross-examination of witnesses.

## Do Not Testify without Refreshing Yourself with Your Reports, Records, Prior Testimony, Deposition, and Other Documents

*Ask a lawyer on your side of the case if he or she sees any problems with your records or reports.*

We have stressed the importance of refreshing yourself in other chapters. It is critical and part of normal preparation. Sometimes the only items of significance that cross-examining lawyers have going for themselves are the inadequacies of the records or reports. If you cannot remember details in the records or reports, it makes you look doubly bad. Memorize details if you must, but at least look them over very carefully. If you have time, ask a lawyer on your side of the case if he or she sees any problems with your records or reports. Review all the documents you have prepared, including your deposition transcript.

## Be Calm, Courteous, and Consistent in Your Demeanor

The best witnesses are those who treat each attorney asking questions in the same manner. The best witnesses and deponents are those who act as helpful and concerned when questioned by the defendant's attorney as they did when questioned by the plaintiff's lawyer—especially in a deposition. Remember to get clarification as to the identity of each participant in the deposition, his or her role, and whom they represent. You do not seek this information for the purpose of treating the attorneys differently but so you can better appreciate where the attorney is coming from. This information will help you see pitfalls in their lines of questioning. Also remember that depositions are used as opportunities to probe you for "hot buttons" to see what will upset or rattle you. Sometimes an attorney tries to wear you down by asking the same question over and over again to see if you will answer it more favorably.

## Loose Lips Sink Ships

Never volunteer information no matter how much you think it will help or needs stating. You can be courteous, calm, and consistent in your demeanor when providing a "yes" or "no" answer. Your goal should be to get on and off the witness stand or in and out of the deposition room as quickly and as unscathed as possible. Volunteering testimony can be the downfall of a witness, especially on crossexamination, and means much more time spent on the witness stand or in an attorney's office. If you believe you must explain your answer, be brief, thoughtful, and responsive to the question that was asked.

*Never volunteer information no matter how much you think it will help or needs stating.*

## Permit Yourself to Be Protected

It is the dream of attorneys to railroad a witness by asking questions that are fast, rhythmic, and innocent to the point that the witness is on a roll. Before the witness knows it, he or she has already answered a question that has been objected to. The judge then overrules the objection and lets the answer stand because the witness has already answered it. The judge may sustain the objection and instruct the jury to disregard the answer after they have heard it. This seldom does much good because jurors' minds are not tape recorders that can erase or delete the information that they receive. Wait a few seconds before you answer. If there is no objection made by an attorney about the improper method of questioning, ask for help yourself. Say, "Your Honor, the attorney is asking questions so quickly I don't have time to consider them and then respond." Slow the questioning attorney down yourself by giving deliberate consideration to every question before you answer.

In a deposition, there is no judge to turn to. If there is an attorney aligned with your client, he or she may be of some assistance if a questioning attorney is getting out of line. If you are without assistance of counsel and you can't get the attorneys to curtail their behavior, politely request on the record that they stop. As a last alternative, politely advise them that you will be unable to continue with the deposition if they continue to ask questions in this manner. Ask the court reporter to provide you with a copy of the transcript of the deposition so you will have it if one of the lawyers files a motion to compel your testimony or for sanctions.

## Testimony File

After you have testified, ask for evaluations from the lawyers, the parties, and even the judge once you have been dismissed from the case. Create a testimony file, and make notes on what you learned and what you can improve next time.

## Juror Observations

When speaking, it is important that you understand your audience. We have compiled a list of general observations about jurors that the mental health professional should keep in mind when testifying before a jury:

- Jurors don't like witnesses who don't answer questions. Being evasive can really irritate jurors, too, and it is better to answer the question even if the answer seems harmful.
- Jurors have a true sense of fairness. Although it is commonly believed that jurors make up their minds about a case in the first 5 minutes of the case, most jurors want to hear all the evidence and listen to what a witness has to say, even the 15th witness called to the stand.
- Jurors don't like witnesses to make forced eye contact with them. Witnesses are often instructed to look at the jurors when they answer a question. Jurors have advised us that this tactic seems too re-

hearsed and unnatural. Occasional eye contact is appropriate but consistent, forced contact is not.

- Jurors don't like witnesses who are too strong or forceful when making their case; for example, "We did *nothing* wrong!" or "We are a *caring* company!" Jurors believe those conclusions are their call to make: "Just give us the facts and we will decide." A mental health professional who comes across too powerfully or forcefully does not appear professionally objective.

- Jurors don't like witnesses who nod their heads, roll their eyes, or make other gestures toward the parties or attorneys at the counsel table. Jurors notice everything that happens in the courtroom and outside the courtroom. Make sure your demeanor and actions are just as appropriate in the hallway outside the courtroom as inside. The jurors will be watching you.

- Jurors don't like witnesses who speculate or guess. It is best to have a sound basis for all opinions given. The jurors are instructed to seek truth and to apply the facts to the law as given to them by the judge. Guesswork is not supposed to be part of that process.

- Jurors don't like witnesses who lose their cool or do not stay focused on the issues in the case. A good rule to remember is that the witness's level of indignation should never rise above the jury's level of indignation. If the case involves a failure to properly diagnose a patient, stay focused on the facts relevant to the case at hand; do not make the case into a crusade to reform the entire health care industry.

- Jurors don't like witnesses who overstate the case. Witnesses on the plaintiff's side are more likely to be guilty of overstatement, for instance, asking for $350,000 in damages for mental anguish.

- Jurors don't like anyone who interjects religion into a case. A holier than thou or preachy attitude will quickly turn off jurors.

- Jurors don't like arrogant witnesses. Think about it; nobody likes to be around or to listen to arrogant people. Humility goes a long way in connecting with jurors.

- Jurors don't like argumentative witnesses. They become impatient and angry with such witnesses who simply won't answer questions that are asked. These witnesses ultimately come across as being too defensive, and their testimony is suspect and might be discounted, dismissed, or disregarded.

- Jurors don't like to be talked down to. There is a common belief that, on average, jurors have an eighth-grade education. That statistic is probably outdated, but even if it is true, there will be people on juries with master's degrees. Talk plainly to the jury but not down to them.

## Answers to Frequently Asked Questions About:

Testifying

Preparation

How do I get to say all I need to say?

Records

### ❓ Question

*One of my long-time clients recently asked me if I would testify on her behalf in a lawsuit she has filed. I agreed to do so at no charge because of her limited financial means but stated that I wanted to meet with her attorney before my court appearance to go over my testimony. Shortly thereafter, the attorney served me with a subpoena that didn't request me to bring my client's records. It is now two days before I am supposed to be in court, and I have not met with the attorney. He has not returned my phone calls. I really want to help my client in this lawsuit because I believe her claims have merit. What do I do?*

### ❗ Answer

You should continue to try to contact the attorney and make yourself available to meet to discuss your testimony. If you do not get an opportunity to meet with the client's attorney before the scheduled time for your appearance, it is best that you do not bring your records into the courthouse with you. You might want to make a photocopy and leave it in your car in case the client's attorney decides at some point that

## Legal Lightbulb

- Be calm, courteous, and consistent in your demeanor.

- Your appearance and mannerisms can be just as important as what you have to say.

- Answer only the question propounded to you. Do not elaborate.

- Never approach the giving of testimony cavalierly and without preparation.

- Create a file to record thoughts and what you have learned for each testifying experience. There will be a next time.

the records would be beneficial and would like to introduce them into evidence. Spend what time you need to review your records for accuracy and to familiarize yourself with the content. Make out a list of questions you think *the attorney should ask you* so you can provide information you believe would be helpful to your client's case. Give that list to the client or the attorney when you get to the courthouse. This procedure should ensure that you are given the opportunity to present to the judge or jury what you feel is important.

We understand your desire to be as helpful to your client as you can, but remember what your true role is. Your job is to provide quality mental health treatment to your client, and you should not be overly concerned about the outcome of her lawsuit. As a professional, you must remain objective and focused on your treatment responsibilities. The verdict or judgment is out of your hands.

## Summary

Unless the mental health professional is an experienced forensic witness, the prospect of giving a deposition or testifying in court is unnerving. By employing a few tips and some common sense, it can be less of an anxiety-inducing experience. Remember that providing quality treatment is your primary role, and although you will prepare and be the best witness you can be, you should not be overly concerned about the outcome of the case. Your goal should be to give objective and professional testimony in a deposition or in court and to get your testimony experience concluded as quickly as possible so you can return to providing quality mental health treatment.

# 15

## Lawyers' Tricks

*Shelly was a 63-year-old psychologist in private practice and an adjunct professor of psychology at the local medical school. She was engaged to testify as a professional expert witness. The basic thrust of her testimony was that two lesbian women could rear a 10-year-old male child as well as a heterosexual couple could.*

*As soon as cross-examination began, she was asked about her present living arrangements. It was revealed that she was living with a 34-year-old man and his child by his former relationship. As this line of detailed questioning continued, she became flustered and upset, finally breaking down into tears. She never anticipated that her personal life would become public information and she would be called on to defend her own living arrangement.*

*What should Shelly have expected?*

When a lawyer refers to the courtroom as theater, the mental health professional feigns shock and surprise. Is not the courthouse the bastion of truth, the final arbiter of what really happened in a conflicted fact situation, and the foundation of all our liberties? Is not the judicial system the guardian of all that is sacred in America? Yes. But the path to all that truth, the protection of liberties, and the guarding of all that is sacred in America is a time-tested process with which we are all familiar either through literature, movies, TV, or our individual experiences. The search for truth and justice is through a maze of procedures and practices that are theatrical, confusing, and often for the purpose of obfuscating the truth. Finally, though, the truth should emerge.

*When the mental health professional is called to the court, the clinician can become the pawn of the two lawyers.*

When the mental health professional is called to the court, the clinician can become the pawn of the two lawyers. To the lawyer who examines the witness on direct examination, the witness is usually a helpful individual who supports the lawyer's client in the client's perception of ultimate truth. The question and answer format is friendly and flows smoothly, with carefully crafted questions designed to support this client's case. Usually there are no surprises. The questions and possible answers are role-played beforehand, and the witness is primed to answer competently and clearly. Few, if any, questions are asked without the answer being known well in advance.

*Witnesses can be questioned concerning their background, history, schooling, education, licenses, and experience as well as their marriages, children, divorces, work or employment history, and any history of addictions.*

However, cross-examination is different. Cross-examination is designed to challenge the witness's credentials, opinions and conclusions, tools of the trade, and the viability of mental health treatment in general. It also challenges the witness's memory of dates and events, whether the witness is being paid, whether the payment might influence judgment, and whether that judgment is prejudiced by individual history, experience, upbringing, or background. Witnesses can be questioned concerning their background, history, schooling, education, licenses, and experience as well as their marriages, children, divorces, work or employment history, and any history of addictions. In summary, when functioning as a witness, the total background, cradle to court, may be subject to cross-examination.

Tricks that lawyers play include:

- **Intentionally mixing up dates:** Be careful of the lawyer who asks for the precise date of an occurrence or episode and then offers a series of dates and asks you to place them in chronological or sequential order. Always couch specifics with words such as "on or about" or "to the best of my recollection," which offer some maneuvering room. On occasion, dates in a clinical file can get confused when entered and are later discovered to be incorrect when compared with collateral information. If an error is made, don't be reluctant to admit to the confusion.

• **Rapid-fire questions:** There must be thinking time between questions and answers. Don't *ever* let the lawyer rush you into thinking that the important matter before the court deserves or justifies a quick answer rather than an accurate response. Take your time. Be sure you understand the question. If not, ask for it to be repeated or clarified. There is no hurry.

• **Leading questions:** A leading question is one that suggests or implies an answer. Sometimes it is the "Do you still beat your wife?" type of question that implies that you used to beat your wife and, by answering the question, an admission that may be untrue is made. Leading questions are allowable and admissible under cross-examination, and the unwary witness may fall into this trap if the question is answered quickly. "I never beat my wife" would be appropriate. "Yes" or "no" would be inappropriate. Demand clarification or tell the court that such a question as this cannot be answered in the manner demanded by counsel.

• **Multiple questions:** Lawyers often get caught up listening to their own voices and ask a series of questions disguised as one question. "Did you go into the house, walk up the stairs, wake up the children, scream at your wife, and then strike her?" In polite conversation, this might be a sensible sentence. On the witness stand, it is objectionable because it is a series of questions, and, as a witness, you have the right to demand that each part of the question be asked separately. One answer to all questions would be inaccurate as well as misleading. Ask that the question be divided into separate questions and seek the help of the judge. The judge will instruct the attorney (who knows this to begin with) that questions capable of an answer should be answered one question at a time, independently, with sufficient time to frame and state an answer.

• **Trapping by jargon:** Between mental health professionals and their colleagues, psychotherapeutic jargon is appropriate as a short-hand method of communicating diagnosis, prognosis, and treatment plans. However, jargon can be devastating if not clearly understood and easily defined in a commonly accepted manner. As elsewhere stated in this book, if a word is used in written memoranda anywhere, it should be capable of explanation from the witness stand by the individual clinician who used it or relied on it as part of the clinical record. The witness must know the layperson's definition as well as the technical one. The judge and each juror must understand what you are saying in terms clear to them.

• **Questions that can't be answered "yes" or "no:"** On cross-examination, the attorney can ask a question and demand a yes or no answer. While many questions can be answered in this manner, many cannot. If a positive or negative answer would be misleading, inaccurate, or confusing, ask the judge for the opportunity to explain the answer. Look at your lawyer and wait for an objection before responding. The lawyer will get the point.

• **Personal and intimate questions:** The lawyer, on cross-examination, has the right to ask personal and intimate questions concerning your failures: in school, in marriage, in the rearing of your children, or in business. The lawyer may probe about your history of arrests, convictions, complaints filed against you, or whether your liability insurance (malpractice) has been denied. He or she may ask you about schools where you applied to serve as an adjunct professor and whether you were accepted, as well as your publishing history. Be prepared for these questions.

• **Attacking the tools of the profession:** If using projective tests, inkblots, or other well-recognized tests, it is important to know the background of the tests, their viability, their level of acceptance, and the professional viewpoints concerning these tests. Be sure to explain some of the negative factors of each particular psychological tool and how consideration was given to those factors in arriving at your conclusions. There are few tools of any trade without flaws.

• **Comparison of texts or publications:** In researching an important case, the lawyer often finds texts, publications, articles in professional journals, or media coverage that supports a point of view different from the view of the testifying witness. Be prepared with answers such as:

"I am familiar with this work, and it can be distinguished in the following manner . . ."

"I believe his research concerned a different group of individuals and does not apply here for the following reasons . . ."

"He has been heard on this subject more recently, and his current view is now _____."

Be prepared to be challenged if any particular text, author, or article is used to substantiate a given point.

## Answers to Frequently Asked Questions About:

A checkered past . . . the reformed sinner

An alcohol or drug past

Detailed reformation

### ? Question

*My past is checkered at best. For many years following college, I drifted in a hazy existence of alcohol and drugs. Finally, I have recovered, returned to graduate school, and now have a PhD in family counseling. I currently have a terrific position with a local counseling center. The staff is aware of my past and feels it is an advantage when counseling with my addictions clients, although I do not always feel it necessary to share my personal struggle with my clients.*

*I have been asked to attend court and testify on behalf of a recovering client, but I am afraid my individual experiences with drugs and alcohol will make me vulnerable to personal attack. I have little to hide from my employer, but will the cross-examining lawyer be able to destroy me?*

### ! Answer

First, arrange a conference with the lawyer who represents your client and tell this lawyer the complete truth. What you tell the lawyer is both confidential and privileged. Give the lawyer the details of your past, and let him or her know you are willing to testify if needed but that you have misgivings. Let the lawyer make the decision as to whether you should be called as a witness.

If the lawyer decides to put you on the stand, he or she will probably have you testify honestly and completely concerning your addictions history. Your testimony will trace this history from the level to which you sank to your current level. It will show how you have beaten your addictions to become a respected, professional member of society. With this open and honest confession before the court, opposing counsel will be hard pressed to attack or harass you. In general, judges and juries forgive reformed sinners and appreciate the new contribution they are presently making to society. Don't be overconcerned about your difficult years.

## Summary

Contested trials are in part theater, but they also are the best method so far devised for resolving conflicts once all efforts to reach an agree-

## Legal Lightbulb

- Don't ever put a lawyer in a position where he or she can be surprised by shocking new information in the middle of a trial. This can be a disaster for the lawyer, your client, and yourself.

- Judges won't allow a lawyer to harass, intimidate, or threaten a testifying witness. However, they will allow wide latitude in the types of questions asked.

- During a trial, the witness can appeal to the court (the judge) for help, but it is the duty of the witness's lawyer to protect the witness from improper questions or inappropriate conduct.

- Rapid-fire questions, demanding yes or no answers, intimate questions, shouting, questioning the tools of the trade, demanding definitions of psychological jargon, and so on are part of a lawyer's bag of tricks.

ment have failed. Certainly, a trial in court is better than a fistfight or a duel. For those involved in this justice system, there are certain risks and hazards. The best approach is to be comfortable with the system and to know its rules.

It is important to know how the system works, the basic rules of evidence that pertain to this trial and to this witness, to the production and explanation of documents, and to the various methods used by lawyers to obtain favorable verdicts and judgments. As in every other facet of life, forewarned is forearmed. By knowing court traditions and procedures, as well as the positions of the various participants and their established roles, the witness is more comfortable in the courtroom and more effective from the witness stand.

# 16

# Challenges to the Expert Witness: The *Daubert* Case

*Carol was a licensed psychologist who considered herself an expert on re-covered memories and the treatment of survivors of childhood sexual abuses. Consequently, when the attorney for a client she treated asked her to appear as an expert witness in a case in which the client was suing an al-leged perpetrator of childhood sexual abuse, Carol had no reservations about accepting the engagement. She prepared diligently and spent hours refining her testimony with the attorney who retained her. When the time came for her courtroom appearance, she confidently walked to the witness stand and was sworn. To her dismay, the opposing counsel made an objec-tion that the court sustained. The jury was sent to its deliberation room, and her attorney began asking her questions in an attempt to have her qualified as an expert witness so that she would be allowed to testify in front of the jury. After an hour of examination, the court ruled that Carol should not be allowed to testify. Carol left the courtroom in total bewilder-ment with hurt pride. What happened?*

Few cases have had the impact of the *Daubert v. Merrell Dow Pharms., Inc.*, 509 U.S. 579, 113 S. Ct. 2786, 125 L. Ed. 2d 469 (1993) (*Daubert*) case, a landmark decision that must be conceptually understood by all mental health professionals as they prepare to testify.

This case, and the appellate decisions that followed, offered spe-cific and detailed instructions to judges about the admissibility of ex-pert testimony. Attorneys and the expert witnesses they call to testify must be familiar with these guidelines. Extensive experience and a good reputation no longer automatically qualify a witness as an expert who will be allowed to testify. Thorough and comprehensive knowledge of the subject matter and the reliability of the science or methodologies employed by the expert are now key.

The material in this chapter is detailed and technical and a direct response to the repeated requests we receive from mental health professionals for a thorough explanation of the origin and significance of *Daubert*.

When issues in a case are complex and beyond the ordinary familiarity of a lay jury or judge, the assistance of persons qualified by skill, knowledge, training, education, or experience has been allowed. The use of and reliance on experts in litigation today have grown tremendously with the advent of technical subjects such as DNA analysis, patented scientific processes, and the role of chemical and pharmaceutical agents in the causation and care of rare diseases.

*The use of and reliance on experts in litigation today have grown tremendously.*

Originally, experts were viewed as impartial specialists who came to trial to explain technical concepts and to shed light on difficult and sometimes esoteric subjects. Over time, with some abuse of the system, this perception changed and experts came to be regarded as advocates for the party that hired them. This practice of providing "opinions for hire" gradually changed the impression of experts from one of respected professionals to that of "hired guns."

At the same time, experts continued to play a vital role in court proceedings. Expert witnesses were still viewed by juries as "unbridled authority figures" who appear more credible than lay witnesses (*E. I. du Pont de Nemours and Co. v. Robinson*, 923 S.W. 2nd 549, 553 [Tex. 1995]). In many cases juries were unable to reconcile conflicting testimony offered by competing experts. Courts traditionally displayed a "let it all in" philosophy believing that it was up to juries to decide the weight to be given to expert evidence. More recently, this approach proved to be inadequate, and courts responded with various reforms aimed at restraining the use of experts and improving fact-finding endeavors as applied to scientific, technical, and other specialized issues.

Challenges to expert witnesses typically are made on one of the following three grounds:

1. Subject matter challenges.
2. Expert qualifications.
3. Lack of reliability of methodology and conclusions.

## Subject Matter Challenges

To be admissible, expert testimony must assist the judge or jury. The expert must have knowledge and experience on a relevant issue that is beyond that of the average juror or the judge and the testimony helps to determine what happened in the case. If an expert witness's testimony is within the common knowledge of the judge and jury, the testimony will be excluded.

The fact that an expert's opinion embraces an ultimate issue (one the jury or judge is being asked to decide—e.g., has Dr. Jones breached his duty of care to the plaintiff?) does not make the testimony inadmissible. Experts will not be allowed, however, to testify on matters considered to be *pure* questions of law (e.g., the existence of a duty of care or the construction of a state statute). Sometimes a court allows testimony that involves a mixed question of law and fact (e.g., practicing a mental health discipline in violation of a state licensing act).

## Expert Qualifications

*There is no specific test to determine whether a particular witness is qualified to testify as an expert.*

A witness may be qualified by knowledge, skill, experience, training, or education to give an expert opinion. Only one of these criteria is necessary for qualification. An expert may be qualified in a particular case by virtue of his or her education even in the absence of actual or considerable experience in a particular area. Conversely, lack of education will not necessarily disqualify an expert who has considerable hands-on experience. There is no specific test to determine whether a particular witness is qualified to testify as an expert. It is the judge's duty to assess the expert's competence, and it is the jury's role to weigh the expert's testimony based on the witness's qualifications and knowledge of the subject matter.

## Lack of Reliability of Methodology and Conclusions

The biggest change in the law governing admissibility of expert testimony has occurred concerning judges' assessments of when experts' opinions are reliable. This element of admissibility has always existed in modern procedural doctrine in one form or another. For years, federal and state courts followed the "general acceptance" test first outlined in 1923 in *Frye v. United States*, 293 F. 1013 (D.C. Cir 1923) (*Frye*). In this case, the court of appeals for the District of Columbia considered the admissibility of evidence derived from a precursor of the polygraph test. The court described the device and its operation and declared:

> Just when a scientific principle or discovery crosses the line between the experimental and demonstrable stages is difficult to define. Somewhere in this twilight zone the evidential force of the principle must be recognized, and while courts will go a long way in admitting expert testimony deduced from a well-recognized scientific principle or discovery, the thing from which the deduction is made must be sufficiently established to have gained general acceptance in the particular field in which it belongs.

This case holding evolved into the rule that expert opinion based on a scientific technique is inadmissible unless the technique is "generally accepted" as reliable in the relevant scientific community. Eventually some courts diverged from this view, concluding that the *Frye* formula had been supplanted by the standards of evidence embodied in the Federal Rules of Evidence enacted in 1975. The issue was finally resolved when the U.S. Supreme Court articulated new "reliability" rules in a series of decisions: *Daubert v. Merrell Dow Pharms., Inc.*, 509 U.S. 579, 113 S. Ct. 2786, 125 L. Ed. 2d 469 (1993), *General Elec. Co. v. Joiner*, 522 U.S. 136, 118 S. Ct. 512, 139 L. Ed. 2nd 508 (1997) (*Joiner*), *Kumho Tire Co. Ltd. v. Carmichael*, 526 U.S.137,119 S. CT. 1176, 143 L. Ed. 238 (1999) (*Kumho*).

## Daubert

In *Daubert*, the plaintiffs were parents who claimed their children's birth defects were caused by their mother's ingestion of Benedictin, a drug prescribed to combat nausea during pregnancy. Merrell Dow, the marketer of Benedictin, moved for summary judgment (a ruling by the court that there is no basis for the case to go to trial), supporting its motion with the affidavit of an expert who stated that no published study had found Benedictin to cause malformations in fetuses. The plaintiffs responded with eight experts who concluded, based on animal-cell and live-animal studies, pharmacological studies, and re-analyses of previously published epidemiological studies, that Bene-dictin can cause birth defects. The federal district court granted the summary judgment finding that the plaintiff's scientific evidence did not meet the *Frye* "general acceptance" standard, and the Ninth Cir-cuit Court of Appeals affirmed. Both courts concluded that an expert opinion not based on epidemiological evidence, in light of the vast amount of data available, was not admissible. The experts' animal-cell, live-animal, and pharmacological studies standing alone could not raise a jury issue as to causation. Further, the reanalyses of prior epidemiological studies were not "generally accepted" within the sci-entific community, as evidenced by the fact that reexaminations had not been published or subjected to the peer review process and were generated solely for use in litigation.

On appeal, the U.S. Supreme Court held that the *Frye* "generally accepted" standard was not the governing standard following the en-actment of the Federal Rules of Civil Evidence, Rule 702, which states:

> If scientific, technical, or other specialized knowledge will assist the trier of fact to understand the evidence or to determine a fact in issue, a witness qualified as an expert by knowledge, skill, experience, training, or education, may testify thereto in the form of an opinion or otherwise.

This rule places limitations on the admissibility of scientific evidence without the application of the "general acceptance" standard of *Frye*. The court explained that "scientific knowledge" as envisioned by the Rule requires an inference or assertion to be derived by scientific method and supported by appropriate validation, meaning that scien-tific knowledge is subject to a standard of "evidentiary reliability." Be-cause evidence or testimony under Rule 702 must also "assist the trier of fact to understand the evidence or determine a fact in issue" and because irrelevant evidence is no help to the jury, scientific evidence must be relevant as well as reliable.

The Supreme Court went on to make some "general observations" for trial judges who are called on to determine whether an expert's testimony involves scientific knowledge that will assist the trier of fact to understand or determine a fact in issue. The Supreme Court explained that there must be a "preliminary assessment of whether the reasoning or methodology underlying the testimony is scientifically valid and of whether that reasoning or methodology can be applied to the facts in issue." The Supreme Court then identified the following four factors (which should not be considered a definitive checklist) that might be helpful to a trial judge's inquiry as to whether expert testimony should be included:

1. Whether the scientific knowledge can be (and has been) tested;
2. Whether the theory or technique has been subjected to peer review and publication;
3. Whether the technique has a known or potential rate of error; and
4. Whether there is general acceptance of scientific technique.

Emphasizing that Rule 702 is flexible, the court added: "Its overarching subject is the scientific validity—and thus the evidentiary relevance and reliability—of the principles that underlie a proposed submission. The focus must be solely on principles and methodology, not on the conclusions that they generate."

## Joiner

An issue unresolved in *Daubert* was the proper standard of review that appellate courts should apply in assessing the district (trial) courts' decisions whether to admit or exclude expert scientific evidence. The plaintiff in *Joiner* brought suit against various defendants after he contracted cancer, allegedly because his work exposed him to polychlorinated biphenyls (PCBs). The plaintiff offered expert testimony to establish his causation theory, but the district court ruled that the testimony was scientifically unreliable and inadmissible. The Eleventh

Circuit Court of Appeals reversed the case, declining to exercise the abuse of discretion standard in reviewing the district court's ruling. The case was then heard by the U.S. Supreme Court, which held that the same abuse of discretion standard that applied to evidentiary rulings generally also applied to the admission or exclusion of expert testimony.

In applying the abuse of discretion standard, the Supreme Court determined that the district court in *Joiner* had not erred in excluding the expert testimony. The court rejected the plaintiff's claim that the district court in barring the testimony had improperly second-guessed the expert's *conclusions* as opposed to considering only the reliability of the expert's *methodology*:

> Respondent points to *Daubert's* language that the "focus, of course, must be solely on principles and methodology, not on the conclusions that they generate." He claims that because the District Court's disagreement was with the conclusion that the experts drew from the studies, the District court committed legal error and was properly reversed by the court of Appeals. But conclusions and methodology are not entirely distinct from one another. Trained experts commonly extrapolate from existing data. But nothing in either *Daubert* or the Federal Rules of Evidence requires a district court to admit opinion evidence which is connected to existing data only by the *ipse dixit* of the expert. A court may conclude that there is simply too great an analytical gap between the data and opinion proffered. That is what the District court did here, and we hold that it did not abuse its discretion in so doing.

## Kumho

Rule 702 applies by its own terms to "scientific, technical, or other specialized knowledge. . . ." *Daubert* made its observations about the Rule's requirements for reliability solely in the context of the "scientific" part of that formulation. That left open for some observers the question of whether the same test would extend to *nonscientific* opinions that were of a "technical" or "specialized nature" (e.g., mental health professional). In *Kumho*, the U.S. Supreme Court clarified this issue by holding that *all* expert testimony is subject to *Daubert's* reliability.

The claim made by the plaintiffs in *Kumho* was that a manufacturing defect in a tire caused a blowout, which in turn caused an accident that resulted in numerous injuries and one death. The tire had been manufactured and installed on the vehicle 5 years before the plaintiffs had purchased it, and, by the time of the accident, the tire had worn bald in certain areas and had undergone prior inadequate repairs to patch punctures. The plaintiffs' expert, who had a master's degree in mechanical engineering and 10 years' work experience at a tire manufacturer as well as prior consulting experience in other tire blowout cases, gave his opinion on the combination of his knowledge of tire failures, a personal theory of the cause of tire failures, and his inspection of the tire at issue. He deduced his conclusions from what he knew and observed: A properly manufactured tire carcass stays bound to its tread; the tread on this tire did not stay so bound and thus was defectively manufactured. The district court excluded the testimony on determining that the expert's method of relying solely on a visual inspection of the tire was unreliable. The Eleventh Circuit Court of Appeals reversed, holding that *Daubert* applied only to "scientific" expert observation.

The U.S. Supreme Court overruled the Court of Appeals holding that the *Daubert* rule was applicable to all opinion evidence offered under Rule 702. The standard seeks to ensure the reliability not only of testimony based on "scientific" knowledge but also that based on "technical" and "other specialized" knowledge, as expressly contemplated by the provisions of the Rule. The overarching goal of *Daubert's* gatekeeping requirement is to make certain that *any* expert, whether basing testimony on professional studies or personal experience, employs in the courtroom the same level of intellectual rigor that characterizes the practice of an expert in the relevant field. Again, this requirement applies to *all* types of expert opinion, even that based primarily on the expert's experience or observations.

## What Do These Cases Mean for Mental Health Professionals?

The judge in a gatekeeper role assesses the expert witness's testimony in light of the Supreme Court's suggested guidelines, namely:

- Whether the scientific knowledge can be (and has been) tested;
- Whether the theory or technique has been subjected to peer review and publication;
- Whether the technique has a known or potential rate of error; and
- Whether there is general acceptance of scientific technique.

In Carol's case, the judge determined that her testimony lacked the necessary evidentiary relevance and reliability to be admissible. The judge may have concluded that Carol's theories about recovered memories:

- Had not been tested or were incapable of being tested;
- Had not been subjected to peer review and publication;
- Did not have a known or potential rate of error; or
- Were not generally accepted in the mental health community.

The cases cited in this chapter are federal cases but are being applied by state courts as well. State courts have been given leeway by the U.S. Supreme Court to include more than just the four *Daubert* factors in making their determinations on the admissibility of expert testimony. In our home state of Texas, for example, the Texas Supreme Court has added two more factors that trial courts should consider: (1) the extent to which the technique relies on subjective interpretation of the expert and (2) the nonjudicial uses that have been made of the theory or technique (*E. I. du Pont de Nemours and Co. v. Robinson*, 923 S.W. 2nd 549 [Tex. 1995]). It is important that mental health professionals become familiar with the interpretations or extensions of *Daubert* made by their home state courts.

In today's courtroom environment, ever-greater scrutiny will be given to the testimony of mental health professionals. In most cases, *Daubert* challenges of a witness will be made during pretrial proceedings well in advance of a trial. Due to the expense involved in hiring expert witnesses, attorneys will have to do a good job of selecting witnesses that the court will approve. Knowledge of a judge and his or her tendencies is crucial because the judge is given such wide discretion in allowing or disallowing expert testimony. The only recourse to a litigant whose witness is denied the opportunity to testify is to raise the

*In today's courtroom environment, ever-greater scrutiny will be given to the testimony of mental health professionals.*

issue on appeal and convince an appellate court that the trial judge committed an abuse of discretion, which is not easy to do.

Expert witnesses and attorneys will have to work more closely together to ensure that the witness's testimony is allowed. Better research must be done to establish peer review, general acceptance, and testing results and to compile a list of supporting publications. Just because an expert qualified in one case does not guarantee the same witness will qualify in another case involving a different judge and facts. (See Appendix B for a short list of federal cases involving *Daubert* challenges of mental health professionals.)

## Answers to Frequently Asked Questions About:

Forensic testimony

Qualifying

Court appointments

### ⁉ *Question*

*I have recently become a licensed professional counselor and would like to do forensic work and court evaluations as well as treat clients in my private practice. My concern is my overall lack of experience. How do I go about getting work?*

### ❗ *Answer*

Your lack of experience does not automatically exclude you from being an expert witness. Your education, training, and license may be enough to qualify you in a given case. If you are appointed by the court to conduct an evaluation, you can usually be assured that the judge will allow you to testify. The judge may not agree with your findings or recommendations, but because he or she appointed you, it is not likely you will be disqualified.

Initially, trying to get hired by attorneys or litigants may be difficult. They will want to be sure your credentials are impeccable and that your methodology is supported by the literature and generally

## Legal Lightbulb

- If a mental health professional wants to get established as an expert witness, pursuing court appointments is an excellent way to begin.

- To be admissible, expert testimony must assist the judge or jury in reaching decisions on facts or issues in the case.

- The expert must have knowledge and experience on a relevant issue that is beyond that of the average juror or the judge.

- The methodology and techniques used by an expert witness to arrive at his or her conclusions and opinions must be reliable and relevant.

- The judge, as the evidentiary gatekeeper, decides whether an expert witness will be allowed to testify in a case.

accepted by the mental health community. Concentrate on securing court appointments to get the experience that will make you an attractive witness for attorneys. Attend legal seminars and hand out your card or brochures to trial lawyers. Network.

## Summary

The current judicial atmosphere requires more than a great resume for a mental health professional to be allowed to testify in front of a jury. The U.S. Supreme Court has laid out guidelines to assist judges in refereeing the battle of the experts, and both federal and state courts are applying them. These guidelines must be applied to all expert testimony. Experts must take care to document the reliability and relevance, including the general acceptance in the expert's professional community, of the methods and techniques employed and that serve as the basis for the expert's conclusions and opinions. The days of an individual merely announcing an extensive educational background or 30 years of service as the basis in and of itself to be allowed to testify in court are long gone.

# PART V

# *THE EXPERT WITNESS'S TOOLS*

Every carpenter or mechanic knows the importance of good tools. If a therapist is going to pursue work as an expert witness, good tools are also essential. An expert witness will need a good resume, a contract that protects the therapist, and a policy that ensures payment of fees for the time and service rendered to a client. A therapist should have these in hand prior to accepting an engagement to perform forensic services, and they should be reviewed regularly and improved on if necessary.

# 17

# The Resume: Your Introduction to the Court

*John Levine was a social worker with a problem: He didn't have an appropriate curriculum vitae for use in court. Instead, he presented the court with a 15-page, single-spaced vita that began with the fact that he was an Eagle Scout and included unimportant details such as his parts in local theater productions. What could have been accomplished with a simple, written, one-page vita delivered to lawyers, the court, and the jury prior to active testimony continued methodically and in monotone intonation for an hour.*

Whenever mental health professionals are called to testify as witnesses, they will be asked certain traditional questions designed to introduce them to the judge and jury. These questions are calculated to indicate that the witness, through learning, training, education, experience, licensing, and continuing education or professional development, has a specialized body of knowledge. This presentation of personal credentials is an important part of the judicial proceeding. The presentation must be handled carefully and resourcefully. The presentation of the witness's life and professional experience sets the tone of the testimony and the level of receptivity of the decision maker. Every mental health professional should have a vita to streamline the process.

*Every mental health professional should have a vita.*

The court resume or vita is not the same as the vita prepared for subsequent employment or to present to colleagues when delivering a professional paper. It is for one purpose only: to convince the judge or jury that the words from the witness stand come from a competent,

*The court resume or vita is not the same as the vita prepared for subsequent employment or to present to colleagues when delivering a professional paper.*

knowledgeable, educated, and trained mental health professional person. A resume should start with the date of college graduation, with significant entries such as degrees earned, major subjects and honors, and initial work experience. Then, as the years go by, each individual accomplishment is added.

Nothing is too small to include on this perpetually updated resume. In the future, depending on the situation when such information is needed, items that are not relevant or material for the presenting purpose can be deleted. The revised vita may contain one to two lines for an introduction, two or three lines for a summary bio for an advertising flyer, one or two pages maximum for a court appearance, or the whole summary for a late-in-life biography.

In putting together the vita, also known as a resume or *curriculum vitae* (CV), consider the following:

- List educational experiences completely. If there is a blemish on the record, for example, you flunked out of a program or failed several courses, either footnote the entry or be prepared to explain what happened. It is usually better to explain the reason for a failure than to allow the opposing counsel to discover it and capitalize on your omission.
- There might be some special research projects that prepared you for this testimony, especially if under the supervision of an agency head or well-known professor. If the material is still current and viable, it can be included.
- Often the witness is a local or national workshop presenter or keynote speaker. If so, include a sampling of speaking engagements with the speech title and a three- or four-word description. Speakers are not invited to speak unless they have some expertise in a subject or have some perceived reputation as being knowledgeable.
- It is not necessary to describe forensic experience in detail. However, opposing counsel is often eager to minimize or trivialize your testimony by implying or stating that, regardless of the facts, you are always on one side or another. In one case, a witness was a frequent speaker in support of Fathers for Equal Rights in custody

conflicts. He was constantly attacked by opposing counsel for having a bias in all custody disputes.

- Other factors might include educational experiences that are only peripherally related to the present case, military service if relevant, particular experience with a particular ethnic or racial group that might give you an insight not possessed by others, a hobby that indicates other interests and avocations, civic interests and activities that might affect or influence a point of view, and so on.
- Review the complete proposed vita with the attorney. Amend the vita in accordance with your understanding of the case and the lawyer's professional input.

See the sample vita form in Appendix B.

## Answers to Frequently Asked Questions About:

The vita

What to include and what not to include

### ❓ Question

*A client recently asked me to appear in court to testify as an expert witness concerning the "best interest of the children." I did believe that custody or conservatorship of the children should be awarded to my client, the mother, so I agreed to appear.*

*However, I have four different vitas: one that I periodically update for purposes of future employment, another that is a brief paragraph or two for introductions when I make a presentation, a third for flyers to be inserted in publicity for workshops and seminars (about two sentences), and a fourth that is a running total of all my achievements since graduate school. This last resume runs about 10 pages and is amended each time I attend a workshop, present, or publish. What should be on a vita that will be presented to the judge to explain and clarify my qualifications as an expert? What will impress the court without boring either a judge or jury with trivia?*

**!** *Answer*

The vita is a useful tool and can save hours of interviews prior to trial and examination and cross-examination in court. A judge would prefer not to have to listen to a long, formal presentation of the witness's accomplishments. Rather, the judge wants a document that summarizes learning, training, education, and experience to date, together with licensing and credentialing certifications by national and state organizations. Any relevant publications you authored would also be appropriate. You may want to put together a fifth vita for court purposes.

## Legal Lightbulb

- The summary of a witness's expertise may be by oral testimony or by introduction of a vita, resume, or *curriculum vitae.*

- The vita must be accurate and precise.

- The lawyer who represents the view opposing yours will probably search and read all publications you have authored. If you have ever written any point of view inconsistent with your testimony today, you will probably be challenged, attacked, cross-examined, and possibly embarrassed. Any prior inconsistent statements, publications, public pronouncements, or interviews are fair game for confrontation.

- Negative matters should not appear on a vita, but they must be explained to your lawyer. The lawyer must be informed of any action, activity, or event that might have a negative effect on your credibility or impact.

- Degrees that have no application to the case at hand need not be included, such as an engineering or art history degree received prior to your entering the mental health profession.

- Any vita submitted for the purpose of establishing credibility will be subject to critical scrutiny. Be careful what you write down; it can come back to haunt you.

## Summary

Specialize your vita for each case. Other information that does not relate to the case should be omitted. If there is doubt, let the lawyer make the decision. The principal goal of the vita is for the judge or jury to conclude that the witness possesses a sufficient body of specialized knowledge to be helpful to the court.

# 18

## Contracts

*Soon after establishing herself in private practice, Karen was contacted by a local attorney to evaluate a client and his relationship with his children in connection with a custody case. Grateful for the engagement, Karen launched into her evaluation spending 15 hours in all. She forwarded her report to the attorney along with a bill for her services. She then sat back and waited for the anticipated check to arrive. Two months later she still hadn't received the check, so she contacted the attorney, who informed her that the client lost the case, discharged him, and owed him past due fees. Furthermore, the attorney advised her that he wasn't obligated to pay her and she should have collected her fees up front from the client. "Didn't you have him sign a contract?" the attorney asked.*

### The Critical Importance of a Contract

*A contract establishes the terms of the relationship and services to be provided as well as the fees to be charged, the method of payment, and the payment schedule.*

Karen's inexperience caused her to fail to protect herself by obtaining a retainer fee up front plus a written and signed contract of employment. A contract establishes the terms of the relationship and services to be provided as well as the fees to be charged, the method of payment, and the payment schedule. Failure to enter into a written client contract makes it difficult to establish the agreement and to determine the extent of the client's or a third party's liability. This written contract should be prepared well in advance and be a standard form prepared by a lawyer for the therapist.

Karen launched into a custody evaluation *assuming* the attorney who requested her involvement would pay. She never dreamed the attorney would not be responsible to compensate her for her time and efforts. Either the client or the attorney who contacted her should have been presented with an attorney-drafted contract for forensic services that made perfectly clear who was to pay, how much would be paid, and when the payment would be made. Getting sufficient funds before providing services is the surest way to be paid. An example of a contract for forensic services is included in Appendix B.

*Getting sufficient funds before providing services is the surest way to be paid.*

Mental health professionals have a duty to obtain and document informed consent from clients to whom services are provided. An exception is a case in which the client is court ordered by a judge or magistrate to participate in the evaluation. The best proof that informed consent has been obtained is through the use of a detailed intake and consent form. Specific information must be disclosed to clients before services are provided. Inserting this information into the intake and consent form makes it extremely difficult for a client or any other person to establish that the mental health professional breached the duty to fully inform the client, for example:

*Mental health professionals have a duty to obtain and document informed consent from clients to whom services are provided.*

Although it is the goal of the undersigned therapist to protect the confidentiality of your records, there may be times when disclosure of your records or testimony will be compelled by law. In the event disclosure of your records or the therapist's testimony is requested by you or any third party or required by law, you will be responsible for and shall pay all the costs involved in producing or copying the records plus the therapist's normal hourly rate for the time involved in preparing for and giving testimony. Such payments are to be made at the time *or prior to* the time the services are rendered by the therapist. Therapist may require a cash deposit for anticipated court appearances, out-of-pocket necessary expenses, and preparation.

## What Should Be Included in a Contract to Provide Forensic Services?

A contract for forensic services should include, but not be limited to, the following provisions:

1. **A description of yourself and your credentials:** Include information about your education, licensing status, restrictions on your license or practice, if any, and, if you are practicing under supervision, the name and address of your supervisor. Inform your client from time to time if supervision changes. State your relationship to any referring entity. Mention your employer if you work for a group or agency, or, if you are in private practice, advise the client of your independent status. If you have been court appointed or engaged by an employer or another third party, this information should be clearly disclosed.

2. **A description of the services you provide:** Tell the client specifically what you will do and what techniques or services will be provided. Explain any testing that will be offered as part of the therapy and how each test will be scored and interpreted. The description of the services should include whether a report will be generated and to whom the report will be disclosed. Let the client know if courtroom testimony is anticipated. The idea is to make sure the client is fully informed, understands what is about to happen and gives informed consent to the treatment as well as a full understanding of the expenses of therapy, testing and courtroom preparation, and appearances.

3. **Procedures for appointments:** Tell the new client how far ahead you schedule appointments and how much notice you expect for a cancellation. Provide the client with specific information on scheduling and canceling appointments, including the times and the numbers to call. *State whether there is a charge for canceled or missed appointments* and the charge for missing scheduled appointments. "No shows" are the thorn in the side of many therapists.

4. **Length and number of sessions:** If a finite number of sessions will be involved in the forensic evaluation, advise the client of the number as well as the amount of time the client can expect to spend with the therapist. Let the client know if additional time will be required for psychological testing. If the number of sessions or the amount of time cannot be, or is not, predetermined, let the client know that as much time will be spent with the client as is necessary to appropriately conduct the evaluation and provide the necessary services and reports.

5. **Relationship between the forensic therapist and client:** It is important that a frank discussion occur with the client to ensure that the client understands that *the forensic mental health professional is not being engaged to provide therapeutic services.* The client should be further advised about dual relationships and boundary limitations and that a personal relationship between the client and the mental health professional can never occur. Advise the client that for your work to be most effective, you must have contact with the client only in the context of the evaluation or any legal proceedings in which you may participate. (How incredibly compromised would the opinion of a mental health professional be if it were shown that he or she had a dual relationship or fuzzy professional boundaries with the person evaluated or on whose behalf testimony was offered?)

6. **Fees/payment:** If the client is responsible for your fees, give him or her accurate information about all charges for the forensic services you will provide including the cost of testing, report generation, and time spent in preparation and testifying. State when payment is due. If a third party is responsible for the fees generated or incurred, advise the client of this fact. State also that if the third party, although contractually obligated to pay, does not pay, the client will be responsible for any fees incurred plus attorney fees if the account is referred to an attorney for collection. Such payments should be made *at the time or prior to the time* the services are rendered. The client should be primarily responsible for all services of any type rendered on his or her behalf. If third parties, such as attorneys, insurance companies, court systems, or investigators are to be responsible for payment, these obligations must be in writing, signed, and preserved.

7. **Confidentiality:** Clients come into a mental health professional's office with the expectation that everything said will be kept strictly confidential and will not be disclosed to any third parties. In reality, however, *absolute* confidentiality *is a myth.* Mental health professionals, including forensic experts, have the duty to explain confidentiality to a prospective client and to *reveal all* the exceptions. HIPAA's Privacy Rule does not impose a new duty in this regard for mental health professionals. Cover the exceptions

to confidentiality thoroughly, list as many exceptions as you can think of, and use the clause "including but not limited to." If you open a practice in a jurisdiction where it is unclear whether you have the right or "duty to warn" or contact an identifiable intended victim, have all your new clients authorize your right to contact any person in a position to prevent harm to the client or a third party. Ask the client to provide you with mail and e-mail addresses and phone numbers of specific persons you can contact if you reasonably suspect the client or any third party is in danger.

8. **Addresses/phone numbers for communication with client:** Be sure to have the client provide you with an address where mail and e-mail can and may be sent and one or more phone numbers (work/daytime, cell, evening, weekend) where you can contact the client if necessary. Check the validity of your client information file at regular intervals. Obtain client consent to contact the client or third persons at the numbers in the client file.

9. **Risks:** Tell all your new clients that you will provide truthful and objective information to the best of your ability and judgment. However, specify that at the conclusion of your evaluation, the client may not like your findings or opinions. It is possible that the client will be negatively impacted by your evaluation. The only expectation a client should have is that you will conduct an honest, objective, and professional evaluation and render opinions accordingly.

10. **Emergencies or therapeutic questions:** Even when presented with information about your forensic role, some clients may call you when an emergency presents itself or when a therapeutic need or question arises. A prompt referral to a competent health care provider, that is, the nearest hospital emergency room, should be provided and should be the only response given.

11. **Therapist's death/incapacity:** Confidentiality survives death— the therapist's as well as the client's. Most states impose a duty on therapists *to plan for these contingencies*, but not all have specific statutory provisions or ethical canons that set out procedures to follow in the event of the death or incapacity of the therapist or the death of a client. One approach is for therapists to state in their wills that all of their records and files are to go to the appro-

priate licensing board in the event of the therapist's death. The therapist's concern is breach of confidentiality. It is not appropriate for a therapist's spouse or any third party not consented to by the client to review files or appointment calendars. A death or disability plan should be conceptualized, implemented, and made available, when needed, to the personal representative of the forensic mental health professional. Provide for the client to consent to having another mental health professional of your choosing take possession of the client's file and contact the client in the event you become unavailable for any reason, incapacitated, or die. If the client wishes, he or she may designate the successor therapist or forensic evaluator as the recipient of the file on the death or disability of the treating professional.

12. **Consent to provide services:** Unless a court order directs a forensic evaluation to occur and for the client to participate, a client must consent for you to provide the forensic mental health services. The consent should authorize you to provide services and state the client's or a third-party payer's obligation to pay. It establishes a contract between you and the client, and it gives you all the rights and duties necessary to provide professional mental health services for compensation. Obtain and document client consent for adults, incompetent adults through their legally appointed guardians, and children consistent with appropriate state law. When the client is a child, make sure you have a signed intake and consent form from a person who has the legal authority to consent for that child. Obtain and retain a copy of any court order that establishes the authority to consent.

Careful consideration should be given to all contractual forms used by a mental health professional in the practice. More than one forensic intake and consent form may be necessary depending on the kind of case involved, the services to be provided, whether a court appointment or order is involved, whether a third party will be obligated for payment of the fees, and so on. An option is to use a general contract, and then insert clauses to apply to specific situations such as play therapy, addictions, communicable diseases, anger management, assertiveness training, and any of a number of special circumstances.

*More than one forensic intake and consent form may be necessary depending on the kind of case involved.*

Consult with a knowledgeable attorney in your area and develop a complete set of forms that will provide you with maximum protection while providing the client with all the information necessary to establish informed consent.

## Answers to Frequently Asked Questions About:

Time in court

Trial time

Scheduling

Rescheduling

### ? Question

*A lawyer just called me. She would like for me to visit with a new client, make an assessment, and then testify concerning my impressions and offer my opinion. She is convinced I will agree with her theory of the case. She also tells me it won't take much time—only a "few hours"—and the case is set next month. She will pay me my usual hourly rate for a whole day plus 20 percent over my usual rate for court time plus all my time when interviewing the client. Is this a good deal?*

### ! Answer

Time in court can never be predicted. It can be conjectured, but never stated with exact certainty. Too many surprise events can occur.

Remember, you will also have to reschedule all clients on the court date; then, if the trial is delayed or postponed, they will all have to be rescheduled again. This is an office nightmare and a huge inconvenience.

If you want to work with this attorney, require a deposit sufficient to cover all your preparation time as described in this chapter, and then create an engagement form with an evergreen balance of $1,000 or more. Bill for additional time if it is required or, when the services are no longer needed, refund the balance on hand.

## Legal Lightbulb

- The contract of a forensic witness is different from that of a therapist-client contract. It must be specifically drafted with courtroom testimony and evaluations in mind.

- One consideration that must be inserted in the contract is the possibility of unrealistic or inaccurate expectations of the evaluee.

- The forms included in Appendix B are for general reference. They must be adjusted and adapted to your practice, your goals, and your needs. They must be reviewed periodically and kept current.

- Client intake and consent forms are the mental health professional's best protection against many ethical and practice-related complaints a client may raise.

## Summary

Remember the old legal maxim that an oral contract is not worth the paper it is written on. If you try to rely on verbal assurances or your perception of what was discussed and agreed on, you may be unsuccessful in your attempts to collect fees, respond to a licensing board complaint, or defend against a malpractice lawsuit. "Get it in writing" should be your mantra in dealing with clients, forensic issues, or therapy. Develop, use, review, and update as needed your quality intake and consent forms. Let these forms be your proof and your first line of defense if a client calls your professionalism into question or refuses to pay a fee.

# 19

# Making Sure You Are Compensated

*Dale, a therapist, has been contacted by a lawyer whose client was in an auto collision late at night when a huge truck jumped the interstate median and hit his car head on. Some five months later, after thousands of dollars in medical expenses, the client is still afraid to drive at night. He may have posttraumatic stress syndrome or some other mental disorder, but to be compensated for this psychological injury, the injured client must produce an expert witness who will testify that the negligence of the truck driver was the proximate cause of the psychological injury. After examining the client, Dale concludes that, indeed, the collision caused the psychological damages, and he is ready, willing, and able to testify to that effect. How can he be sure he is compensated for his time?*

## The Agreement or Contract of Employment

*Arrangements should be made in advance for compensation.*

To our knowledge, mental health professionals do not take vows of poverty. Generally, unless the circumstance is a voluntary pro bono activity, the clinician called to court either voluntarily or involuntarily should be paid. Arrangements should be made in advance for compensation at the provider's usual rate plus, perhaps, an additional 10 percent or 20 percent for the inconvenience of going to court plus lost billing opportunities. A mental health professional should be compensated for more than just time on the witness stand. Time spent in reviewing records, doing research, consulting other professionals if appropriate, and preparing to testify should be included.

Because Dale will examine the client but not necessarily treat him, the contract should be specifically drafted for court-related services beginning with the initial examination and ending when the services are no longer needed. This (preferably lawyer-created) employment form or agreement should contain a contract including compensation for the following:

- Time spent conducting an investigation of the client and/or surrounding circumstances.
- All courtroom preparation including reading and reviewing the file, reviewing actual and potential examination and cross-examination questions including role-playing the potential testimony with counsel, and getting reacquainted with the rules of evidence as they pertain to the introduction of admissible mental health testimony.
- Checking the latest statutory and case law in this area of litigation and in this jurisdiction.
- Out-of-pocket expenses for incidentals such as mileage and copying documents.
- Court time including travel time, parking, waiting for the trial to begin, or waiting to be called as a witness.
- Telephone calls, computer time, lawyer conference time, and conferences with colleagues, which may be necessary from time to time.
- Establishing, keeping, and maintaining professional service logs for all time dedicated to this particular case.
- Review of current literature or literature search concerning the subject of the suit.
- Any other time when the therapist is obligated to devote time and energy to this litigation instead of other pursuits.

*Note:* It should be clear that this witness will be paid for testimony only, plus the time and effort expended in preparing for and attending the trial. Compensation is based on time and time only, and this time will be substantiated by time sheets, electronic logs, or other methods designed to indicate the dates of service, the hours devoted to the client, and the various times and descriptions of the services rendered. There should be no relationship between the amount due and the outcome of the trial—no contingencies, percentages, or bonuses, just straight time. Testimony is immediately suspect when payment is in any way related to the outcome of the case or the amount ultimately recovered.

## How to Secure Payment

If therapists are going to spend time and energy in preparation and then put their reputation and professionalism on the line during examination and cross-examination while testifying, they should be appropriately compensated. Not receiving the agreed fee from a client or an attorney who retained the therapist is a very disturbing experience that should be avoided. With forethought and firmness, the collection of one's fee can be dramatically improved, regardless of the outcome of the client's legal matter.

### Trust Fund Deposit

*The best method to guarantee payment is to demand an advance sufficient to cover anticipated expenses.*

The best method to guarantee payment for services to be rendered is to demand and require a trust fund deposit in the form of an advance sufficient to cover the anticipated expenses of the therapist. The client or the client's lawyer would make this deposit to compensate the mental health professional. For example, estimate the time needed for all the activities required in the preceding section and multiply the hours by the professional's hourly rate. Require that this sum be deposited with you with the understanding that if the case is settled or if the actual time is less than the estimate, the excess sum on deposit will be promptly refunded to the client or the client's lawyer if the lawyer advanced the funds. The deposit is a deposit only and is *refundable*. Any unused portion belongs to the person who made the deposit. Perhaps the contract for services could be drafted so the sum is *nonrefundable*. This is a negotiable point between the parties.

## Deposit and Bill as Earned

Sometimes lawyers and clients are unwilling or unable to make a substantial deposit, but the therapist would still like, for other reasons, to testify. In this situation a deposit can be negotiated, and the agreement will provide that the lawyer or client will be billed as the case progresses with payment due 10 to 20 days after the billing. The agreement should provide that if the bill goes unpaid for a specific period of time, the employment will be considered terminated and the therapist will retain any deposit as payment for services to date.

*Note:* If the bill goes unpaid for an unreasonable period of time, the attitudes of all parties become frayed and often hostile. Prompt payment should be required and termination of services enforced if payment is not received within the period of time specified in the agreement.

## Bill Periodically as Earned

Billing periodically is sensible, yet not as secure as getting all fees and expenses upfront. It entails billing as services are rendered with the possibility that, should the case be determined early by some legal maneuver such as a summary judgment or the client decides to dismiss the case, loses enthusiasm for litigation, is embarrassed by it, or feels that life would be better if the case were in the past rather than in the future, the client might abandon the proceeding, leaving the whole process without compensating the therapist or anyone else. Bill as you go is risky business, because at any given time there is an unpaid bill. It also means, in some sense of the word, that the therapist is financing the litigation and, as the bill grows greater, the possibility of payment is more dubious.

Bill as you go, without a deposit, is the payment method of last resort. It benefits the client and the client's lawyer without any substantial benefit to the provider. If this method is used, make sure that there is a time line and that payment is due 10 to 20 days after billing or else services will terminate. If payment is not due until the case is settled and/or money received, the contract should provide that the

*Bill as you go, without a deposit, is the payment method of last resort.*

client and the lawyer hold any monies received in trust for the therapist and pay the therapist immediately on receipt of payment from the payer. Get the stipulation in writing that the lawyer would make payment as soon as the settlement check is received from the paying party. Anecdotal stories abound concerning clients who receive money and then figure a plausible, self-serving excuse so they don't have to pay the mental health witness who testified in their behalf.

### Evergreen Account

The evergreen account is a common approach taken by attorneys undertaking legal representation of a client. Essentially, it is a deposit that must be maintained at a certain level. The account is billed on a regular basis. The therapist is paid out of the deposit, which is maintained in a separate or trust account. It is the responsibility of the client or the lawyer to keep and maintain the account at an agreed-on level by making periodic deposits as needed. As the therapist earns fees for services, he or she transfers money from the trust account to his or her regular fee or money earned account. The client or lawyer is then obligated under the agreement to replenish the account to bring it up to the agreed-on level. In that sense, it is evergreen or always sufficiently funded. When all services or anticipated services are terminated, sums remaining in the evergreen account are refunded to the depositor. This arrangement ensures that the clinician always has money on deposit for future services and that sizable accounts receivable are not accumulated.

*Unpaid accounts receivable almost always create friction between the provider and recipient of mental health services.*

Unpaid accounts receivable almost always create friction between the provider and recipient of mental health services. Writing off a small amount is an acceptable business risk. Large amounts, which are due and payable from a client, are a blow to the mental health of the mental health professional.

### The Unpaid Bill

As fully explored in *Portable Lawyer*, second edition, there is no nice way to recover an unpaid bill. Suing a client or former client usually produces a counterclaim or cross-action, which frequently makes the amount due and owing superfluous. Therapists who turn clients over to collection agencies or file suits in small claims court spend more time trying to collect the fee than they did in earning it.

If there is an unpaid amount due:

- The therapist *might* be paid if the case is resolved in favor of the client.
- The therapist will *probably not be paid* if the client loses the case and there is no recovery.
- Often, when a case is lost and there is no recovery, the only amount the therapist is paid is the deposit. The remainder due is written off as an unrecoverable account receivable.

## Answers to Frequently Asked Questions About:

Contract for testimony, if needed

Scope of compensation

Method and time of payment

No connection with outcome of litigation

**?** *Question*

*I have a lawyer-drafted contract for therapeutic services, which includes all the requisites of my state licensing law. What I do not seem to have is a clause in my intake form or contract for therapeutic services that pays me if I am called into court by subpoena or subpoena duces tecum involuntarily. My client might insist I appear in court, or, on occasion, my client's spouse or some other party may subpoena me for either a deposition or an appearance for a hearing. Can I get any protection where there is at least a possibility of being paid? If so, by whom am I paid?*

**!** *Answer*

You can have a contract with your own client whereby, in the event you are called into court either voluntarily or involuntarily by subpoena issued by the client or the client's lawyer, the client agrees to pay you in accordance with your set or agreed-on rate. It can further provide that you are paid using any of the designated methods set out earlier, that is, a trust fund deposit, deposit plus monthly billing, evergreen account, or any acceptable method of payment. Then at least you have a contract for payment, and the client is legally obligated to pay you. Whether the client does in fact pay you is another matter, which must be handled on a case-by-case basis, depending on the circumstances.

It would be wise to include in the contract that should you receive a subpoena to appear and testify in the client's case from any other person, the client will compensate you for your time and efforts. Here, the possibility of payment is a little more dubious. Although you have nothing to gain and much inconvenience if subpoenaed into court by someone with whom you are not associated, the client may not feel obligated to pay since the client did not initiate your appearance. Thus, even though the client signed the contract of engagement, he or she may be reluctant to hand you a check, especially if the client feels, justly or unjustly, that you did not help his or her case.

*The worst settlement is often better than the best lawsuit.*

Treat this area gingerly. The best advice is to put every guarantee for payment you can think of, with the help of your lawyer, in the contract. Then, if you are not paid, discuss the next step with counsel. Try negotiation, conciliation, mediation, and gentle persuasion. If, after all the options for peaceful settlement are used and the client and no one else seem to feel you are entitled to compensation, before commencing litigation, see if a discount will elicit some percentage of the amount due. If not, seek and accept the advice of your attorney. The worst settlement is often better than the best lawsuit.

In the contract, make sure you will be paid for your time and expenses as set out in this chapter and that there is a set time for payment. The contract should provide that you will be paid regardless of the outcome of the litigation in which your client is engaged and that you will be paid promptly after the bill is mailed and received, unless you are to be paid under other contractual methods.

## Legal Lightbulb

- Witnesses who testify in response to a subpoena are rarely compensated even if they have a contract for payment, but they have legal recourse if they choose to pursue it, and clients are sometimes inclined to pay if they have signed a contract that obligates them to pay.

- Compensation should be for all time devoted to a case, plus expenses and staff time.

- The best method of payment is full payment in advance. The worst method is to be paid after the case is over and all services have been completed.

## Summary

Every mental health professional can, at some time, be called or subpoenaed as a witness. If there is no contract or agreement, there is no obligation on behalf of the person issuing the subpoena to compensate the potential witness for the time and inconvenience spent in preparation, waiting, and finally testifying.

In many cases, years after the treatment commenced and terminated and long after the file was closed, a dispute arose, and the clinician, who may have moved on to a new job or retired, was subpoenaed into court along with the client's file. Unless obligated by contract, there is no compensation for this inconvenience.

The time to review intake and consent forms and client-therapist contracts is now, before the subpoena is served. Create language in all your forms to be signed by the client, so that if you are involved in any litigation because of your association with the client, he or she is obligated to pay for your time, toil, and effort.

# 20

## What to Do If You Are Sued

*I am in a doctoral program in clinical psychology and have been in personal treatment for about 3 years with three different therapists. I need about $35,000 to complete the program before I receive my degree, finish supervision, become licensed, and begin making a professional income. I understand from my course work that I am entitled to a copy of my clinical records and progress notes from each of my three treating therapists. If I get copies of my records from all therapists, would you look them over to see if there is any way to sue any of them so I could get the funds to complete my degree? Surely, in 3 years, one of them did something wrong or was careless. All I want is for you to review the record carefully and determine if there is some act of professional negligence worthy of a claim. I will be happy to pay you 50 percent of anything you recover from the insurance companies or the therapists. Should I send the files over?*

This is not fiction, but a call actually received in the office a few years ago. The dialog is substantially correct. The case, the client, and the contingent fee were refused, and nothing more has been heard from the potential client. There is no way of knowing whether this prospective client ever engaged an attorney or whether other lawyers also declined the case. This call illustrates the rationale or genesis of some malpractice litigation, the possible mind-set of a would-be plaintiff.

### The Plaintiff

Mental health professionals are vulnerable. They can be not only sued in a civil suit for money damages in malpractice litigation but also indicted for criminal acts in the criminal court system. They can also be disciplined by licensing boards in the administrative law system. In addition, most national organizations have ethics committees that oversee their members, and if an ethical violation occurs, they terminate membership or eject the member. They also, in many cases, record the violation and publish it periodically in their journals and newsletters with the name of the violator in bold type. Here we outline most, but not all, actionable violations that might cause a person to file a complaint or lawsuit against a mental health professional.

*Most national organizations have ethics committees, and if an ethical violation occurs, they terminate membership.*

## Areas of Vulnerability Leading to Complaints

A sampling of acts of omission and commission that might lead to a violation in which the practitioner becomes a defendant in a judicial, administrative, or criminal conflict follows:

### Acts of Omission

- Failure to have a contract or intake form that outlines the duties of the therapist, the duties and obligations of the client, and the exceptions to confidentiality.
- Failure to refer the client to another therapist when there is a conflict of interest.
- Failure to refer the client to another therapist when the provider has exceeded his or her own level of known competence, licensing authority, or degreed credentials.
- Failure to consult with an expert or more knowledgeable colleague when the limits of competence have been reached or when the provider does not know or realize his or her own level of competence and treats a client with a problem that is beyond the level of the therapist's learning, education, training, experience, or license.
- Failure to order a particular test, physical or psychological, when indicated.
- Failure to timely answer calls or requests for help or services made to an answering service or answering machine.
- Failure to make a referral to a person or entity who is capable of professionally treating the client.

- Failure to take all the necessary and appropriate steps authorized in your jurisdiction in homicide or suicide cases.
- Failure to appropriately supervise a client or intern.
- Failure to appropriately document the diagnosis, treatment plan, prognosis, and informed consent.
- Failure to obtain a new consent form as the treatment plan changed or if a new approach is needed and required.
- Failure to timely deliver client records when requested by a client.
- Failure to train support and office staff properly concerning ethics, confidentiality, HIPAA, dealings with other therapists, professional courtesy, methods of transferring files, telephone procedures, and responsibilities.
- Failure to seek and obtain state- and license-mandated continuing education units.
- Failure to renew a license in accordance with state procedures.
- Failure to know about or use the latest modalities for treatment.
- Failure to fully inform the client of the risks of treatment, alternative treatments available, or the possibility of the use of medications.
- Failure to maintain client records for the appropriate length of time.
- Failure to properly qualify opinions in written reports and while testifying.

*Acts of Commission*

- Engaging in an inappropriate dual relationship with a client.
- Entering into a business relationship with a client.
- Becoming a friend with a client.
- Accepting gifts from a client.
- Trading out or exchanging services with a client.
- Failure to make the proper diagnosis.
- Paying or receiving payment for client referrals.
- Failure to have a death plan in place in the event of the death of the therapist or the client.
- Maintaining files in an unsecured manner or location.
- Having a computer or fax machine repaired without providing for the confidentiality of client files.
- Treating a client without the necessary consent.

- Having sex with a client, a client's spouse or former spouse, or any member of the client's family.
- Disclosing client information without client consent, a court order, or other legal basis.
- Rendering opinions about persons they have not personally evaluated or without properly qualifying the opinions about the person.

## The Therapist as a Defendant

Once there is any legal process whereby the mental health professional must defend himself or herself, steps must be taken. The following checklist would be helpful to any named defendant as soon as a hint of conflict arises:

*Steps for Self-Protection*

- Whenever any process is served, call the lawyer and the malpractice carrier at once. Fax them what you received, and do nothing without their informed input. The malpractice liability carrier will provide you with legal representation as needed.
- When a suit is filed, a *defendant's original answer* or other defendant's motion or pleading is appropriate. A letter from a licensing board or from a national or local organization requires a timely written response. If litigation, there is a formalized format. Regardless of the document or form of the notice received, the response is important and has profound implications. It must be handled correctly in the time indicated and in the approved manner.
- Review the problem with *your* lawyer. Review the facts of the case, the nature of the complaint, the issues involved, and the possible options. Have a copy of your clinical file available to share with your lawyer.
- Review any previous complaints received from the client, both oral and written. Make a note of anything that may have been said or any message you may have received that was insignificant at the time but which, in retrospect, is more important and relevant now that a complaint has been filed. Arrange the notations in chronological order so they indicate a time line history of the relationship.

*Once there is any legal process whereby the mental health professional must defend himself or herself, steps must be taken.*

*Perhaps your colleague can see a quick end or satisfactory resolution to the controversy before it escalates out of control.*

- Review the clinical file or progress notes. Organize the file and determine whether it is correct as written or whether any corrections or amendments should be made.
- Talk to a colleague. Use no names, and talk of the case as a hypothetical situation so the colleague can't be involved later as a fact witness. Ask him or her to assume certain facts and then to offer input. Perhaps your colleague can see a quick end or satisfactory resolution to the controversy before it escalates out of control.
- If recommended by your lawyer and your colleague, contact and place your malpractice insurance liability insurance carrier on notice. Make sure you fulfill every requirement of your insurance policy so the company will have no excuse to either decline or deny coverage or provide you with a defense.

## Avoiding Litigation

Steps to avoid litigation that can save time, expense, and emotional conflict include:

1. **Negotiation:** Sometimes a call can ameliorate the problem and settle the dispute. Anecdotal evidence indicates that the client often wants the attention of the therapist or a simple explanation that was not forthcoming. A call, a free exit session, a letter of understanding (without admitting any liability or negligence), or referring the client to some literature will calm the nerves and massage the wounded ego.

2. **Mediation:** Mediation is a formalized and organized meeting of the parties in which a trained, neutral individual listens to both parties, finds common ground, and determines whether the parties themselves can reach an acceptable accommodation that is a win-win solution. Parties who have had an opportunity to vent and state their cases to each other can, once the smoke clears, settle their disputes with the helpful and trained input of a creative mediator. Usually, having found expression for their grievance, both parties will make the necessary adjustments to come to an agreement.

3. **Conciliation and arbitration:** In conciliation, the parties each have their lawyers negotiate and seek to conciliate their differences. If they cannot reach a settlement, they withdraw and other lawyers are engaged to litigate. In arbitration, the parties appoint a third, neutral party to hear the disputes and, by contract, the parties agree to abide or honor the decision of the paid arbitrator. In effect, this third-party, informal arbitrator, who may or may not be a judge or a lawyer, listens to the dispute and makes a decision.

4. **A professional panel:** Several jurisdictions and national organizations, in the interest of public relations and settling disputes quietly, have ethics committees that set up professional panels to review cases involving disputes between members and clients or consumers. Each group is different. The local branch might have to be encouraged to assemble a group of professionals, set a hearing date, establish rules and guidelines, and have a hearing with all parties agreeing in advance to abide by the panel ruling. This process might be mediation by another name, but it is offered as an in-house solution when mental health professionals are involved in conflicts with the consuming public.

If alternative dispute resolution fails, there is always litigation. The mental health professional becomes a defendant in an adversarial trial, and the client, the consumer of mental health services, becomes the plaintiff. Thus, the parties enter into court.

## The Mental Health Professional as a Litigator/Defendant

Preparing for trial as a defendant is not much different from preparing for trial as an expert witness. The therapist must be prepared to defend every action and contact with the client from the initial communication to the conclusion of the treatment. If the alleged negligence is untrue or unsupportable, it must be resisted using every legal and ethical method available. If the negligence is provable, the defense strategy, from the standpoint of the defendant, is to minimize the risk or exposure. Use the following checklist in preparing for trial:

*Preparing for Trial Checklist*

1. Did you properly prescreen the plaintiff, and, if not, can you explain why you limited the prescreening process?

2. Can you explain the initial diagnosis, how it changed from time to time, and how the treatment plan was amended to reflect the ever-changing diagnosis?

3. How did medications affect the treatment process? Can you explain your general understanding of the medications taken by the client?

4. Review your entire clinical record with your attorney. Is there any entry that requires explanation? If so, be prepared to enlighten the judge or jury in court.

5. Have there been depositions taken, requests for the production of documents, requests for admissions, interrogatories (written or oral), letters written to the court, or pleadings filed? If so, read all these documents. Point out to your lawyer any information that you feel should be underlined. Don't assume the lawyer has absorbed every point contained in your clinical notes and all the documents before the court.

6. Is there any jargon or psychobabble that requires explanation and clarification? Be prepared to explain it in court.

7. Are you clear exactly what the plaintiff is complaining about, and can you systematically refute the allegations? If the allegations can't be refuted, can you and your lawyer figure out a manner to explain any damaging evidence so that the end result is more favorable?

8. Have you worked with your lawyer to determine the questions you want your lawyer to ask you? Did you furnish the "ask me abouts" described in other chapters in this book?

9. Review your "in court" conduct with the lawyer. Practice for both examination and cross-examination. Role-play, and work at it until you are satisfied and comfortable.

10. Review your court demeanor with the lawyer. Rehearse conduct in the courthouse; in the hall; entering the courtroom; sitting at the counsel table; approaching the witness stand; testifying; reacting to mean, hostile, insulting, and abrasive questions; leaving the stand; and leaving the courthouse.

11. Practice courtroom manners. Nod good morning to the lawyers, the court reporter, the bailiff, the court clerk, the jurors, and the judge. Effusive greetings are not appropriate. Maintain dignity at all times.

12. Think about your final reaction whichever result occurs. React with dignity.

13. When the case is complete, review the trial in its entirety with your lawyer. The lawyer can explain the consequences of either winning or losing and can clarify the next steps in the litigation process. The end of the trial is not always the end of your involvement. You are a party to the litigation until the final stage of the conflict. Your lawyer will shepherd you through this difficult situation.

## Answers to Frequently Asked Questions About:

Responding to a fake complaint

Handling the unreasonable client

Controlling your emotions

### ❓ Question

*I have just received a phone call from a client complaining about my treatment. In my opinion, my therapy over the past year was clinically competent and appropriate. This client is borderline and has accused all her former therapists of incompetence and sexual boundary violations and was involuntarily terminated by two previous clinicians. (I did not discover this history until well into her therapy.) Her outrageous claims are so preposterous that I am inclined to tell her to simply stop making these claims or I will recommend she seek a new therapist. But I know better. What should I do?*

### ❗ Answer

Keep your cool. At this time quietly contact a colleague, your lawyer, your malpractice liability insurance carrier, and your therapist. After brainstorming a little, perhaps call in this woman, offer a free session, let her vent, and tell her that perhaps the mix was not appropriate for a clinical relationship due to conditions beyond the fault of either you or her. Give her a list of three to six other licensed and degreed professionals, and tell her to interview them carefully, remembering that with her background in mental health, she needs a specially competent clinician and one who can understand her problems in all their ramifications. Offer to cooperate at no charge with any person she chooses. Armed with this list, maybe she will undertake the project of locating a new treating provider and your troubles will be over.

If she persists in calling or harassing you, then have either your malpractice carrier or your lawyer run interference for you. Perhaps either or both of them can dissuade her from proceeding further. They might even suggest mediation. If they do, educate yourself concerning mediation processes and procedures, and make an effort to solve the problem through mediation. If some settlement should be made, they can structure it with the least expense and with no admission of negligence or liability of any type. Leave it to the professionals.

Upset, borderline clients are a very dangerous class of client. They have to be handled with kid gloves and treated with overwhelming respect and courtesy. If handled gruffly or without sensitivity, the angry, unstable client will become a lifetime enemy and future litigant, and the consequences to your peace of mind and your practice will be unpleasant and drastic. Remember the maxim: *A bad settlement is better than a good lawsuit.*

## Summary

Every mental health professional should be able to practice in peace. No suits would ever be filed by unhappy clients, no complaints would ever be filed with licensing boards or national or state organizations, and no client would ever approach a prosecutor or district attorney with a criminal complaint against the mental health services provider.

To think that such will be the case is a combination of naiveté and overzealous optimism. There are risks in every profession. Some of

## Legal Lightbulb

- Any complaining client is to be handled very carefully. The idea is not to win an argument but to solve a problem.

- Your attorney, the malpractice carrier, an insurance adjuster for the carrier, or a mediator is better suited to negotiate with an unhappy client. A representative can better state your position and bring the matter to an agreeable accommodation and close.

- *Don't admit any liability,* negligence, wrongdoing, or failures on your part.

- Every named defendant must have professional representation.

- Every official document received is important and must be referred to an attorney for a timely response.

- Unofficial documents or casual phone calls or e-mails that indicate an unhappy client must be taken seriously.

these risks, such as malpractice, can be insured against, and others, such as complaints to the board, can be partially covered. However, criminal complaints cannot be insured at all. Should a therapist be named in a criminal action, the therapist is on his or her own.

When the mental health professional becomes the defendant, the same rules of professionalism apply as in the other chapters of this book. The file must be prepared, the defendant must be prepared, and the case must be prepared.

# PART VI

# *OTHER EXPERT WITNESSES*

Mental health professionals work in many different capacities, and even though they are not engaged in providing psychotherapy, they may become involved with the legal system. A common example of this kind of professional is the school counselor. Other mental health professionals specifically hold themselves out to be forensic experts and actively seek legal engagements. The chapters in this section offer suggestions for these professionals to assist them with their interaction with our legal system.

# 21

# The School Counselor as a Courtroom Witness

*Susan, an elementary school counselor employed by the school district, had never been to court. In fact, she did not know that counselors ever went to court. Joan and John were elementary schoolchildren with school problems. During their three previous years in elementary school, Susan had counseled with the children and had visited with their parents individually and jointly. On several occasions, though careful not to call it therapy, she assembled the family of four for a frank discussion of family issues and problems that led to school misbehavior and study difficulties. The mother was compassionate and willing to adjust to Susan's suggestions. The father was angry, belligerent, and hostile, and at the end of one session harshly told Susan, "We'll do our job, you better do yours!" The school problems continued unabated and, in fact, got worse.*

*Just as the semester ended, Susan was informed that the parents of Joan and John were getting a divorce and were contesting custody. Susan received a subpoena to testify.*

When two individuals contest primary custody for the same child or children, each party inevitably seeks the counsel and ultimately the testimony of an expert. Usually, regardless of the discipline of the expert, whether professional counselor, social worker, psychologist, psychiatrist, or marriage and family therapist, the potential witness is hired to make an investigation, offer a recommendation to the court, and render an opinion. If the opinion is favorable to the client, the potential witness is engaged to appear in court and testify on behalf of the client. If the opinion is lukewarm or unfavorable, the client and the client's attorney continue the search for a more enthusiastic source of support, that is, witnesses who will bolster and shore up their case. They are not looking for clinical objectivity and total professionalism; rather, they are searching for favorable witnesses who will be supportive of their position in the case. Usually, these witnesses are paid by the party to the litigation who summoned or subpoenaed them to court. While it is more implied than expressed, paid witnesses are usually suspect.

### Enter the School Counselor—the Unpaid, Professional, and Believable Witness

*The school counselor can always be subpoenaed to testify in any case in which a student or a parent becomes an issue or participant in litigation.*

The school counselor can always be subpoenaed—even during retirement—to testify in any case in which a student or a parent becomes an issue or participant in litigation. The counselor may be called as a lay witness to testify about words or actions that were observed or heard, or he or she may be qualified as an expert and asked to answer hypothetical questions or offer clinical opinions to the judge or jury.

Judges and juries often have great faith in the testimony of school counselors. They know that, unlike paid witnesses, the counselor has only one thought in mind: the best interest of the child. School counselors are usually not compensated for appearing as witnesses when their court appearance is in response to a subpoena. In addition, few school counselors have experience in the unfriendly and adversarial atmosphere of a courtroom. Counselors acting in their professional capacity are by inclination and training "helping professionals" who are not used to having their opinions, conclusions, training, schooling, experience, or education challenged.

*School counselors are usually not compensated for appearing as witnesses when their court appearance is in response to a subpoena.*

Unfortunately, Susan must testify about her recollection of the counseling sessions with the children as well as about her sessions with the parents if asked and ordered by the court. Susan, in preparation for the trial, should review all her case notes and school records as well as any personal, "sticky paper" memoranda so that there are no forgotten contacts or encounters such as phone calls in the middle of a busy day that she dismissed as soon as the call was terminated but that were significant in the eyes of the parent who participated.

If a school counselor has retired or resigned when asked to appear for a case, he or she is under no obligation to do more than to appear, be sworn, and testify. The retired counselor does not have to locate either the file or the file custodian or record keeper. If the attorney wishes to examine the student file, the attorney must locate the record. Retired counselors cannot refuse to be involved, but they can limit their involvement to appearing or showing up and testifying both for the trial or a deposition. They cannot be compelled to locate files or testify to anything they can't recollect. They need not meet with the attorneys in advance of the hearing if they choose not to. If they wish to be paid, they should have a written contract in advance of the trial or deposition and should further insist on a cash payment up front in an amount that will be anticipated as a reasonable fee for the services to be rendered. (See contracts in Appendix B.)

## Trial Preparation for the School Counselor

As soon as the school counselor has any notice that litigation is possible, he or she should take the following steps as applicable to the circumstances of the litigation:

1. **Notify the principal and supervisor (if any) at once.** The principal always wants to be aware of any school-related events, and the supervisor might like the opportunity to review the counselor's file, diagnosis, treatment plan, prognosis, and recommendations.

2. **If supervisors have ultimate responsibility for the file, give them the opportunity to review the file before it is presented to the court.** The school counselor may have been the only contact with the student and parents, but if there is a supervisor, he or she must be informed of any litigation or subpoenas and given an opportunity to examine any documentation that is to be brought before the court.

*A supervisor must be informed of any litigation or subpoenas and given an opportunity to examine any documentation that is to be brought before the court.*

3. **Notify the parents involved.** Tell the parents that you have been called by a lawyer or served with process. Tell them you continue to be their child's school counselor and are available for consultation within the limits, protocols, or parameters of the counseling profession. Make sure they understand that you are not an advocate of any litigant; rather, you are a school counselor and will answer questions put to you in court to the best of your ability. Be sensitive to implied or express threats, and if any are forthcoming, call your attorney or the school district's lawyer. Obtain a waiver of confidentiality from the parents so you can freely talk to attorneys, the parties, your principal, teachers, or staff about the children. Try to get the waiver of confidentiality in writing.

4. **Review the entire file carefully.** Remember, parents and sometimes individuals *in loco parentis* have the right to review educational records, and usually the school counselor's records are a part of the child's educational records. Review them carefully and critically for errors. Have you come to any conclusions noted in the file that, in retrospect, should be reconsidered? Is this file complete and correct, or will it look inadequate when seriously examined through the critical eyes of the parents or their attorneys?

5. **Create a curriculum vita (CV) if you don't have one.** Significant time can be saved if the counselor has a previously prepared CV, resume, or vita that outlines education and experience. This version of the CV should indicate the education, experience, and work history of the counselor as it pertains to counseling and the case before the court. Degrees, workshops attended, continuing education, professional experience and development, internships, graduate programs, or special studies should be included.

6. **Make copies of any documents you think may be introduced into evidence.** When a school counselor appears in court with the counseling record, it is *always advisable* to have two extra copies. Bring two copies so that if anyone wishes to introduce the documents into evidence as an exhibit, a copy may be substituted for the original and the counselor can return to school with the original file intact. It is a hassle to retrieve an original file introduced into evidence.

7. **Back up any conclusions with the literature or consultations.** On occasion, during the course of counseling, a school counselor reaches conclusions that require a referral of a child and the parents to a specialist, such as a tutor, an outside psychologist, psychiatrist, anger management expert, or a curriculum coordinator. When you do refer, make sure there is adequate documentation in the file to substantiate your decision to involve any of these specialists.

8. **Arrange a role play or rehearsal with a lawyer.** This advice is helpful at all times, but it is especially useful the first or second time the school counselor is drawn into the courtroom. Court appearances can make even seasoned participants anxious. Ask the school to retain an attorney to prepare you for trial. If the system will not, see if there is legal aid or a free volunteer service in the area or call the pro bono division of the local bar association. The local law school might also provide this service. (Don't be surprised if some time in the future you receive a call from someone who helped you with the case who has a counseling problem and seeks and expects a return favor.) Review what you will be expected to respond to in examination and in cross-examination. Anticipate questions about any difficult judgment calls you have made, and be prepared to defend your decisions.

9. **Extend professional courtesy.** A subpoena compels an individual to appear. A subpoena duces tecum compels the individual to appear and to bring stated documents. If the documents are not accessible, as in the case of a retired school counselor, announce to the court that the records requested are not in your possession or available to you. You will then be excused from producing them. You must still appear, be sworn, and testify.

10. **Request professional courtesy.** Judges know that it is inconvenient for active school counselors to leave their jobs and students to appear in court. They also know it is intrusive for retired individuals to spend their retirement time sitting on a bench in the courthouse waiting to be called as a witness. Therefore, it is appropriate to call the court, the bailiff, the lawyer who issued the subpoena, or the court clerk and ask for professional courtesy.

Indicate that you are ready, willing, and able to testify and can attend the court on, for example, one-hour notice, and give your phone number. Then you can continue as usual until the call to appear in court on one-hour notice. This arrangement is far better than appearing, being sworn, and waiting hours to be called as a witness. Physicians have been accorded this professional courtesy for years. School counselors and, indeed, any mental health professional, should be accorded the same consideration.

11. **Act professionally.** When called to court, the counselor should dress professionally, appear on time, report to the court, and, when waiting, sit quietly in the hall, greeting lawyers, clients, colleagues, and friends who happen to be in court with a nod and a smile. Professional credibility is lost if there are effusive hugs in the hall, loud greetings in the hearing and sight of the judge or jury, or other conduct that can be characterized as unprofessional.

12. **Don't argue, make jokes, or be glib.** Answer the questions as best you can, and don't argue with the lawyer no matter how appealing the temptation. If the lawyer does not ask the right questions, let the other lawyer or the judge bring out the evidence. Occasionally, there is some humor in the courtroom, but it is rare. Save the humor for your friends.

13. **When it's over, thank everyone and leave.** When your part of the trial is over, simply thank the court, thank the lawyers, and nod to the parties to the case. Don't linger. Follow the court's instructions, if any, and don't discuss the case even with your family, spouse, or best friend.

## The First Court Experience

The first court appearance can be intimidating and daunting. Little in school preparation grooms the counselor for this first experience. If there is time, visit the courtroom before the court date. If you are familiar with the layout, when the day comes, you can walk briskly across the room, go to the witness chair, be sworn, and begin the process. The ordeal will still be a little frightening, but you will be somewhat desensitized and will do just fine. Testify as best as you can, and be proud of your contribution to the process.

## Special Thoughts for the School Psychologist

The preceding steps are also relevant to a school psychologist. The school psychologist, however, has several additional burdens that must be considered:

1. **Carefully review jargon.** Many words in the file will have technical meanings. The school psychologist must be familiar with all technical jargon in the student record and be prepared to discuss these terms in lay language.

2. **Document medications.** Occasionally, the school psychologist will visit with a student who is taking medication. Where the medication, prescription or otherwise, in any way alters the conduct or behavior of the child, make a note in the clinical file describing the effects of the medication. If the effects are in doubt or if there are many side effects, consult with the school nurse. The psychologist must always be prepared to testify about school conduct with medication. Psychotropic drugs can have a profound effect on school conduct and affect behavior considerably. (See *PDR: Drug Guide for Mental Health Professionals*, Thomson, Psychotherapy Finances, TherapyShop.com 800-869-8450.)

3. **Include the diagnosis, treatment plan, and prognosis.** The clinical file should always contain a statement of the problem, treatment plan suggested by the psychologist, and the anticipated result of the psychologist's treatment. The end result of the behavioral modification, if any, should also be included. If tests are used, the psychologist must be familiar with the test and the reason for the test and must be able to explain the test result or outcome.

4. **Get parent permission.** Some jurisdictions require written parental consent before conducting a psychological examination, test, or

treatment unless related to child abuse reporting. If parental permission is required in your state, make sure this written permission is included in the student psychological record.

## Answers to Frequently Asked Questions About:

What to keep in a student file

Who has access to the file

If a subpoena duces tecum is served, what is brought to court

Once in court, who has a right to view the student file

### ❓ Question

*I am a school counselor and am required to maintain a confidential record of all contacts with students. How complete should the records be and how much detail is required? Does my principal have the right to read the file? Occasionally, I get served with papers to appear in court, and usually there is a subpoena duces tecum attached. What do I bring, and to whom do I deliver it when I get there? Often, a pushy lawyer demands the right to examine the file before I am sworn. Do I have to make the student file available to the lawyer? Can I keep the file locked up until it is time to testify and wait until the judge orders me to do something with the file?*

### ❗ Answer

The student file should include any significant act that pertains to the student and that affects the counseling and educational process. Because all students and files are different, there is no objective yardstick that defines with particularity exactly what should be contained in every file. Review the published protocols and requirements of the school itself and the school district. Consult the appropriate mental health texts for technical documentation requirements. Make notations that are relevant and that are required by the state licensing law and national professional organizations.

Don't use slang or racial epithets, slander students, report harmful hearsay statements that do not pertain to the student, include information about third parties that do not apply to this student, use vocabulary or jargon that you do not understand or cannot explain, itemize or include unsubstantiated conclusions, use curse words, include matters that are extraneous to the student file, or include gratuitous comments or information. Try to include and document the facts you heard, felt, saw, or concluded as a result of your counseling consultations and experience.

National organizations such as the National Association of Social Workers, the American Counseling Association, and the American School Counselors Association provide only general advice on what to include, such as: records necessary for rendering professional service; accurate records of the dates of counseling treatment intervention, types of counseling treatment intervention, progress or case notes, and billing information; and records to facilitate the delivery of services and to ensure continuity of services provided to clients in the future. (See *The Portable Ethicist for Mental Health Professionals*, Bernstein & Hartsell, p. 181, John Wiley & Sons, 2000, and check latest national organization revisions.) In any given case, the judgment of the school counselor or psychologist determines the verbiage in the clinical or educational record. However, many school districts have written protocols when student homicide or suicide is the presenting problem. These problems must be independently researched. Each district has its own procedures.

Individuals may peruse the file on a "need to know" basis. Generally, the principal can look at any file. The school nurse can view parts of the file that pertain to student or school health, and teachers can be told parts of the file that are relevant to the learning experience of a particular child with a particular problem. Parents generally have a right to view their children's educational records. The school psychologist can consult about mental health problems as can the supervisor. The president of the PTA, a school board member, or the head of any other support group has no right to see a student file, nor do they have any authority to receive a briefing about a particular student. Should any unauthorized person request information, ask him or her to seek and obtain the principal's prior permission and possibly a court order authorizing disclosure. Ask the person to sign a hold harmless agreement, which makes him or her responsible for any unauthorized disclosure.

If you are served with a subpoena duces tecum for all the school records and they are in your possession and control, bring them to court. *Let no one see a file until you are ordered to do so by the court.* Remember, make a copy anyway, so you can leave the court with the original student record in your possession. Then, if the court orders you to produce and deliver the file to any third party such as the lawyers for either side, deliver the copy. Making a student file available either by orally disclosing information or by delivering the file to an unauthorized person is a serious and actionable breach of confidentiality.

## Summary

We receive more questions from school counselors and psychologists about subpoenas than any other professional area. The reason? Few are trained in undergraduate or graduate school to understand the judicial system. When a court appearance is mandated, it often takes time away from what the counselor considers his or her primary duty: counseling. Nevertheless, as infrequently as it occurs, it is part of the treatment and personal educational process when it does occur. And, as an important part of the professional service, the witness must be thoroughly prepared, knowledgeable, confident, and competent.

# 22

# The Forensic Expert

*Clinton, a licensed marriage and family therapist, was well known in judiciary and litigation circles. He had testified in numerous trials but never in a high-profile case until he was asked to testify in a case involving a Hollywood celebrity. He knew there would be extensive press coverage and he would come under intense scrutiny.*

*Clinton realized this case would have a significant impact on his forensic practice. It could lead to numerous future engagements should he be perceived as knowledgeable, competent, and persuasive. How should he prepare?*

## Checklist for Trial Preparation

You are prepared for trial when you have complied with all the requirements of the eight R's. Use this checklist to begin preparations for every case. Many of the chapters in this book have checklists for more specific information (e.g., the vita). When applicable, refer to those chapters to augment the eight R's:

*The Eight R's*

1. **R**esearch the subject matter.
2. **R**esearch the literature that supports your opinions and conclusions.
3. **R**esearch the literature that contradicts your opinions and conclusions.

4. **R**esearch the opposing experts.
5. **R**esearch opposing counsel.
6. **R**esearch the judge.
7. **R**esearch the courthouse climate.
8. **R**eview for examination and cross-examination carefully.

## Research the Subject Matter

The approach to problems may be different now from when you had your last student practicum. New theories of practice have been developed, and new techniques have been established. Furthermore, many clients are on medications that were developed only in recent years, therefore:

- Thoroughly research the subject matter at hand. What is this case about, and what are the ramifications?
- Are there collateral issues, such as sex, food, elder or child abuse, genetic predispositions, or drug or alcohol addiction?
- Does sexual dysfunction play a part in the problem at hand, or is there some religious affiliation that might lead to unusual conduct that must be explained to be understood? Are these conditions that require clarification?
- Are any of the parties taking medications, and what are the effects and side effects of those medications?
- Is there recent literature that might affect the problem before the court? (A quick search online might reveal a recent breakthrough that would indicate that the entire matter has to be reevaluated.)
- Are there any unanswered questions that must be answered to have a thorough understanding of the case?
- Have you completely reviewed the mental health history of the individuals before going to court? Can you testify with a reasonable degree of certainty that you have a professional understanding of all parties before the court and about whom you may testify? Have

*Thoroughly research the subject matter at hand.*

you made an effort to obtain all psychological data available for
your review?
- Can you explain the technical problems in lay terms, remembering
that neither the judge nor the jurors are experienced mental health
professionals?

## Research the Literature That Supports Your Opinions and Conclusions

In today's court proceedings, opinions should be supported by well-
recognized literature, studies, outcome results, or other evidence.
Supporting evidence includes journal articles, texts, reference works,
interviews, learned treatises, or other indications that support
the point of view of the witness. Not all professionals will be cross-
examined critically, but forensic experts cannot afford to be unprepared without the backup to defend their conclusions, therefore:

- A literature search is basic and necessary to support a point of view.
- Opinions alone are of little weight.
- Any modern sources of information should be accessed. Old
college texts that have not been updated are not necessarily
relevant.
- If there are ethnic considerations in the case, make sure the literature considers this ethnic group in the research.

## Research the Literature That Contradicts Your Opinions and Conclusions

Every mental health professional has lived through the waxing and
waning of various theories that make the talk show circuit, sell countless books, and, then, a short time later, are shown to be unsound and
are forgotten. Literature and published works that contradict the principle or theory to which the witness currently subscribes probably exists, therefore:

- Review the literature that supports and contradicts your present position.
- Be prepared to refute, distinguish, or diminish conclusions contrary to yours.
- There is no harm in acknowledging that a particular issue is still somewhat unsettled among practicing professionals. Research continues in all areas of mental health.

## Research the Opposing Experts

In most litigation procedures, each lawyer has to provide opposing counsel and the court with a list of proposed witnesses and/or experts. As soon as the witness list is disclosed to you, search for the opposing expert's interviews, publications, presentations, and teaching credentials. Try to attend one of his or her speeches. In addition:

*Search for the opposing expert's interviews, publications, presentations, and teaching credentials.*

- Ask the opposing expert to mail you a vita or biography.
- Conduct an Internet search of the opposing expert.
- Make a complete list of publications where the expert is cited.
- Note whether the expert has a resounding theme in the publications that might imply that his or her research is slanted toward one conclusion.
- Find out if the expert testifies for only one kind of client.
- Determine whether the expert is a "hired gun expert" or whether he or she also practices.
- Search for problems with the publications of the opposing expert that might be helpful to your lawyer.

## Research the Judge

Every judge has special personality traits and judicial demeanor. Often these personality traits are well known to the legal and mental health community. For example, certain judges, in divorce cases, are incensed by adultery. Others might feel that when adultery occurs, both parties have made a contribution to the problem. Other judges feel that reasonable child discipline can include spanking, while others feel that discipline can effectively be carried out without hitting. In criminal cases, some judges feel environmental issues are important in assessing punishment, while others feel that every crime is a crime regardless of the youthful environment or social history of the criminal. In preparing for trial, knowing the attitude of the judge is important. Questions and answers can be customized to reflect the sensitivities of the court, therefore:

- Investigate the judge carefully. Omit statements that will offend the court, and include testimony that the judge will find persuasive and credible.
- Remember that the judge at the trial level is supreme arbiter.
- Be prepared to answer complicated mental health questions without the use of psychobabble or technical jargon. Know the technical terminology, but be able to explain it in lay terms.

*Be prepared to answer complicated mental health questions without the use of psychobabble or technical jargon.*

## Research Opposing Counsel

Like judges, lawyers have reputations within the community. Spend a little time researching the opposing counsel. Your own lawyer is a good place to start. Then, talk to other people in the legal and mental health community. The witness can't change the lawyer's tactics, but with advance knowledge the edge of sharp questions can be blunted. In addition:

- Ask friendly lawyers and mental health professionals about opposing counsel.
- Learn what to anticipate when the time comes for cross-examination.
- Role-play projected cross-examination and prepare possible responses.

## Research the Courthouse Climate

The forensic expert should check out the courtroom, the parking facilities, the restrooms, the cafeteria, and the general layout of the route from entering the building to testifying to departing from the witness chair. Learn the path so it can be traveled with dignity.

In addition, be aware that mannerisms suitable for one court may not be appropriate for another. (One of the authors, wearing shorts in the middle of a Texas summer while delivering papers to the court clerk for filing, once appeared in court by mistakenly entering the wrong courthouse door in a rural county. The judge glimpsed him and called him before the bench, berating him for showing a lack of respect for the court. Casual was not the custom in this deep East Texas town!) Each court has its own character and personality. To determine the personality of a court:

*Mannerisms suitable for one court may not be appropriate for another.*

- Ask a local lawyer and a local mental health professional about "how things are done" in their city.
- Check with the locals about the reception of mental health professionals and how they are received as expert witnesses.
- Be respectful, considerate, and sincere.

## Review for Examination and Cross-Examination Carefully

There should never be any surprises in direct examination. Be sure to provide your lawyer with a list of questions that are important for you to be asked. It is important to review the questions that can be anticipated under cross-examination. Every lawyer with trial experience can reasonably predict the questions that might be asked. Review the trial plan and the weak points in your testimony, and give some thought to the best method to respond to questions that are designed to render your testimony meaningless on cross-examination. In addition:

- Insist that the client provide you with a seasoned lawyer (not a legal assistant or paralegal) to prepare you for examination and cross-examination at least a week before trial.
- Read several articles or books concerning courtroom testimony.

## Advantages and Disadvantages of Forensic Work

Just about all activities a person gets involved in will have its pluses and minuses. Forensic work for therapists is no exception, and one who pursues this work will quickly experience this. Understanding the advantages or disadvantages will make the therapist a better forensic expert and witness.

### Advantages of Forensic Work

- You work with knowledgeable lawyers.
- You set your own fees as a professional person and insist on a *deposit in advance* to cover your estimated expenses for preparation, research, and trial.
- There are no "no shows."
- You don't have to work with managed care and insurance companies.
- The time is blocked out. Trials and testimony usually are reasonably predictable and, unlike therapy, are not spread over a lengthy period of time.
- You are compensated for travel, research, preparation, court and consultation time, plus all out-of-pocket expenses.
- If you are really good, you may be "discovered" and become another Dr. Phil.
- The publicity may catapult you into fame and fortune.
- When the case terminates, your services are terminated. There is no obligation to continue therapy of any type unless you care to do so and create an obligation to continue in some capacity.

### Disadvantages of Forensic Work

- You work with knowledgeable lawyers and opposing counsel who are poised to challenge your conclusions, history, credentials, and credibility.
- Trial preparation is a lot of work. It includes personal homework as well as anticipating the "game plan" of the opposition.
- The testimony is in open court and available to the public, your clients, and curious reporters. Therefore, any error of language or judgment becomes a matter of public record.

- There is no confidentiality when testifying from the witness stand.
- While word of mouth is a fundamental way to build a practice, a flagrant error can ruin a practice.

## Answers to Frequently Asked Questions

Building a forensic mental health practice

Making contacts with the legal community

Obtaining referrals from lawyers and other mental health professionals

Obtaining publicity

### ❓ Question

*I have just testified in court and enjoyed the experience. How can I make myself known in the forensic area?*

### ❗ Answer

There are numerous, time-tested methods to create and foster a practice in the forensic area. The best way to start is to contact the local and state bar associations and determine all the continuing legal education courses on courtroom testimony. Take some of these courses, and pass out your card to every lawyer you meet. Tell the lawyers you are in the process of acquiring expert witness skills. Send them relevant digested publications and announcements if you feel that the information would be helpful to them. Don't send out a deluge that includes all the articles you read and journals to which you subscribe, just an occasional article or tidbit—enough to keep your name before the legal community.

If there is a local law school, visit with the dean or faculty members, and explain your new interest. They will advise you whether you could audit a course that would help prepare you for court or expand your knowledge of the legal system. They can steer you to the formal and informal courses that will be most helpful, meanwhile introducing you to the next generation of lawyers.

Write for legal and mental health journals, newsletters, and other publications. These periodicals are always looking for something different. If you have writing talent, patience, and can face occasional rejection, submit brief articles to bar journals and specialized bar section reports. There is no compensation for this type of endeavor, but your colleagues will assume technical background and expertise. A resume with publications indicates a step above the crowd.

Make yourself available to the local bar association or branches of the bar. Offer to, without compensation, speak to lawyers about mental health problems and how they can be discussed in a trial in a way that makes sense to a judge or jury. Lawyers are anxious to pick the brains of knowledgeable mental health professionals and will appreciate insight.

Discretely select a public relations person. If you publish, speak, offer a demonstration, go on a talk show, or participate in any other activity, see that the word gets out. The news about your accomplish-

## Legal Lightbulb

- Experts cannot usually be sued for testimony from the witness stand as long as it is their justifiable opinion and is truthful. However, if the testimony shows a lack of expertise in the field for which they were hired, a complaint can be made to the licensing board on the basis of lack of professionalism.

- Clients and attorneys expect more from an expert who solicits forensic work.

- Research and study the other experts who testify in the kinds of cases you want to participate in.

- Keep a notebook to record what you learn from each testifying experience. Once the case is concluded, ask for feedback from the client and attorney you worked with as well as the judge and jurors.

ments and appearances should be ethical, in good taste, and with future forensic employment in mind.

## Summary

Forensics is a subspecialty of the mental health profession. While most mental health professionals enter the helping professions to do clinical work and provide services to clients within their specific discipline, forensic work transcends specialties and may be applied to all areas of expertise encompassed by the general field of mental health.

In forensic work, the goal is to review the facts, assess the admissible evidence, and testify concerning the judgment, observations, and conclusions of the forensic expert. Without this expertise, the court would be less able to reach a fair, just, and informed judgment.

# Appendix A
# Useful Web Sites

American Academy of Child and Adolescent Psychiatry: http://www.aacap.org

American Academy of Experts in Traumatic Stress: http://www.aaets.org

American Art Therapy Association: http://www.arttherapy.org

American Counseling Association: http://www.counseling.org

American Dance Therapy Association: http://www.adta.org

American Music Therapy Association: http://www.musictherapy.org

American Psychiatric Association: http://www.psych.org

American Psychological Association: http://www.apa.org

American Medical Association: http://www.ama-assn.org

American School Counselor Association: http://www.schoolcounselor.org

Art Therapy Credentials Board: http://www.atcb.org

Association for Marriage and Family Therapists: http://www.aamft.org

Clinical Social Work Federation: http://www.cswf.org

Guide for Mental Health Professionals: http://www.pohly.com/admin_mh
.html#Internet

National Association of School Psychologists: http://www.nasponline.org

National Association of Social Workers: http://www.naswdc.org

National Institute on Alcohol Abuse and Alcoholism:
http://www.niaaa.nih.gov

United States Department of Health and Human Services:
http://www.hhs.gov

U.S. Dept. HHS: Office for Civil Rights: http://www.hhs.gov/ocr

# Appendix B

# Useful Forms

The forms included in this appendix are for general reference. They must be adjusted and adapted to your practice, your goals, and your needs. They must be reviewed periodically and kept current.

**Example of a Motion to Quash Subpoena**

CAUSE NO. XXXXXXXXX

| | | |
|---|---|---|
| IN THE INTEREST OF | : | IN THE DISTRICT COURT |
| | : | |
| MATTHEW JAMES ANDERSON | : | 322ND JUDICIAL DISTRICT |
| AND | : | |
| ERIC JAMES ANDERSON, | : | DALLAS COUNTY, TEXAS |
| MINOR CHILDREN | : | |

**MOTION TO QUASH SUBPOENA**

This Motion to Quash Subpoena is brought by ANN NICOLE BROWN, Movant, a licensed professional counselor practicing in Dallas County, Texas. In support, Movant would show the following:

1. Movant was served with a subpoena issued at the request of SUSAN SIMONE ANDERSON to appear for a deposition at the Law Offices of William McKinley at 10:00 A.M. on June 10, 2_____ and to produce all records and documentation pertaining to the evaluation and treatment of BENJAMIN THOMAS ANDERSON.

2. Movant objects to the subpoena, and without admitting the existence of a professional relationship between Movant and BENJAMIN THOMAS ANDERSON or the

existence of any of the records or documentation described in the deposition subpoena, asserts that there is no legal basis to compel testimony from Movant or production of such information if it in fact exists. Specifically, if it exists such information
would be protected from disclosure under applicable Texas law and 42 CFR Part 2—
Confidentiality of Alcohol and Drug Abuse Patient Records.

3. Movant is ready, willing, and able to cooperate with all orders made by this court
but respectfully requests the court to quash this subpoena.

Movant prays for relief according to the terms of this Motion. Movant prays for attorney's fees and costs.

Respectfully submitted,

_____

**THOMAS L. HARTSELL, JR.**

State Bar Number 09170300
6440 North Central Expressway
Suite 402
Dallas, Texas 75206
(214) 363-0555
**ATTORNEY FOR MOVANT**

### FIAT

Please be advised that a hearing on the foregoing motion has been scheduled for
8:30 A.M. on June 9, 2_____.

SIGNED this 5th day of June, 2_____.

_____

JUDGE/Clerk

### CERTIFICATE OF SERVICE

I hereby certify that a true and correct copy of the foregoing has been delivered to all
parties or attorneys of record, in accordance with the Texas Rules of Civil Procedure.

_____

**THOMAS L. HARTSELL, JR.**

### Example of a Motion for Entry of a Protective Order

CAUSE NO. XXXXXXX

| | | |
|---|---|---|
| IN THE MATTER OF | : | IN THE DISTRICT COURT |
| | : | |
| THE MARRIAGE OF | : | |
| ROBERT JAMES HORTON | : | |
| AND | : | |
| KAREN LESLIE HORTON | : | 302ND JUDICIAL DISTRICT |
| AND IN THE INTEREST OF | : | |
| MELINDA CHRISTINE HORTON, | : | |
| A MINOR CHILD | : | DALLAS COUNTY, TEXAS |

### MOTION FOR ENTRY OF PROTECTIVE ORDER

This Motion for Entry of Protective Order is brought by ANN NICOLE BROWN, Movant, pursuant to the Texas Rules of Civil Procedure. In support, Movant would show the following:

### I.

Movant is a licensed mental health professional and was served with a subpoena issued by KAREN LESLIE HORTON to appear in court to testify in this cause on June 10, 2_____ at 9:00 A.M. and to produce all records and documentation pertaining to the evaluation and treatment of ROBERT JAMES HORTON.

### II.

Movant requests the court to enter a protective order on the following grounds:

1. Movant is scheduled to depart on a prepaid vacation with her husband on June 9, 2_____ and to require Movant to appear in court on June 10, 2_____ would cause undue hardship and expense to Movant. Movant requests that the court enter a protective order freeing Movant from her obligation to comply with the

subpoena completely or, in the alternative, allowing her to testify when she returns from her vacation.

2. Without admitting the existence of a professional relationship between Movant and ROBERT JAMES HORTON or the existence of any of the records or documentation requested, Movant asserts that such information sought by KAREN LESLIE HORTON to the extent it exists is privileged and confidential. If the court determines that Movant must testify and that privileged information should be disclosed in this case, Movant requests the court to enter a protective order detailing the nature and extent of the information to be disclosed and limiting its disclosure and use to the matter set for hearing before the Court. In addition Movant requests that the court order that any records or documentation that Movant is compelled to disclose in this case, together with all copies, be returned to the court until all appeals are concluded and thereafter to be delivered to Movant.

3. Movant is ready, willing, and able to cooperate with all orders made by this Court.

Movant prays for relief according to the terms of this Motion. Movant prays for attorney's fees and costs.

Respectfully submitted,

_____

**THOMAS L. HARTSELL, JR.**

State Bar Number 09170300
6440 North Central Expressway
Suite 402
Dallas, Texas 75206
(214) 363-0555
**ATTORNEY FOR MOVANT**

## FIAT

Please be advised that a hearing on the foregoing motion has been scheduled for 8:30 A.M. on June 7, 2_____.

SIGNED this 5th day of June, 2_____.

_____

JUDGE/Clerk

## CERTIFICATE OF SERVICE

I hereby certify that a true and correct copy of the foregoing has been delivered to all parties or attorneys of record, in accordance with the Texas Rules of Civil Procedure.

_____

**THOMAS L. HARTSELL, JR.**

## Example of a Qualified Protective Order

### CAUSE NO. XXXXXX

| | | |
|---|---|---|
| IN THE MATTER OF | : | IN THE DISTRICT COURT OF |
| THE MARRIAGE OF | : | |
| BETTY SUE CANNON | : | COLLIN COUNTY, TEXAS |
| AND | : | |
| MICHAEL THOMAS CANNON | : | 219TH JUDICIAL DISTRICT |

### PROTECTIVE ORDER
Psychiatric Records

1. On this day came on to be considered by the court the request for protection from disclosure of certain documents and records, which have been inspected by the court in camera, and shall hereinafter be referred to as Court's Exhibit "A—Psychiatric Records of MICHAEL THOMAS CANNON, Respondent" and held by the court Reporter, and hereinafter referred to as "confidential documents."

2. The court orders the said "confidential documents" to be discoverable and orders them to be disclosed pursuant to the following terms and provisions.

3. The said "confidential documents" shall not be used or shown, disseminated, copied, or in any way communicated to anyone for any purpose whatsoever who is not a "Qualified Person" as defined in this order without the written permission of Respondent or by further order of this Court.

4. Except with prior written consent of Respondent or upon further order of this Court, said "confidential documents" shall be shown, or the contents thereof disclosed, only to the following persons (herein referred to as "Qualified Persons") by the parties or by their representatives:

(a) the parties' counsel of record in this action;

(b) employees of such counsel assigned to and necessary to assist such counsel in the preparation or the trial of this action;

(c) independent experts and consultants retained by the parties whose assistance is necessary for the preparation or trial of this specific action;

(d) the Court; and

(e) the Guardian Ad Litem, if one is appointed.

5. Each Qualified Person, as described in (a) through (e) above to whom the parties or their representatives intend to deliver, exhibit, or disclose any such "confidential document" or material contained therein shall be advised of the terms of this Order, shall be given a copy of this Order, and prior to any disclosure, shall agree in writing before a notary in the form attached hereto as Exhibit "1" to be bound by the terms as if they were parties' counsel. The agreements shall be filed with the Court, together with a copy to the court Reporter.

6. The court Reporter, or any other such agent or clerk of the court in whose charge the "confidential documents" are entrusted for safekeeping, shall maintain a list of all persons to whom such agent, reporter, or clerk provides any such document or material contained therein, and that list shall be available for inspection by counsel for the parties and by the Court.

7. All "confidential documents" provided to any Qualified Person as provided herein shall be returned to the court as soon as such Qualified Person has reviewed or otherwise evaluated the "confidential documents" so provided, but in no event shall such "confidential documents" remain out of the Court's custody for two weeks after a final decree has been signed by the Court.

8. No copies shall be made of the "confidential documents" or material contained therein, deposited with the court except as provided in paragraph 5 without the prior written approval of the Respondent or further order of this Court.

9. To the extent that such "confidential documents" or information obtained therefrom is used in the taking of depositions, such "confidential documents" or information and the transcript pages of the deposition testimony dealing with the protected "confidential documents" or information shall remain subject to the provisions of this Order.

10. Promptly after the conclusion of this action, all "confidential documents," all copies of "Confidential Documents," and all excerpts there from shall be returned to counsel for Respondent.

11. The parties or "Qualified Persons" shall not under any circumstances publicize or disseminate in any manner either the contents of the "Confidential Documents" or the fact that the parties have obtained "Confidential Documents" from the Respondent.

12. After termination of this litigation, the provisions of this Order shall continue to be binding, except with respect to those "confidential documents" and information that become a matter of public record. The parties hereto and persons agreeing to be bound by this Order agree this court retains and the court thus orders that it shall have

jurisdiction over the parties and recipients of the "Confidential Documents" for purposes of any necessary enforcement of the provisions of this Order following termination of this litigation.

13. This Order shall be binding upon the parties hereto, upon their attorneys, and upon the parties and their attorneys' successors, executors, personal representatives, administrators, heirs, legal representatives, assigns, subsidiaries, divisions, employees, agents, independent contractors, or other persons or organizations over which they have control.

SIGNED this _____ day of _____, 20_____ .

_____
Judge Presiding

I,_____ have read the Protective Order—Psychiatric Records in Cause No. XXXXXXXX and agree to be bound by the terms set forth therein.


_____


STATE OF TEXAS
COUNTY OF COLLIN

SWORN TO AND SUBSCRIBED TO before me on this the _____ day of _____, 20_____, to which I certify my hand and seal of office.


_____
Notary Public in and for
State of Texas

My commission expires: _____

## Authorization for the Use and Disclosure of
## Protected Health Information

I, Harold Cross (Social Security No. 123-45-6789, Date of Birth 6/4/59), the undersigned client of Susan A. Jones, L.P.C., do hereby authorize Susan A. Jones L.P.C., my treating mental health provider, to disclose any and all protected health information in my file, including but not limited to her psychotherapy notes, to the following persons upon request to include deposition or record production subpoenas:

Thomas L. Hartsell Jr., Attorney at Law, who represents me in connection with my divorce case, Cause #2003-1456-Y, now pending in the 330th Judicial District court of Dallas County, Texas; and Barton E. Bernstein, Attorney at Law, who represents my wife, Sharon Cross, in this same divorce suit.

This information is to be provided at my request for use by said attorneys only in connection with the child-related issues presented in my above-referenced divorce suit. This authorization shall expire upon the entry of a final decree of divorce in my above-referenced divorce suit and the conclusion of any and all appeals.

**I acknowledge that I have the right to revoke this authorization in writing at any time to the extent Susan A. Jones, L.P.C., has not taken action in reliance on this authorization. I further acknowledge that even if I revoke this authorization, the use and disclosure of my protected health information could possibly still be compelled by court Order under state law as indicated in the copy of the Notice of Privacy Practices of Susan A. Jones, L.P.C., that I have received and reviewed.**

**I acknowledge that I have been advised by Susan A. Jones, L.P.C., of the potential of the redisclosure of my protected health information by the authorized recipients and that it will no longer be protected by the federal Privacy Rule.**

**I further acknowledge that the treatment provided to me by Susan A. Jones, L.P.C., was not conditioned on my signing this authorization.**

Signed this _____ day of _____, 20_____


_____

**Harold Cross, Client**


_____

**Social Security Number**

_____

Address

_____

Phone Number

I acknowledge that I received a copy of this signed authorization from Susan A. Jones, L.P.C., on this _____ day of _____, 2_____.

_____

**Harold Cross**

## Checklist for Deposition Testimony

1. Subpoena duces tecum
   a. Ever see before today?
   b. All efforts to comply
   c. All responsive documents brought? If not, why not? Instructed not to by attorney?
   d. All documents reviewed? Relied upon? Consulted? Form the basis of any opinions?
   e. (Mark as exhibits)

2. Background
   a. CV attached as exhibit
   b. General qualifications
   c. Certifications, licensing
   d. College, university
   e. CV data accurate? Overstated? Inaccurate?
   f. Membership in professional societies
   g. Requirements for membership
   h. Payment of dues
   i. Publications
   j. Anything pertaining to subject of case?
   k. Point to any professional literature written by someone else that supports your opinions in this case
   l. What business activities are you currently engaged in?
   m. What types of employment have you had in the past?
   n. What percentage of your income is derived from consulting and testifying in litigation matters?
   o. What percentage of your work is for plaintiffs versus defendants?

3. Prior testimony
   a. Number of depositions
   b. Number of trials
   c. Number for plaintiff/petitioner

    d. Number for defendant/respondent

    e. Styles of cases

    f. Attorneys involved

    g. Opinions and issues in cases

4. Criminal history

    a. Have you ever been arrested? Convicted? Misdemeanor? Felony?

    b. Was it related in any way to your profession?

    c. What was the charge?

    d. When did that happen?

    e. In what county was that case filed?

5. Party to suits

    a. Have you ever been sued?

    b. Why?

    c. When?

    d. Where? Style?

    e. What was the outcome?

6. Resume problems

    a. Ever received a written reprimand at work?

    b. Ever left a job because your competency was called to question?

    c. Ever left a job because of disciplinary reasons?

7. Bias and special interests

    a. Fee for testimony?

    b. Frequency of testimony in support of party that retained you or its attorneys?

    c. Portion of total income derived from expert witness services?

    d. Greater hourly rate for testimony at trial than for case-review time or deposition testimony?

    [To show profit motive to support plaintiff's or defendant's case]

    e. Nature of defense coaching or instructions on how to respond to cross-examination questions

    f. Testifying history: Ever provided expert services on behalf of any plaintiff or defendant?

8. Profit motive in testifying for party retaining you
   a. How much will you be paid to testify today in support of plaintiff/defendant?
   b. How many other times have you appeared as an expert witness to support plaintiffs/defendants?
   c. Have you appeared as a plaintiff's/defendant's expert in support of other plaintiffs/defendants?
   d. How many other plaintiffs/defendants have you testified for?
   e. What percentage of your total income comes from testifying in favor of plaintiffs/defendants?
   f. Do you charge these plaintiffs/defendants more for the hours you spend in case review than for your hours of actual testimony at trial and in deposition?
   g. Did the plaintiff's/defendant's lawyers in this case instruct or coach you on how to respond to this cross-examination?
   h. Have you ever—even once—testified in support of a plaintiff/a defendant in a case?

9. Contact in this case
   a. First contacted when?
   b. By whom?
   c. What story told to you?
   d. What asked to do?
   e. Were you given a maximum budget?
   f. Have you asked plaintiff/defense attorneys to do anything or provide anything that was denied to you?
   g. What was provided to you?
   h. What third parties did you consult with?
   i. Speak to plaintiff/defendant or to anyone else?
   j. What texts did you consult and what research did you do?
   k. What documents were generated?
   l. Correspondence, e-mails, and reports?
   m. All communications with plaintiff/defense attorney employees?
   n. Tell plaintiff/defense attorney employees any weaknesses in case?

10. Prior work for these attorneys
   a. How many cases for this attorney or any member of his or her firm?
   b. For defense or plaintiff?

    c. Styles of cases?

    d. Depositions or trials?

    e. Similar issues as issues in this case?

    f. Opinions?

    g. Total dollars for testimony over the years

    h. Socialize with attorney's or firm employees?

11. All work done in this case

    a. What?

    b. When?

    c. Why?

    d. All documents reviewed?

    e. All sources consulted?

    f. Ever speak to plaintiff, defendant, or any witnesses?

    g. Any further work recommended to plaintiff's/ defendant's attorneys?

    h. Plan any further work?

    i. Total hours spent on case?

12. Reports in this case

    a. What reports did you prepare?

    b. Drafts or revisions? Why or why not? At whose request?

    c. Destroy any drafts? At whose instruction?

    d. No opinions outside of report?

    e. With whom have you discussed report?

    f. What was said?

    g. Notes and correspondence re: report? With whom? Why?

13. Confining opinions to report

    a. All opinions, point by point

    b. Any opinions not in report?

    c. Why not in report?

    d. Know that both plaintiff/defendant and jury rely upon thoroughness and accurateness of your report?

    e. Realize that when you prepared the report?

    f. You saw the reports from the plaintiff's/defendant's expert, didn't you?

g. Each of those reports was several pages long and contained very detailed opinions and conclusions and mental impressions that supported their opinions

h. You did not include all your opinions, did you?

i. Did plaintiff's/defendant's lawyers tell you what to include in your report?

14. All bases of your opinions
    a. All documents and materials that form a basis for your opinions?
    b. All information, treatises, and authoritative texts that form a basis for your opinions?

15. What happens if we vary your assumptions?
    a. Agree that your assumption that _____ occurred forms a basis for your opinion that _____
    b. You are making that assumption in this case because _____ ?
    c. If we change that assumption and assume instead that _____ occurred, what does that do to your opinion?
    d. Why?

16. Other plausible scenarios
    a. You have testified that _____ occurred. You would agree that _____ is equally plausible?
    b. Why not?
    c. Can you exclude my scenario with reasonable certainty?

17. Authoritative texts and articles
    a. Recognize _____ as authoritative in your field?
    d. What texts do you consider to be authoritative?

18. *Daubert* issues (see Chapter 16 for discussion of *Daubert*)
    a. What areas do you believe you are an expert in?
    b. On what basis?
    c. All training and experience that qualifies you in each area?
    d. Ever been challenged on *Daubert* grounds before?
    e. Where? When? Result?
    f. Has your testimony ever been struck by any judge on *Daubert* grounds?

g. Where? When? Result?

h. Ever had challenge denied by any judge on *Daubert* grounds?

i. Where? When? Result?

j. Agree you are not an expert in:

    1. _____

    2. _____

    3. _____

k. Not trained or certified in any of the above areas?

1. Not qualified to opine concerning any of the above areas?

m. Ever rendered an opinion re: _____ outside the litigation setting?

n. When? Where?

o. Ever authored any peer-reviewed journal re: _____ ?

p. Any peer-reviewed journals advocate _____ ? Which ones? _____ Did you author any? _____

q. As specifically as possible, what was the *methodology* you used in arriving at your opinions?

r. How was your methodology tested?

s. Is your methodology generally accepted? How do you know?

t. What is the rate of error of your methodology?

u. Has the methodology been peer-reviewed?

v. To what extent does the methodology rely on your subjective interpretation?

w. What are the nonjudicial uses that have been made of your methodology?

x. What did you do to validate your methodology?

y. What did you do to determine what the error rate is in your methodology?

19. Criticisms of plaintiff's/defendant's experts

a. Ever heard of _____ or _____

b. Ever work with/against them?

c. Are they well qualified? If not, why not?

d. Details of all criticisms of them and their opinions

e. Criticize any of their assumptions?

f. Criticize any of their opinions?

g. Criticize any of their methodology?

h. Their methodology not peer-reviewed? Not reliable? Why not?

i. Agree that your opinions are consistent with theirs in the following respects: _____

20. Any opinions not yet discussed
    a. Plan to provide any opinions at trial that we have not yet discussed?
    b. Understand this is my only day to discover your opinions in person before the trial?

21. Further work
    a. Plan any?
    b. What?
    c. Why?
    d. Who told you to do the work?
    e. Discuss with plaintiff/defense attorney?
    f. When are you going to do the work?
    g. Why not done before?

22. Trial
    a. You will be there?
    b. Discussed your presence at trial with plaintiff/defense attorney?
    c. What were you told?

23. Closing concessions
    a. You're not 100 percent certain regarding _____?
    b. You could be wrong?
    c. It *is possible* that _____?
    d. If we change your assumption that _____ occurred, then your opinion changes?
    e. You are not saying that _____, but only that _____?

### Checklist for Direct Examination for Courtroom Testimony

The checklists in this appendix are not a complete review, but rather serve as a quick assessment to remind the potential witness that in every trial there are events to remember, dates that will be questioned, and, depending on the nature of the case, technical information, theories, and conclusions that will be questioned.

Prior to any trial, fill in the blanks by reviewing the clinical file or progress notes, consulting
with colleagues, visiting with attorneys as appropriate, and researching any topic that is relevant to the case.

If a witness is fully prepared, the questions will be quick and gentle. If a witness is ill prepared or lacks mastery of the facts or theory, the cross-examination will be exhaustive and brutal. This is aggravation the provider can easily do without.


### DIRECT EXAMINATION CHECKLIST

#### Personal background

- Name
- Home address
- Business address
- Citizenship
- Age/date of birth
- Military record


#### Profession or occupation

- Type of professional (mental health discipline—describe profession in lay terms)
- When and where licensed or certified, if applicable?
- Place of former employment
- Certification or licensing
- By whom?
- Qualifications necessary for certification? Licensing?
- Recertification or relicensing

## Educational background

- Undergraduate (where, when, degree achieved)
- Graduate (where, when degree achieved)
- Postgraduate (where, when, degree achieved)
- Courses or training

## Professional training

- Internship or fellowship (where, when)
- Nature of internship or fellowship (where, when)
- Specialty or subspecialty
- Name and description of field
- Nature or training
- Degrees/awards
- Years of experience
- Number of same type of tests administered
- Number of cases included with same or similar theory and techniques

## Associations and affiliations

- Name of professional memberships (international, national, state, local)
- Requirements for membership
- Offices held
- Institution affiliated with
  —Where, how long, nature of affiliation
  —Accredited?
  —Title held with institution
  —Hours spent per week, month, and so on

## Academic positions

- Where, how long
- Duties
- Courses taught (specialty area)
- Amount of time spent (week, month, etc.)

## Research projects

- Where, duration
- Sanctioned by whom?
- Subject

## Clinical positions

- Describe clinical position
- Where (hospital, county, federal or state agency)
- How long in clinical position?
- Duties/title
- Funded by

## Published papers, articles, and writings

- Field (e.g., psychology)
- List and describe publication and date
- Any publication pertaining to the condition, testing, or issues of the parties in this case?
- Other research interests

## Experience as expert witness

- Number of court appearances in past 10 years
- Number of consultations involving litigation
- Testified for attorney on either side?
  —How many times?
- Type of cases, generally
- How learned of present case

## Relationship to litigation

- Party
- Employed by party?
- Blood relation?
- Acquainted with anyone in case?

- Contractual relationship with anyone in case?
  —With whom?
  —Substance of contract?
- Financial interest in outcome?
- Personal interest in outcome?

## Financial interest in case

- Total compensation paid
  —Professional services
  —Expenses
  —Other
- Basis of compensation
  —Hourly *rate/flat* fee
  —Time in preparation
  —Time in testimony
  —Contingent on outcome?
- Usual charges for same or similar case

## Introduction to facts

- Date first contacted
- By whom?
- Who related facts?
- Content of oral facts related
- Written material relating to facts:
  —Identify document
  —Custody of document

## Source of knowledge of facts

- Extent of personal observation and experience
- Other sources:
  —From what source?
  —Received by whom?

- Efforts to obtain information:
  —Describe
  —Sources tried
  —Dates and times
  —How obtained?
- Avoidance by opposing party?
- Reasons for avoidance

## Consultation and conversation about facts

- Date, time, location
- Mode of communication (phone, person, etc.)
- Persons present:
  —Whom
  —Circumstances
  —Relationship to parties
- What was said?
- Notes or record of conversation?
- Cooperation by person tested/evaluated?
- Lack of cooperation by opposing party?

## Written statements and reports

- Date, time
- Content
- By whom?
- To whom?
- Relationship to parties
- Substance of statement
- Reason for obtaining

## Treatises and articles read in preparation of testimony

- Identify treatises
- Author, subject, nature, and so on of treatises
- Relied on as authoritative?

### Writings, records, and data read in preparation of testimony

- Identify
- Author, subject, nature, and so on
- Original or copy
- Custodian (then and now)
- Experts' familiarity with types of writings, records, and documents
  —Relied on as authoritative?
  —When first reviewed
  —When last reviewed
  —Time spent in reviewing
- Whether expert relied on writings, records, documents in formulating opinion
  —To what extent?

### Examination/evaluation in preparation for trial

- Dates and locations of exam/evaluation/parties
- What was done at exam/evaluation?
  —Primary purpose
  —Person conducting exam/evaluation/testing
- Reason for exam/evaluation/test
- Time spent during each exam/evaluation/test
- Persons present
- Tests given/administered/conducted:
  —Name
  —Description (give a succinct and complete explanation of the type and test administered and customary procedure)
  —Purpose of test
  —Person who performed testing
  —Person who supervised testing
  —Explain scientific theory underlying test
  —Scientific theory of test valid?
  —Technique applying theory valid?
  —Technique properly applied in this case?
  —Scientific theory and technique accepted as valid in scientific community?

—Names, authors, and so on of literature that support or reject theory and techniques used

—Explain (in lay terms) the equipment/material, if any, utilized in testing

—Explain scoring (computerized?)

—Accuracy of scoring

—Accuracy of equipment at time test was performed/scored in this case

- Explain potential rate of error (both human and mechanical)
- Explain chain of custody procedure
- Establish complete chain of custody (from start to finish)
- Any information that distorts tests or results

## Opinions

- Based on above, this test performed in accordance with acceptable standards and procedures?
- Accuracy of this test
- Results of test performed in this case
- State opinion on relevant fact(s)

## Basis for opinion

- Factual basis for opinion in this case (related facts, test data, etc.)
- Theory on which opinion in this case is based
- Explain different schools of thought on subject as it applies to this case
- Why this theory is accurate or reliable in this case
- Explain margin of error in opinion, if any, in this case

## Consultation with other experts relating to data or opinion

- Name, address of persons consulted regarding procedure or test results, their occupations
- Training and specialization of persons consulted
- Information exchanged and other experts' familiarity with current subject

## Checklist for Cross-Examination

### Education

- Accredited school?
- Lack education of peers in area of specialty?
- Lack education to join certain professional associations?
- State of knowledge in field at time educated
- Poor grades or performance in school?
- Fellowship or internship terminated for misconduct or incompetence?

### Licenses

- Failed licensure test?
- Suspended or revoked?
- Has a licensing board ever placed you under supervision? Why?
- Has any licensing board or other entity placed restrictions on your license?

### Certification

- Failed specialty exam?
- Not permitted to sit for specialty exam?

### Professional memberships

- Refused or revoked?

### Experience

- Not qualified in area material to case? No writing or research in area of specialty?
- Practice is concentrated in area different from issues involved in this case?
- Subspecialty is not most appropriate for case?
- Practical, not theoretical, and you are aware of underlying theories?
- Experience is purely theoretical?
- Previous work has been criticized by other members of profession?
- Skill in formulating opinion lacks superiority to that of recognized authorities?
- Experience does not contribute to validity of conclusion?
- Bases opinion on invalidated theories?

- Opinions, in past, not capable of being proved correct?
- Failed to keep abreast of recent developments and literature?

## Bias or interest

- Professional witness—always fixed point of view?
- Usually testify for one side?
- Make substantial part of income from testifying?
- Social, family, business, professional connection with opposing party?
- Number of times you and attorney refer clients to each other? You were informed of what opinion should be *before* employed?
- Unreasonable fees?
- Paid witness?
- Contingency fee for testimony?
- If not yet paid:
  —What is expected fee?
  —What method to determine change in the fee?
- Research and testing confined to theory in which you are only one who believes it to be valid?
- Methodology was developed by you and not recognized by anyone else in field?

## Inadequate preparation

- Hypothetical expert—no first-hand knowledge?
- Made no independent verification of chain of custody or how data obtained?
- In normal practice, you would never give conclusion, without full investigation of facts?
- Examined opposing party only for purpose of testifying—not comparable to professional opinion?
- Cannot remember pertinent facts without looking at file to refresh memory?

## Insufficient basis for opinion

- Reliance solely on subjective data without confirmation by objective findings?
- Examination of parties, facts, and evidence too brief (compare time spent by client's expert)?
- Inadequate or inappropriate test performed?

- Failed to examine pertinent data or to review relevant documents or evidence?
- Failed to consult with other authorities to confirm conclusions?
- Test interpretation open to question?
  —Results were borderline?
  —Data employed was too recent, too old, or incomplete?
  —Accuracy or data not conclusively established—no double-checking?
  —Conflicting opinions or interpretation possible?
  —Data not obtained by recognized means?
- Failed to consider recent developments?
- Scientific theory of test invalid?
- Technique applying theory invalid?
- Technique was not properly applied?
- Scientific theory and technique not scientifically accepted?
- High potential rate of error in testing or results?

**Incorrect opinion**

- Theory is uncertain or not generally accepted by relevant scientific community?
- Issue at trial is at theoretical stage rather than established level?
- By nature, opinion is speculative?
  —Issue falls into gray area and not capable of being answered?
  —Issue, at trial, is subject of controversy in field and opinion is not wholly accepted by profession?
  —No basis for believing theory is superior to other theories?
  —Pure speculation that your testing methods are superior to alternative methods?
- Opinions and explanations are not generally accepted?
- Facts on which opinion is based are equally consistent with different opinion?
  —Other experts may have different opinions based on same facts?
  —Lack of current scientific data prevents conclusive opinion to issue?
- Personal judgment or bias played major role in testimony?
- Opinion primarily based on history or *data* assumed and never verified?
- If facts varied, opinion would change significantly?
- Contaminated or distorted data?
- Break in chain of custody of evidence/testing?
- Scoring equipment not properly checked or maintained.

# List of Federal Cases Involving *Daubert* Challenges of Mental Health Professionals

| Case Claims | Type of Expert | Holding/Basis | Evidence Sought |
| --- | --- | --- | --- |
| *U.S. v. Mazzeo* 2000 *U.S. App. Lexis* 8847 (2nd Cir. 1/21/2000) | Misappropriation of postal funds | Psychiatrist on issue of false confessions | Exclusion of testimony as being unreliable was not manifest error because expert admitted that he spent only 1 hour 20 minutes with the defendant and that he had not conducted any of the available tests designed to measure the extent to which a person is likely to make false confessions. |
| *Calhoun v. Yamaha Motor Corp., USA* 350 F. 3rd 316 (3rd Cir. 2003) | Product liability (Jet ski) | Psychologist | The psychologist was allowed to testify that children in stressful situations would confuse jet ski throttle with bicycle brakes and accelerate when they intended to brake, but was not allowed to opine that people in emergency situations tend to react by clenching their fists. |
| *French v. Wal-Mart Stores, Inc.*, 1999 U.S. App. Lexis 20054 (4th Cir. 8/23/1999) | Negligence | Rehab counselor | Admission of testimony was not an abuse of discretion. |
| *Volger v. Blackmore*, 352 F. 3d 150 (5th Cir. 2003) | Wrongful death suit (Auto accident) | Thanatologist and "grief expert" | Admission of evidence was not an abuse of discretion because defendants did not raise a proper challenge to the witness's credentials or to the reliability of her testimony. Defendants challenged only whether such testimony was necessary to aid the jury in understanding grief due to loss of a loved one. The district court did not abuse its discretion in finding that the testimony was relevant and its probative value outweighed any prejudicial effect. |
| *Tyler v. Union Oil Co. of California*, 304 F.3d 379 (5th Cir. 2002) | Age discrimination case | Psychologist | Admission of evidence was not an abuse of discretion |
| *Skidmore v. Precision Printing & Packaging, Inc.*, 188 F. 3d 606 (5th Cir. 1999) | Title VII | Psychiatrist | Admission of testimony was not an abuse of discretion. (Case reversed vacated and remanded on other grounds.) |
| *United States v. Katz* 178 F. 3d 368 (5th Cir. 1999) | Criminal (Child pornography) | Tanner Scale of Human Development test | Criticized trial judge for devoting too much time (i.e., better part of 5 days) on *Daubert* hearing to determine the reliability of testimony "involving a well-known test that is applied in a straightforward manner." The court stated that much more complex hearings are customarily conducted in a few hours. |

| Case Claims | Type of Expert | Holding/Basis | Evidence Sought |
|---|---|---|---|
| *United States v. Langan,* 263 F. 3d 613 (6th Cir. 2001) | Criminal (Bank robbery) | Psychologist on the issue of the reliability of eyewitness identifications | Exclusion of testimony that eyewitness's identification could have been mistake as the result of "unconscious transference" was not an abuse of discretion because theory was unreliable. |
| *Newsome v. McCabe,* 319 F. 3d 301 (7th Cir.2003) | Civil rights case | Psychologist | Admission of report was not an abuse of discretion |
| *Walker v. Soo Line R.R.,* 208 F. 3d 581 (7th Cir. 2000) | FELA case (Plaintiff struck by lightning on work platform) | Psychologist | Psychologist allowed this expert to testify regarding plaintiff's post-accident IQ. The trial court, however, did not allow this expert to testify as to plaintiff's functioning prior to the accident. The court of appeals concluded that all of this expert's testimony should have been admitted. |
| *Bryant v. City of Chicago,* 200 F. 3d 1092 (7th Cir) cert. denied, U.S. _____, 121 S. Ct. 64 (2000) | Title VII case | Psychologist | Admission of testimony was not an abuse of discretion. |
| *Tyrus v. Urban Search Management,* 102 F.2d 256 (7th Cir. 1996), cert. denied, 520 U.S. cert. denied, 520 U.S. 1251 (1997) | Racial discrimination | Psychologist | Exclusion of testimony was an abuse of discretion because trial court failed to apply Daubert criteria. |
| *Smith v. Rasmussen,* 249 F. 3d 755, 2001 U.S. App. LEXIS (8th Cir. 2001) | Social Security action (Failure to fund sex change operation) | Psychiatrist | Trial court allowed testimony regarding general psychiatric principles and basic diagnostic criteria, but excluded opinions concerning gender identity disorder and the potential treatment options therefore as unreliable. Court of appeals found no as unreliable. Court of appeals found no error. |
| *Jenson v. Eveleth Taconite Co.,* 130 F.3d 1287 (8th Cir. 1997), cert. denied, 524 U.S. 953 (1998) | Sex discrimination case | 6 psychiatrists and psychologists on causation | Exclusion of expert testimony was an abuse of discretion. The court of appeals found the proffered testimony to be both reliable and relevant. |
| *Wilson v. Muckala,* 303 F.3d 1207 (10th Cir. 2002) | Sexual harassment case | Psychiatrist | Testimony from psychiatrist regarding the general veracity of witnesses was not appropriate. |

## Trial Vita (Sample Form)

PREPARED FOR CAUSE # _____ , JONES V. SMITH

Name

Address

Phone and fax number

Chronological educational experience: (years, institutions attended, degrees conferred)
- 
- 

Relevant employment: (years, job title, brief job description)
- 
- 

Special studies or seminars attended that are relevant to Jones v. Smith
- 
- 

Seminars presented that contained information relevant to Jones v. Smith
- 
- 

Articles, monologues, books, or other publications by the witness: (dates of publication, name of publication, title of article or book, or other description)
- 
- 

Special studies authored by the witness, whether published or unpublished:
- 
- 

Previous courtroom experience if relevant to this case:
- 
- 

Other factors not yet included that might be helpful to the court or jury if included in the vita

## Employee Evaluation Information and Consent Form

### Therapist

The undersigned Therapist is a licensed psychologist engaged in private practice providing psychological evaluations for clients on a fee for service basis.

### Evaluation Services

The Therapist, using her knowledge of development and human behavior and her education, training, and experience as a psychologist, will do an evaluation, including appropriate psychological testing, of the person designated for the evaluation (hereinafter referred to as "Evaluee") and will provide the client (hereinafter referred to as "Employer") and the Evaluee with a copy of her written report. The Therapist further agrees to make herself available on a reasonable basis to discuss the report and the evaluation with the Employer and the Evaluee. The evaluation is dependent on the cooperation of the Evaluee and the consent of the Evaluee as indicated by Evaluee's signature below.

### Appointments

Appointments are made by calling (XXX) 555-2222 Monday through Friday between the hours of 9:00 A.M. and 5:00 P.M. Please call to cancel or reschedule at least 24 hours in advance or you, the Evaluee, will be charged a "missed appointment fee" of $_____ for failing to cancel the appointment 24 hours in advance.

### Cancellations

Cancellations must be received at least 24 hours before your scheduled appointment; otherwise, Employer may be charged a fee for that missed appointment. The Evaluee is responsible for calling to reschedule an appointment and for paying promptly for missed appointments.

### Number of Visits

The number of sessions needed depends on many factors and will be discussed by the Therapist. The time necessary to properly and accurately evaluate the Evaluee will be discussed, and such time as is required will be spent on the evaluation.

## Length of Visits

Sessions are generally two to four hours but may take longer for psychological testing.

## Relationship

There is no intent on the part of the Therapist, Evaluee or Employer for the Therapist to enter into a therapeutic relationship with the Evaluee. *The Therapist's role and relationship is limited solely to performing the psychological evaluation and submitting the written report to the Employer and Evaluee.* Serious boundary violations by the Evaluee will result in a termination of the evaluation and all earned fees shall be retained by the Therapist or paid by Employer. The employment by therapist is for evaluation and for the report to the employer only, and not for therapy.

## Payment for Services

The Employer is responsible for advance payment for the evaluation that is covered by letter agreement between the Employer and the Therapist. Although it is the goal of the undersigned Therapist to protect the confidentiality of Evaluee's records, there may be times when disclosure of these records or testimony will be compelled by law. Confidentiality and exceptions to confidentiality are discussed below. In the event disclosure of Evaluee's records or testimony is required by law, the Employer will be responsible for and shall pay the costs involved in producing the records and the Therapist's normal hourly rate for the time involved in any courtroom procedures including giving testimony. Such payments are to be made at the time or prior to the time the Therapist renders the services. The Therapist may require a deposit for anticipated court appearances and preparation.

## Confidentiality

Discussions between a Therapist and a patient are confidential. No information can be released without the patient's written consent unless mandated by law. Possible exceptions to confidentiality include but are not limited to the following situations: child abuse, abuse of the elderly or disabled, abuse of patients in mental health facilities, neglect, financial exploitation, sexual exploitation, AIDS/HIV infection and possible transmission, criminal prosecutions, child custody cases, suits in which the mental health of a party is in issue, situations where the therapist has a duty to disclose, or where, in the therapist's judgment, it is necessary to warn, notify, or disclose; fee disputes between the therapist and the client; a negligence suit brought by the client against the therapist; or the filing of a complaint with a licensing board or other state or federal regulatory authority. **FOR FURTHER INFORMATION, REVIEW THE NOTICE OF PRIVACY PRACTICES FURNISHED TO YOU BY YOUR THERAPIST IN CONJUNCTION WITH THIS EMPLOYEE EVALUATION INFORMATION AND CONSENT DOCUMENT.** If you have any questions regarding confidentiality, you should bring them to the attention of the Therapist when you and the Therapist discuss this matter further. By signing this information and consent form, you, the Evaluee, are giving your consent to the undersigned Therapist to share your confidential information with the Employer and to all others mandated by law, and you are also releasing and holding harmless the undersigned Therapist from any departure from your right of confidentiality that may result.

### Risks of Evaluation

The evaluation of the Therapist may be unfavorable or damaging in some manner to the Evaluee. By signing this information and consent form, Evaluee acknowledges this possibility and advises the Therapist that he or she wishes to go forward with the evaluation and submission of a written report to the Employer and releases the Therapist from all liability for the unfavorable or damaging consequences to Evaluee as a result of the evaluation, the written report, and lawful disclosure of the confidential information revealed to, discovered by, or learned by the Therapist in the course of the evaluation. The possibility of an unfavorable evaluation is an accepted risk of the evaluation process.

### After Hours Emergencies

Your Therapist is *not* available to respond to emergency calls from you. In the event you experience an emergency requiring the attention of a mental health professional, you should present yourself immediately for treatment at a hospital emergency room nearest to you.

### Consent to Evaluation

I, the Evaluee, agree to submit to a psychological evaluation by the undersigned Therapist and further agree that the therapist prepare a written report to be delivered to the

Employer and to myself. I further agree that the undersigned Therapist can share with the Employer all notes, test reports, or other information, both verbal or written, that is revealed to, discovered by, or learned by the Therapist during the course of the evaluation. I understand and agree that I will participate in the evaluation and cooperate with the Therapist at all times and will sign all necessary releases for the Therapist to secure information necessary to complete the evaluation. I understand that the evaluation is voluntary on my part and that I may stop the evaluation by the undersigned Therapist at any time even though it may have implications for me with respect to my relationship with the Employer.

By signing this Employee Evaluation Information and Consent Form, the undersigned Employer and Evaluee acknowledge that they have both read and understood all the terms and information contained herein.

_____            _____

**EMPLOYER**                       DATE

As witnessed by:

_____            _____

**THERAPIST**                      DATE

_____            _____

**EVALUEE**                        DATE

As witnessed by:

_____            _____

**THERAPIST**                      DATE

## Home Study Information and Consent Form

### Therapist

The undersigned Therapist is a licensed social worker engaged in private practice providing home studies upon referral from family law courts for clients on a fee for service basis.

### Evaluation Services

The Therapist, using her knowledge of development and human behavior and her training and experience as a social worker, will do a home study of the persons, including children, designated for the home study in the attached court order. The parties will be hereinafter referred to as "Evaluee" and will provide the court and any attorney representing an Evaluee with a copy of her written report. The Therapist further agrees to make herself available on a reasonable basis and prior notice to provide in-court or deposition testimony. The home study is dependent on the cooperation of the Evaluee and the consent of the Evaluee as indicated by Evaluee's signature below.

### Appointments

Appointments are made by calling (214) 555-2222 Monday through Friday between the hours of 9:00 A.M. and 5:00 P.M. Please call to cancel or reschedule at least 24 hours in advance or you will be charged the "missed appointment" fee of $ _____ for failing to cancel the appointment 24 hours in advance, to be paid by Evaluee prior to the next session.

### Cancellations

Cancellations must be received at least 24 hours before your scheduled appointment; otherwise Evaluee may be charged an additional fee of $200.00 for that missed appointment, which must be paid before the home study will continue. The Evaluee is responsible for calling to reschedule an appointment.

### Number of Visits

The number of sessions needed depends on many factors and will be discussed by the Therapist. The time necessary to properly and accurately evaluate the Evaluee will be spent on the evaluation.

## Length of Visits

Sessions are generally two to four hours in length but may take longer for psychological testing. Visits by the Therapist to Evaluee's home should be expected. Evaluee will be expected to make the subject children available upon request from the Therapist.

## Relationship

There is no intent on the part of the Therapist or Evaluee for the Therapist to enter into a therapeutic relationship with the Evaluee or any children of Evaluee. *The Therapist's role and relationship is limited solely to performing the home study and submitting the written* report to the court and the attorney representing an Evaluee. Serious boundary violations by the Evaluee will result in a termination of the home study, and all earned fees shall be retained by the Therapist. The reasons necessitating termination of the home study will be reported to the referring Court.

## Payment for Services

Pursuant to the attached court order, each Evaluee is obligated to pay $700.00 to Therapist prior to commencement of the home study. Once the home study report is filed with the court, any party that subpoenas Therapist to give in-court or deposition testimony shall be responsible to compensate Therapist for her time expended in responding to the subpoena at the rate of $125.00 per hour. A deposit of $375.00 shall be paid to Therapist in advance of the date set for the Therapist's court or deposition appearance. Although it is the goal of the undersigned Therapist to protect the confidentiality of Evaluee's records, there may be times when disclosure of these records or testimony will be compelled by law outside the scope of the legal proceeding in which the home study is being conducted. Confidentiality and exceptions to confidentiality are discussed below. In the event disclosure of Evaluee's records or testimony is required by law outside the scope of the legal proceedings in which the home study is being conducted, the Evaluee will be responsible for and shall pay the costs involved in producing the records plus the Therapist's then normal hourly rate for the time involved in giving testimony. Such payments are to be made at the time or prior to the time the services are rendered by the Therapist. The Therapist may require a deposit for anticipated court appearances and preparation.

## Confidentiality

Discussions between a Therapist and a patient are confidential. No information can be released without the patient's written consent unless mandated by law. Possible exceptions to confidentiality include, but are not limited to, the following situations: child abuse, abuse, neglect and exploitation of the elderly or disabled, abuse of patients in mental health facilities, sexual exploitation, AIDS/HIV infection and possible transmission, criminal prosecutions, child custody or conservatorship cases, suits in which the mental health of a party is in issue, situations where the therapist has a duty to disclose, or where, in the therapist's judgment, it is necessary to warn, notify, or disclose; fee disputes between the therapist and the client; a negligence suit brought by the client against the therapist; or the filing of a complaint with a licensing board or other state or federal regulatory authority. **FOR FURTHER INFORMATION, REVIEW THE NOTICE OF PRIVACY PRACTICES FURNISHED TO YOU BY YOUR THERAPIST IN CONJUNCTION WITH THIS HOME STUDY INFORMATION AND CONSENT DOCUMENT.** If you have any questions regarding confidentiality, you should bring them to the attention of the Therapist when you and the Therapist discuss this matter further. By signing this information and consent form, you, the Evaluee, are giving your consent to the undersigned Therapist to share your confidential information with the referring court and any attorney representing an Evaluee and to all others mandated by law, and you are also releasing and holding harmless the undersigned Therapist from any departure from your right of confidentiality that may result from such disclosure.

## Risks of Evaluation

The home study of the Therapist may be unfavorable or damaging in some manner to the Evaluee. This is a usual and customary risk of all home studies. By signing this information and consent form, Evaluee acknowledges this possibility and advises the Therapist that he or she wishes to go forward with the home study and submission of a written report to the court and any attorney representing an Evaluee and releases the Therapist from all liability for the unfavorable or damaging consequences to Evaluee as a result of the home study, the written report, and lawful disclosure of the confidential information revealed to, discovered by, or learned by the Therapist in the course of the evaluation.

## After Hours Emergencies

Your Therapist is not available to respond to emergency calls from you. In the event you experience an emergency requiring the attention of a mental health professional, you should present yourself immediately for treatment at a hospital emergency room nearest to you or to a therapist of your selection.

## Consent to Evaluation

I, the Evaluee, agree to submit to a home study by the undersigned Therapist and further agree that she prepare a written report to be delivered to the court and to any attorney representing me or another Evaluee. I further agree that the undersigned Therapist can share with the court and any attorney representing me or any other Evaluee all notes, reports, or other information, both verbal and written, that are revealed to, discovered by, or learned by the Therapist during the course of her home study. I understand and agree that I will participate in the home study and cooperate with the Therapist at all times and will sign all necessary releases for the Therapist to secure information necessary to complete the home study. I understand that the home study is being conducted pursuant to a court order and that my refusal to participate or cooperate will be reported to the referring court and may result in adverse action being taken against me.

By signing this Home Study Information and Consent Form, the undersigned Evaluee acknowledges that he or she has both read and understood all the terms and information contained herein.

_____          _____

EVALUEE                          DATE

As witnessed by:

_____          _____

THERAPIST                        DATE

## Contract for Forensic Services and
## Information and Consent Form

### Therapist

The undersigned Therapist is a licensed psychologist engaged in private practice providing psychological evaluations and courtroom testimony for clients on a fee for service basis.

### Evaluation Services

The Therapist, using her knowledge of development and human behavior and her education, training, and experience as a psychologist, agrees to conduct an evaluation, including appropriate psychological testing, of the person designated for the evaluation (hereinafter referred to as "Evaluee"). If a written report is requested, the Therapist will provide the undersigned client (hereinafter referred to as the "Responsible Party") and the Evaluee with a copy of her written report. The Therapist further agrees to make herself available on a reasonable basis to discuss the report and the evaluation with the Responsible Party and the Evaluee. The evaluation is dependent on the cooperation of the Evaluee and the consent of the Evaluee as indicated by Evaluee's signature below. The Therapist further agrees to make herself available for deposition by any party, and to testify at any court proceedings, in the suit in which the Therapist's services have been engaged.

### Fees for Services

The Responsible Party agrees to pay the Therapist $_____ per hour for each hour spent by the Therapist on the evaluation of the Evaluee, research, necessary consultation with collateral sources, report writing, testimony preparation, time spent in consultation with the Responsible Party and/or the Evaluee, depositions, courtroom testimony, travel, and time spent waiting to testify. In addition, the Responsible Party agrees to reimburse the Therapist for any out-of-pocket expenses incurred in providing services to the Responsible Party and/or the Evaluee, which may include, but are not limited to, photocopying, facsimile charges, long distance phone charges, parking fees, psychological tests, and scoring.

The Responsible Party agrees to pay a nonrefundable retainer fee of $ _____ to the Therapist upon the execution of this agreement. IT IS UNDERSTOOD AND AGREED THAT NO SERVICES WILL BE PROVIDED BY THE THERAPIST PRIOR TO RECEIPT BY HER OF THIS RETAINER FEE. The Therapist agrees to provide periodic billing statements to the Responsible Party detailing the work performed and the balance of the retainer fee that has not been earned. If the original retainer fee is exhausted before the conclusion of the litigation or matter in which the Therapist has been engaged, upon notice by the Therapist of the depletion of the original retainer fee paid, the Responsible Party further agrees to pay within seven (7) days an additional retainer fee of $ _____. However, this additional deposit shall be refundable to the Responsible Party if it is not earned by the Therapist.

## Appointments

Appointments are made by calling (XXX) 555-2222 Monday through Friday between the hours of 9:00 A.M. and 5:00 P.M. Please call to cancel or reschedule at least 24 hours in advance or the Responsible Party will be charged a "missed appointment fee" of $ _____ if the Evaluee fails to cancel the appointment 24 hours in advance.

## Relationship

There is no intent on the part of the Therapist, Evaluee, or Responsible Party for the Therapist to enter into a therapeutic relationship with the Evaluee. *The Therapist's role and relationship is limited solely to performing the psychological evaluation and submitting a written report to the Responsible Party and Evaluee if requested and to testify by deposition or in court.* Serious boundary violations by the Evaluee will result in a termination of the forensic services and all retainer fees shall be retained by the Therapist and any fees earned but not covered by the retainer shall be paid by the Responsible Party. The employment by therapist is for evaluation, report generation if requested, consultation and testimony only, and not for therapy.

## Confidentiality

Discussions between a Therapist and a patient are confidential. No information can be released without the patient's written consent unless mandated by law. Possible exceptions to confidentiality include but are not limited to the following situations: child abuse,

abuse of the elderly or disabled, abuse of patients in mental health facilities, neglect, financial exploitation, sexual exploitation, AIDS/HIV infection and possible transmission, criminal prosecutions, child custody cases, suits in which the mental health of a party is in issue, situations where the therapist has a duty to disclose, or where, in the therapist's judgment, it is necessary to warn, notify, or disclose, fee disputes between the therapist and the client; a negligence suit brought by the client against the therapist; or the filing of a complaint with a licensing board or other state or federal regulatory authority. **FOR FURTHER INFORMATION, REVIEW THE NOTICE OF PRIVACY PRACTICES FURNISHED TO YOU BY THE THERAPIST IN CONJUNCTION WITH THIS EMPLOYEE EVALUATION INFORMATION AND CONSENT DOCUMENT.** If you have any questions regarding confidentiality, you should bring them to the attention of the Therapist when you and the Therapist discuss this matter further. By signing this agreement form, you, the Evaluee, are giving your consent to the undersigned Therapist to share your confidential information with the Responsible Party and to all others mandated by law, and you are also releasing and holding harmless the undersigned Therapist from any departure from your right of confidentiality that may result.

## Risks of Evaluation

The evaluation of the Therapist may be unfavorable or damaging in some manner to the Evaluee. By signing this information and consent form, Evaluee and the Responsible Party acknowledge this possibility and advise the Therapist that they wish to go forward with the evaluation and release the Therapist from all liability for the unfavorable or damaging consequences to Evaluee or Responsible Party as a result of the evaluation, written report, testimony and lawful disclosure of the confidential information revealed to, discovered by, or learned by the Therapist in the course of the evaluation. The possibility of an unfavorable evaluation is an accepted risk of the evaluation process.

## After-Hours Emergencies

The Therapist is *not* available to respond to emergency calls from you. In the event you experience an emergency requiring the attention of a mental health professional, you should present yourself immediately for treatment at a hospital emergency room nearest to you.

## Consent to Evaluation

I, the Evaluee, agree to submit to a psychological evaluation by the undersigned Therapist and further agree that if requested, she prepare a written report to be delivered to the Responsible Party and to myself. I further agree that the undersigned Therapist can testify at deposition or in court if called to do so by any party in the case in which the Therapist's services have been engaged and that the Therapist can share with the Responsible Party and necessary third parties in connection with deposition or courtroom testimony all notes, test reports, or other information, both verbal or written, that is revealed to, discovered by, or learned by the Therapist during the course of her evaluation. I understand and agree that I will participate in the evaluation and cooperate with the Therapist at all times and will sign all necessary releases for the Therapist to secure information necessary to complete the evaluation. I understand that the evaluation is voluntary on my part and that I may stop the evaluation by the undersigned Therapist at any time even though it may have implications for me with respect to my relationship with the Responsible Party.

By signing this Contract for Forensic Services and Information and Consent Form, the undersigned acknowledge that they have both read and understood all the terms and information contained herein and are in agreement with same.

_____          _____

RESPONSIBLE PARTY                 DATE


_____          _____

THERAPIST                         DATE


_____          _____

EVALUEE                           DATE

# Index

## A

Abuse, child/elder/disabled, and confidentiality, 63–64
Admissibility of expert testimony, 140–150
  challenges to:
    qualifications as expert, 142
    reliability of methodology and conclusions, 143
    subject matter, 142
  federal cases:
    *Daubert* case, 143–145
    *Joiner* case, 145–147
    *Kumho* case, 146–147
  implications for mental health professionals, 147–149
Advocate, lawyer's function as, 26
Alternative dispute resolution (ADR), 6, 26, 74
Amendments, Fifth and Sixth, 14, 22
Angry clients. *See* Conflict(s), resolving; Alternative dispute resolution (ADR)
Answer, in civil process, 4–5
Appeals:
  civil process, 8
  criminal process, 12
Appointments, procedures for, 160

Arbitration, 179
Arraignment, in criminal process, 10
Arrest, 9
Association form, 28
Attachment order, 87–89
Attorneys. *See* Lawyers

## B

Bail, 9–10
Bench trial, 6
Billing. *See* Payment/fees
Booking, in criminal process, 9

## C

Checklists:
  for cross-examination, 235–237
  for deposition testimony, 221–227
  for direct examination for courtroom testimony, 228–234
  for trial preparation (eight R's), 198–199
  for trial preparation as a defendant, 180–181

Child abuse (exceptions/limitations to confidentiality), 63
Child in need of supervision, 14
Civil litigation process, 4–8
    alternative dispute resolution (ADR), 6, 26, 74
    answer, 4–5
    appeal, 8
    bench trial, 6
    discovery, 5–6
    filing petition, 4
    jury trial, 6–8 (see also Testimony; Trials)
        closing arguments, 7
        jury deliberation and verdict, 7–8
        jury instructions, 7
        jury selection, 7, 34
        opening statements, 7
        witness testimony and cross-examination, 7
    postjudgment motions, 8
    preliminary motions, 5
    service of process, 4
Clients:
    angry (see Conflict(s), resolving; Alternative dispute resolution (ADR))
    getting payment from (see Payment/fees)
    problem issues for, in deposition, 109
    relationship with therapist, 161
    traits of (having lawyers ask about, in direct examination), 101–102
    unreasonable, 181

Closing arguments, 7
Compensation. See Payment/fees
Competence, professional, 54–57
Complaints:
    angry clients (see Conflict(s), resolving)
    areas of vulnerability leading to, 175–177
        acts of commission, 176–177
        acts of omission, 175–176
    filed with licensing board, 50, 73
Computer records, attempts to obtain, 6
Conciliation/arbitration, 179
Confidentiality, 62–68
    abuse (child/elder/disabled) and, 63–64
    breach of, 51–52
    child abuse and, 63
    contracts and, 161–162
    court orders, for providing records/information, 16, 81
    criminal cases and investigations and, 65
    death (client, therapist) and, 66, 162, 163
    depositions and, 106–107
    drug/alcohol treatment records, 87–88
    duty to warn, 64
    ethics and, 58–59
    exceptions/limitations to, 63–67
    group/couples/family therapy and, 65

malpractice suits and
complaints before the
licensing board, 66
mental health condition and,
64
office staff and, 64
oral explanations of
limitations to, 66–67
parent-child relationship and,
64
school counselors, 65
subpoena and responses to
subpoena, 65
waiver/release from, 64, 81, 85
Conflict(s), resolving, 71–78
clients filing complaint with
licensing board, 73
clients filing malpractice suit,
72 (*see also* Malpractice
lawsuits)
clients publicly attacking
competence,
professionalism, and
personal life of mental
health professionals,
73–74
clients venting/forgetting,
72
depressed clients who don't get
better, 76–77
handling the angry client,
71–74
methods of diffusion:
lawyer-supervised and
carefully drafted letter,
74
mediation or other ADR, 74
office visit(s) with third
party present, 74

not offering to return fees, 74
resolving posttrial conflicts,
74–75
reviewing file, 75
risk management, 72
Conflict of interest, 53–54,
58–59, 118
Consent:
informed (ethical principle),
50–51
release from confidentiality,
64, 81, 85
Consent forms:
contract not to testify, 21–22
lawyer-drafted form, intake
and consent to treatment,
28, 163, 165
sample contract for forensic
services and information
and consent form,
249–252
sample employee evaluation
information and consent
form, 241–244
sample home study
information and consent
form, 245–248
Contact information in
contracts, 162
Contract(s), forensic, 158–165,
249–252
content, 159–164
addresses/phone numbers
for communication
with client, 162
confidentiality, 161–162
consent to provide services,
163
credentials, 160

Contract(s), forensic,
  (*Continued*)
  death/incapacity of
    therapist, 162–163
  emergencies or therapeutic
    questions, 162
  fees/payment, 119, 161,
    166–168
  length/number of sessions,
    160
  procedures for
    appointments, 160
  relationship between
    forensic therapist and
    client, 161
  risks, 162
  scheduling/rescheduling, 164
  services provided, 160
  critical importance of,
    158–159, 165
  outcomes/results not
    guaranteed, 77
  sample, 249–252
  school counselors, 189
  versus therapist-client
    contract, 165 (*see also*
    Consent forms)
Contract not to testify, 21–22
Copying documents/client files,
  16, 111–112, 115–116, 190
Counselor, lawyer's function as
  (versus advocate), 24
Court(s):
  researching personality/
    climate of, 202–203
  trials (*see* Testimony; Trials)
  types of, 3–4
Court appearance subpoena,
  86–87

Court orders, for providing
  records/information, 16, 81
Credentials. *See* Qualifications,
  expert
Criminal cases:
  appeals, 12
  arraignment, 10
  arrest, 9
  bail, 9–10
  booking, 9
  confidentiality and, 65
  expungement, 12–13
  plea bargain, 10
  preliminary hearing, 10–11
  pretrial motions, 11
  sentencing, 12
  steps in criminal process, 8–13
  trial, 11–12 (*see also*
    Testimony)
Cross-examination:
  checklist for, 235–237
  defined, 7
  lawyers' tricks in, 133–139
    attacking tools of the
      profession, 136
    comparison of texts or
      publications, 136–137
    intentionally mixing up
      dates, 134–135
    leading questions, 135
    multiple questions, 135
    personal/intimate questions,
      136, 137–138
    questions that can't be
      answered yes or no,
      136
    rapid-fire questions, 135
    trapping by jargon,
      135–136

questions to expect, 37,
117–118
reviewing for, 203
Curriculum vitae (CV),
153–157, 240
content, 154–156
court resume versus
employment resume,
153–154
educational experiences, 154
forensic experience, and biases
revealed, 154–155
lawyer review of, 155
multiple versions of, 155–156
sample form, 155, 240
school counselors, 190
special research projects, 154
Custody cases, crucial
importance of court
appointed forensic
evaluator, 1–2

**D**

Dates:
approximate, 125
lawyer's trick of mixing up,
134–135
*Daubert v. Merrell Dow Pharms.*,
140–141, 143–145,
238–239
Death:
confidentiality surviving, 66
of therapist, in contract,
162–163
Defendants:
civil cases, 4
criminal cases, 10

therapists as (*see* Malpractice
lawsuits)
Deposit(s), and billing as earned,
169
Depositions:
checklist for, 221–227
judge not present, 112, 128
juvenile cases, 14–15
preparing for, 105–113
confidentiality, 106–107
consult, 108–109
consulting with attorney,
108–109
copying files, 111–112
logistical problems,
109–110
payment for, 110
problem issues for client,
109
problem issues for mental
health professional,
110–111
reviewing client file,
107–108
role-play, 111
reviewing, in preparation for
trial, 116, 126
subpoenas, 86, 91–92
by written interrogatory, 5
Direct examination. *See also*
Testimony; Trials:
checklist for, 228–234
what to expect, 35–36
Disabled, abuse of the, 63–64
Disclosure of protected health
information:
authorization form, 219–220
(*see also* HIPAA Privacy
Rule)

Disclosure of protected health
    information (*Continued*)
    court order required for, 16, 81
    ethics (*see* Confidentiality)
Discovery, 90–96
    background, 90–91
    civil process, 5–6
    compensation, 95
    deposition with subpoena
        duces tecum, 91–92
    extra legal (learning about the
        expert informally),
        94–95
    interrogatories, 93
    legal advice and, 93
    motion for production of
        documents, 92–93
    record production subpoena,
        92–93
    requests for admissions, 94,
        116
    subpoenas, 86, 92
Divorce, lawyer's function in
    preparing for, 25–26
Drug/alcohol treatment records,
    confidentiality of, 87–88
Dual roles, 53–54
Duty to warn, 64

**E**

Elder abuse, 63–64
Emergencies, in contracts, 162
Employee evaluation information
    and consent form, 241–244
Ethics, 49–61
    avoiding harm, 52–53
    competence, 54–57

complaints, 50, 73
    acts of commission,
        176–177
    acts of omission, 175–176
    confidentiality, 51–52, 58–59
    conflict of interest, 53–54,
        58–59
    dual roles, 53–54
    informed consent, 50–51
    loss of objectivity or impartial
        judgment, 57
Evaluations, asking for (from
    jurors/lawyers/parties/
    judges), 128
Evergreen account, 170
Expert witnesses, 32–39
    challenges to admissibility of
        testimony, 140–150
        based on qualifications as
            expert, 142
        based on reliability of
            methodology and
            conclusions, 143
        based on subject matter, 142
        *Daubert* case, 143–145
        implications for mental
            health professionals,
            147–149
        *Joiner* case, 145–147
        *Kumho* case, 146–147
    compensation for (*see*
        Payment/fees)
    establishing forensic practice,
        149–150
    forensic contracts, 158–165
    forensic experts, 198–207
    kinds of, 32–33
    lawsuits against, 174–183
    versus lay witness, 33–35

qualifications, 33, 142
resources:
    forms (*see* Forms)
    web sites, 209–211
resumes (*see* Curriculum vitae
    (CV))
roles, 34–35
    cross-examination
        testimony, 37
    direct testimony, 35–36
    jury selection assistance, 34
    witness preparation
        assistance, 34
school counselor as, 187–197
Expungement, 12–13

## F

Federal cases involving *Daubert*
    challenges of mental health
    professionals, list of,
    238–239
Fees. *See* Payment/fees
Fifth Amendment, 14, 22
Files:
    client:
        copying, 16, 111–112,
            115–116, 190
        organizing, 114–115
        reviewing and correcting,
            75, 107–108, 114, 126,
            178
    student, 189, 190
Forensic work:
    advantages, 204
    building forensic mental
        health practice, 149–150,
        205–206

    disadvantages, 204–205
    forensic expert versus
        reluctant treating
        professional, 18–22
Forms, 165, 211–252
    authorization for use and
        disclosure of protected
        health information,
        219–220
    contract for forensic services
        and information and
        consent form, 249–252
    contract not to testify,
        21–22
    employee evaluation
        information and consent
        form, 241–244
    forensic, 29
    home study information and
        consent form, 245–248
    lawyer-drafted form, intake
        and consent to treatment,
        28, 163, 165
    motion for entry of a
        protective order,
        213–215
    motion to quash subpoena,
        211–212
    qualified protective order,
        216–218
    trial vita, 240

## G

Governors' pardon authority, 12
Group/couples/family therapy,
    and confidentiality, 65
Guessing, in testimony, 126, 129

# H

Harm, avoiding, 52–53
Hearings, in juvenile cases, 14
HIPAA Privacy Rule, 80–89
Home study information and
    consent form, 245–248
Honesty, in testimony, 123–124

# I

Informed consent, 50–51
Insurance carriers, malpractice,
    28–29, 30, 177, 178, 182
Intake/consent forms, 28, 29,
    165. *See also* Forms
Intake officer, juvenile cases, 14
Interrogatories, 5, 93, 116

# J

Jargon:
    lawyers' tricks: tricking by,
        135–136
    reviewing, 193
*Joiner* case, 145–147
Judges:
    not present at depositions,
        112, 128
    researching the, 201–202
    system of justice, 3–17
Judicial system, 1–2, 3–17
    civil litigation process, 4–8
    criminal case process, 8–13
    expert witnesses, 32–39
    juvenile cases, 13–15

lawyers, functions of, 24–31
therapists involvement in,
    18–23
Juries:
    deliberation and verdict, 7–8
    instructions, 7
    observations about, 128–130
    selection, 7, 34
Juvenile cases, 13–15
    depositions, 14–15
    hearings/outcomes, 14
        child in need of
            supervision, 14
        juvenile delinquent, 13, 14
        status offender, 14
    proceedings determinations,
        13
    referrals, 13

# K

*Kumho* case, 146–147

# L

Lawsuits against mental health
    professionals. *See*
    Malpractice lawsuits
Lawyers, 24–31
    cultivating list of specialized,
        29–30
    functions:
        as advocate, 26
        as counselor, 24
        in divorce preparations,
            25–26

need for, by mental health
professionals:
conflicts of interest, 118
drafting letters to angry
clients, 74
malpractice suits, 177, 182
preparing for depositions,
108–109
preparing for trials,
118–119
preparation of documents
needed by mental health
professionals, 27–29
association forms, 28
forensic forms, 29
intake and consent to
treatment forms, 28
lease forms, 27
malpractice or professional
liability insurance,
28–29
managed care contracts,
27
specialized forms, 29
referrals to, 29–30
tricks of (*see* Cross-
examination)
Lay (nonexpert) witness,
33–34
Leading questions, 135
Lease documents, 27
Licensing board, complaints filed
with, 50, 73
Literature, researching:
contradicting your opinions/
conclusions, 200–201
supporting your opinions/
conclusions, 200

**M**

Malpractice insurance carriers,
28–29, 30, 177, 178, 182
Malpractice lawsuits, 72,
174–183
areas of vulnerability leading
to complaints, 175–177
acts of commission, 176–177
acts of omission, 175–176
avoiding litigation:
conciliation and arbitration,
179
mediation, 178
negotiation, 178
professional panel, 179
confidentiality and, 66
controlling your emotions,
181–182
handling unreasonable client,
181
plaintiffs, 174–175
preparing for trial, 179–181
responding to fake or
unsubstantiated
complaint, 181
reviewing clinical file or
progress notes, 178
reviewing previous complaints,
177
role of lawyer, 177, 182
role of malpractice insurance
carrier, 177, 178, 182
steps for self-protection,
177–178
talking to colleague(s), 178
Managed care contracts, 27
Mannerisms, 203

Mediation, 74, 178
Medications:
    documenting, 193
    researching, 199
Mental health/condition,
    confidentiality and, 64
Mental health professionals:
    contract not to testify, 21–22
    as defendants in lawsuits (*see*
        Malpractice lawsuits)
    as expert witnesses:
        forensic experts
            (volunteers), 18–20
        preparing for testimony (*see*
            Testimony; Trials):
        reluctant treating
            professionals, 18–19,
            20–21
    lawyers and, 27–29 (*see also*
        Lawyers)
    legal documents needed,
        27–29
        association forms, 28
        forensic forms, 29
        intake and consent to
            treatment forms, 28
        lease forms, 27
        malpractice or professional
            liability insurance,
            28–29
        managed care contracts, 27
        specialized forms, 29
Methodology, challenges to, 143
Motions:
    for entry of a protective order,
        213–215
    postjudgment (civil process), 8
    preliminary (civil process), 5
    pretrial (criminal process), 11

for production of documents,
    92–93
to quash subpoena, 211–212

N

Negotiation, 178

O

Objectivity, loss of, 57
Office staff, and confidentiality,
    64
Opening statements, 7
Opposing counsel, researching,
    202
Opposing experts, researching,
    201
Oral explanations of exceptions/
    limitations to
    confidentiality, 66–67

P

Pardons, 12
Parents:
    confidentiality, exceptions/
        limitations to, 64
    notification, 190
    permission, 193–194
Payment/fees, 166–173
    angry clients and, 74
    contract (intake/consent
        form), 15–16, 29, 119,
        161, 166–168, 171–172
    for copies of records, 111–112

deposition, 110
items/services for which
    compensation is
    expected, 167
methods of securing payment,
    168
    advance payment, 173
    billing periodically as
        earned, 169–170
    deposit and bill as earned,
        169
    evergreen account, 170
    trust fund deposit, 168
outcome of litigation and,
    171–172
subpoenas and, 21–22, 172, 173
unpaid accounts, 170–171
Personal/intimate questions, 136
Personality of a court,
    determining, 202–203
Petitions, filing, 4
Plain subpoenas, 84, 92
Plaintiffs, 174–175
Plea bargain, criminal process,
    10
Postjudgment motions, in civil
    process, 8
Practice association form, 28
Preliminary hearings, criminal
    process, 10–11
Preliminary motions, civil
    process, 5
Preparing for testimony. See
    Testimony; Trials
Presidential pardon authority, 12
Pretrial motions, in criminal
    process, 11
Proceedings determination,
    juvenile cases, 13

Production requests, complying
    with and reviewing, 116
Professional courtesy,
    extending/requesting,
    191–192
Professionalism on the witness
    stand, 192
Professional panel, 179
Professional referrals, 29–30
Protective orders:
    qualified, 83, 85, 216–218
    sample, 216–218
    sample motion for entry of,
        213–215
    trial preparation, 116

## Q

Qualifications, expert:
    challenges to, 142 (see also
        Daubert v. Merrell Dow
        Pharms.)
    in forensic contracts, 160
    questions to have lawyer ask
        in direct examination,
        99–100
    resume (see Curriculum vitae
        (CV))
Qualified protective orders, 83,
    85, 216–218. See also
    Protective orders

## R

R(s), eight, 198–203
    researching courthouse
        climate, 202–203

R(s), eight *(Continued)*
  researching judge, 201–202
  researching literature that
    contradicts your opinions/
    conclusions, 200–201
  researching literature that
    supports your opinions/
    conclusions, 200
  researching opposing counsel,
    202
  researching opposing experts,
    201
  researching subject matter,
    199–200
  reviewing for examination and
    cross-examination
    carefully, 203
Rape/murder, juvenile cases, 13
Recognizance, own, 9
Record subpoena or discovery
    request, 86
Referrals:
  juvenile cases, 13
  lawyers, 29–30
Reimbursement. *See* Payment/fees
Religion, 129
Reluctant treating professionals
    (as expert witnesses),
    18–19, 20–21, 22
Requests for admissions, 94,
    116
Research:
  collateral, 37
  preparation for trial (eight
    R's), 198–203
  reference to, 37–38
Respondents, 4
Resume. *See* Curriculum vitae
    (CV)

Risk(s):
  angry clients, and
    management of, 72
  in contracts, 162
Role-play, 111, 117, 191


**S**


School counselors, 65, 187–197
  confidentiality and, 65
  contracts, 189
  credibility as witnesses, 188–189
  curriculum vitae (CV), 190
  extending/requesting
    professional courtesy,
    191–192
  first trial experience, 192–193
  notifying parents, 190
  notifying principal and
    supervisor at once, 189
  parental notification, 190
  professionalism, 192
  role-play/rehearsal with
    lawyers, 191
  subpoenas, 188–189
  trial preparation, 189–192
School psychologists, 193–194
  documenting medications,
    diagnosis, treatment plan,
    and prognosis, 193
  getting parental permission,
    193–194
  jargon review, 193
Sentencing, step in criminal
    process, 12
Service of process, 4
Sexual dysfunction, 199
Slander/libel, 73–74

Status offender, 14
Student files, 189, 190, 194–195
Subject matter:
    challenges, 142
    researching, 199–200
Subpoenas, 79–89
    attachment of witness, 87–88
    compensation and, 21–22,
        172, 173
    confidentiality and, 65, 81,
        85, 87–88
    qualified protective orders, 83,
        85
    recommended procedure when
        served with, 84–87
    responding to, 87–88
    sample motion to quash,
        211–212
    school counselors, 188–189
    types of:
        court appearance (trial),
            86–87
        deposition, 86
        duces tecum, 84, 91–92
        plain, 84, 92
        record, 86
    waiver of confidentiality form,
        85

**T**

Testimony, 7, 69
    courtroom (see Cross-
        examination; Trials)
    direct examination, checklist
        for, 228–234
    documenting (creating file,
        after your testimony), 128

lawyers' tricks, 133–139
    preparing "ask me" questions
        for the lawyer, 97–104
        categories (three), 99–102
        critical/exceptional events,
            100–101
        outstanding traits of the
            client, 101–102
        professional qualifications/
            studies/training,
            99–100
    preparing for depositions,
        105–113
    requesting evaluations from
        jurors/lawyers/parties/
        judges, 128
    versus therapy, 41, 43–48
    tips, 47, 123–132
    what to expect, 35–36
Texts/publications, comparison
    of, 136–137
Therapist(s):
    checkered past of, 137–138
    death/incapacity of, 162–163
    differing roles, 43–48
        forensic therapist, 44–46
            (see also Forensic work)
        treating therapists, 43–44
    as expert witnesses (see Expert
        witnesses; Testimony)
    lawsuits against (see
        Malpractice lawsuits)
    obligation to testify, 46–47
    taking Fifth Amendment, 22
Trials:
    bench/jury, 6–8
    checklists:
        for cross-examination,
            235–237

Trials *(Continued)*
> for deposition testimony,
>> 221–227
> for direct examination for
>> courtroom testimony,
>> 228–234
> for trial preparation (eight
>> R's), 198–199
> for trial preparation as a
>> defendant, 180–181
> civil process, 6–8
> criminal process, 11–12
> preparing for, 114–120 (*see
>> also* Cross-examination;
>> Testimony)
> attending pretrial lawyer
>> conference and role-
>> playing, 117
> checklist for (eight R's),
>> 198–199
> complying with and
>> reviewing production
>> requests, 116
> considering protective
>> orders, 116
> contacting the client,
>> 115
> copying the record,
>> 115–116
> engaging personal lawyer,
>> 118–119
> expecting certain questions
>> in cross-examination,
>> 117–118
> organizing the file,
>> 114–115
> reviewing record of the
>> client, 114

> reviewing requests for
>> admissions,
>> interrogatories, and
>> depositions, 116
> school counselors, 189–192
Trust fund deposits, 168

**U**

Unpaid accounts, 170–171

**V**

Vitae. *See* Curriculum vitae
> (CV)
Volunteering information, 127

**W**

Waiver of confidentiality form,
> 85
Warrant, arrest, 9
Web sites, useful, 209–211
Witnesses:
> assistance in preparing, 34
> expert (*see* Expert witnesses)

**Y**

Yes/no questions:
> lawyers' trick, 136
> requests for admissions, 94,
>> 116